THE PSYCHOLOGY OF MEN IN CONTEXT

What does it really mean to say that boys will be boys, men are from Mars, or that contemporary men are in crisis? Does modern psychology support or refute these notions? And how is psychological theory and research about boys and men used in society?

The Psychology of Men in Context is an essential introduction to the field which challenges readers to examine psychological research on men, masculinity, and gender, and consider its impact on daily life, through everyday speech, popular media, political rhetoric, and more.

The authors offer a range of lenses for studying masculinity, including biology, social learning, social constructionism, feminism, and intersectionality. Demonstrating how these frameworks can be used to understand research on pressing topics such as violence, health, and relationships, the book also considers masculinity in its broader philosophical and historical contexts, equipping readers with the tools needed to connect the psychology of men with other areas of social science. Exercises and prompts to help students relate the research to their own lives are included throughout.

Designed for students at undergraduate and graduate level, but suitable for anyone curious about understanding the field from a more critical social scientific perspective, *The Psychology of Men in Context* is a valuable introduction to the history, current scholarship, and social implications of the psychological study of men and masculinity.

Michael E. Addis, PhD, is professor of psychology at Clark University. He has authored numerous scientific articles and books on a variety of topics related to men's mental health and clinical psychology. Dr. Addis is a fellow of the American Psychological Association and past president of the Society for the Psychological Study of Men and Masculinities.

Ethan Hoffman, MA, is a doctoral student in clinical psychology at Clark University. He received undergraduate and master's degrees from Wesleyan University. His research focuses on the social psychology of mental health beliefs, men's rhetoric about depression, and the history of clinical and social psychology.

"With *The Psychology of Men in Context,* Addis and Hoffman provide a truly innovative contribution appropriate for scholars, clinicians, or anyone interested in the field. This creative, accessible book allows readers to consume the latest research-informed conclusions in an easy to digest, real-world manner. What I most appreciate is the rare combination of depth and scope in the topics covered, placing each within the context of pressing social concerns. The writing is engaging in a way that allows readers to use concepts from the scientific literature to generate their own insights and conclusions. It is this balanced, thoughtful, and engaging style that makes *The Psychology of Men in Context* an instant classic."

Aaron Rochlen, PhD, professor of counseling psychology
and counselor education, Department of Educational Psychology,
The University of Texas at Austin

"*The Psychology of Men in Context* is a highly readable, accessible text that brings a fresh perspective to the psychology of gender and the psychology of men specifically. The authors' focus on the history of research on men and masculinities is especially novel, and their discussion of this research—which occurs at the front end of the book—provides important context for current debates and lines of inquiry related to the psychology of men. In addition to covering expected but necessary territory (biological and social contextual components of gender, for example), the text also delves into important yet less frequently explored topics related to the psychology of men, including intersectionalities (race, culture, social class) and methodologies. Peppered throughout the book are engaging points for consideration which draw the reader's attention to critical points for contemplation and discussion. Key terms are highlighted throughout, making this text especially appropriate for introductory or mid-level courses on gender."

Abbie E. Goldberg, PhD, professor of psychology and director
of Women's and Gender Studies at Clark University

"An excellent book that goes 'under the hood' of the social, political, and scientific aspects of the psychology of men. Addis and Hoffman discuss complex issues in accessible language, making this text a must-have for anyone interested in learning about the history, science, and applications of this field."

Ryon C. McDermott, PhD, University of South Alabama

"This book is not afraid to tackle the difficult questions. It provides students with the tools needed to critically engage with complicated and emotionally-charged topics. The focus on context evades simplistic or reductionist thinking and demands that students consider their own lives while critically evaluating contemporary psychological research. My students have asked for a book like this — one that does not offer easy answers, but forces all of us to take responsibility for the social forces shaping gender and masculinity."

Kate Richmond, PhD, Muhlenberg College

THE PSYCHOLOGY OF MEN IN CONTEXT

Michael E. Addis and Ethan Hoffman

Routledge
Taylor & Francis Group

NEW YORK AND LONDON

First published 2020
by Routledge
52 Vanderbilt Avenue, New York, NY 10017

and by Routledge
2 Park Square, Milton Park, Abingdon, Oxon, OX14 4RN

Routledge is an imprint of the Taylor & Francis Group, an informa business

© 2020 Taylor & Francis

The right of Michael E. Addis and Ethan Hoffman to be identified as
authors of this work has been asserted by them in accordance with sections
77 and 78 of the Copyright, Designs and Patents Act 1988.

Library of Congress Cataloging-in-Publication Data
A catalog record for this title has been requested

ISBN: 978-1-138-58933-9 (hbk)
ISBN: 978-1-138-58934-6 (pbk)
ISBN: 978-0-429-49171-9 (ebk)

Typeset in Minion
by Swales & Willis, Exeter, Devon, UK

CONTENTS

ACKNOWLEDGMENTS

We would both like to thank our numerous colleagues at Clark University for sustaining such an intellectually rich and supportive environment. In particular, this book would not have been possible without the curiosity and commitment of an exceptional group of doctoral students over the last two decades: Josh Berger, Geoff Cohane, Doug Gazarian, Jon Green, Jon Jampel, Emma Kironde, Mariola Magovcevic, Abigail Mansfield, Jennifer Primack, Chris Reigeluth, Joe Schwab, David Slatkin, Matt Syzdek, and MySha Whorley. We would also like to thank the numerous undergraduate students who provided feedback on drafts of this book. A special thank you goes out to Jessica Chadwick for the laborious efforts she put into transcribing our conversation about the philosophy of science, and Mathilde McAlpin, for her work formatting references and providing research assistance.

Michael would also like to acknowledge the support and influence of several colleagues around the country. In particular, Chris Kilmartin, Fred Rabinowitz, Aaron Rochlen, Ron Levant, and Ryon McDermott are all influential scholars who have been willing to share their ideas and perspectives on the field over the years. In addition, Barry Walsh has been both an inspiration and a true friend. I had some doubts two years ago when we agreed that I should write a book on the psychology of men and you should write one on the history of Katsina carvers. But we both did it!

This book would not have been possible without the love and support of my life partner, Kelly Dolen. Your belief in the project has been unwavering, as has your willingness to whip out a 14-point motivational scale, a well-timed reflection, or a simple reality check. Thank you for bearing witness.

Finally, it has been a true pleasure to work with my co-author Ethan Hoffman. This book has been a genuine collaboration, whether it was reading and writing numerous drafts of chapters, hunting down references, or dialoguing on the philosophy of science over pints of beer. In my opinion, you are exactly the kind of psychologist the field needs, and I look forward to witnessing your journey through it.

Ethan would like to thank all the teachers and colleagues that have offered their guidance and support. I would be remiss if I did not specifically thank my former advisor, Jill Morawski, as well as the Science in Society Program at Wesleyan University, for preparing me to think critically about gender, philosophical, and historical issues in psychology.

Throughout the process of writing this book, I have been lucky to count on the emotional and intellectual support of my partner, Alexandra Khristich: *мая, родная, милая, и рациональная.* You have never failed to offer warmth, intellectual debates on feminist epistemology, or a 5,000-piece Bruegel puzzle in order to keep life both silly and serious. To my mother, Deborah, and late father, Jon: thank you for always believing in me and for making my education a priority. This book would not have been possible without you. To my sister Olivia: your poetry, intellect, and love inspire me to never stop trying to become a better writer, thinker, and brother.

I am, last but not least, deeply grateful that my mentor and co-author, Michael Addis, invited me to join him in writing this book. I especially appreciate your willingness and ability to balance your roles of educator and co-writer over the last two years—nurturing my development as a psychologist, writer, and human being all the while treating me as your partner. Thank you for your faith, support, patience, and humor over the last four years. You've shown me that it is possible to get down in the weeds of research without sacrificing critical, reflective, and big-picture thinking about social science. For that and more, I look up to you as an intellectual father.

PART ONE
Entering the Territory

1

INTRODUCTION

(The Psychology of Men) in Context/The Psychology of (Men in Context)

In 2005, a small group of researchers, educators, and therapists affiliated with the American Psychological Association (APA) began developing a series of guidelines for mental health practice. Their goal was to identify the most cutting-edge research findings and clinical approaches specifically relevant to boys and men. The project came on the heels of other APA documents focused on women and girls (2007), lesbian, gay, and bisexual individuals (2012), and racial and ethnic minorities (2017). Each of these populations were assumed to face specific, and possibly unique factors influencing their physical, emotional, and interpersonal well-being. For example, sexism and unrealistic gender role expectations are particularly salient for girls and women, whereas racism, discrimination, and homophobia are likely to have significant psychological effects on racial and sexual minorities respectively. What about boys and men?

The guidelines were 13 years in the making and were not finalized and released to the public until late 2018 (APA, 2018), right around the time we were putting the final touches on this book. Among the general principles identified in the guidelines were the following:

Psychologists strive to recognize that masculinities are constructed based on social, cultural, and contextual norms.

(p. 6)

Psychologists understand the impact of power, privilege, and sexism on the development of boys and men and on their relationships with others.

(p. 9)

Psychologists strive to encourage positive father involvement and healthy family relationships.

(p. 12)

Psychologists strive to reduce the high rates of problems boys and men face and act out in their lives such as aggression, violence, substance abuse, and suicide.

(p. 15)

Psychologists strive to build and promote gender-sensitive psychological services.

(p. 17)

For those familiar with the newer psychology of men (e.g., Levant & Wong, 2017) there was nothing particularly shocking about the guidelines; they articulated several of the most common and basic assumptions driving theory, research, and clinical practice focused on boys and men. But surprisingly, their publication was followed by several weeks of widespread national and international media coverage. Psychologists working in the field of men and masculinity were inundated with requests for radio interviews, television appearances, and op-eds.

Media attention is not unheard of for psychologists working on issues related to gender. But two things stood out in this case. First, the sheer pace and volume of coverage was unprecedented. Second, publication appeared to tap straight into a seemingly deep divide between those who saw the guidelines as potentially helping men by liberating them from restrictive gender roles, and those who saw them as an attack on traditional manhood, if not on men themselves. Consider the following headlines culled from the internet:

New American Psychological Association guidelines declare 'traditional masculinity' harmful to boys and men.

(*The Blaze*, January 8, 2019)

The APA says traditional masculinity hurts boys. Of course it does. The problem isn't that traditional masculinity is being attacked and eroded. The problem is that it continues to exist.

(*Fatherly*, January 14, 2019)

Men can take it: reactions to the APA guidelines on men and boys.

(*Psych Central*, January 24, 2019)

Manhood as mental disorder.

(*American Conservative*, January 7, 2019)

Our interest in these kinds of reactions—the ways psychological theory and research related to men and masculinity are consumed by society—provided a major motivation for writing this book. We believe that the psychology of men cannot be understood without considering its historical, current, and potential future contexts; where did the psychology of men come from, what is it doing now, and where might it be headed? Thus, the title of this book can be understood partly as "(The Psychology of Men) in Context."

The psychology of men is neither a historical accident nor simply a set of scientific facts waiting to be discovered. Rather, the theories and research that comprise the field are collections of reactions to historical developments such as the rise of the women's movement, the gradual erosion of White, middle-class, male privilege, and the increasing cultural recognition that gender is at least as much socially constructed and learned as it is driven by genetics and the evolutionary history of the human species.

Academic, political, and clinical work in the psychology of men is also motivated by a desire to intervene in social problems involving men and gender. There is an extensive list of socially significant issues that call for a psychology of men. Why are men four times more likely than women to take their own lives but far less likely to seek help from mental health professionals? Why are the overwhelming majority of violent crimes committed by men? How do homophobia and misogyny affect the ways we raise boys and young men? These are provocative questions. It is therefore not surprising that the psychology of men stirs up strong reactions in politically engaged corners of society. Put another way, the theories, ideas, and research findings in this book are consequential in not only academic terms; they are also products of knowledge that are consumed, digested, transformed, debated, and put to use by interested actors and groups in society.

With this in mind, consider the idea that masculinity is a historically changing set of gender roles and ideologies rather than an essential part of every man—a premise supported by a large body of research that figured prominently in the APA guidelines. Here is how one media commentator on a daily news program in the U.S. characterized the idea:

This is what's so dangerous about this report: it's political theory. It has nothing to do with science. And it's also bigotry, right? There's a suggestion that masculinity—and that would mean all men, because you're dealing with the issue of testosterone, the nature of what it is to be male—are prone to violence or homophobia or sexual violence or sexual harassment. Women involve those things as well. Women can be violent. Women can do sexual harassment. It's a remarkable pathology they're using. These are guidelines to all psychologists saying that "when you treat men and boys you should presume that they're suffering from an illness." And it's also interesting that they're using the phrase "traditional masculinity" which implies that it's taught, that it's not the very nature of men. And, of course, I think that scientists would disagree, when you're dealing with the impact of estrogen and testosterone that there is a manliness and a masculinity that's involved. I tell you, the things they're complaining about: if we didn't have men's courage and focus and determination we would be living in caves right now. The modern world is the result of the male framework of wanting to move forward and create things, and I think it is obscene and everyone should complain that those attributes of men are being determined to be negative and something that is either a sickness or mental illness or wrong or even artificial.

(Tammy Bruce, *Fox and Friends,* January 10, 2019)

In contrast, the APA (2019) issued the following the news release in defense of the guidelines:

Research ... shows that men and boys who are taught to bury their feelings are less willing to seek help for psychological distress. As a consequence, many boys and men who need help aren't getting it. The guidelines are intended to change that fact. By making the guidelines widely available, APA hopes that more men and boys get the message that it's not only OK to seek help, but also shows strength ....

Psychologists who treat men and boys already know that their male clients aren't stereotypes. They have feelings, needs and desires. They're adaptable. They possess many positive masculine characteristics. The guidelines are designed to give psychologists a framework to help men and boys embrace their masculinity in ways that are helpful, rather than harmful, to their health and quality of life.

How are we to make sense of these apparently irreconcilable characterizations of a single document? One option might be simply to consult the original source. We could read the guidelines carefully and try to determine when its contents are being accurately portrayed and when they are being misrepresented. Although this approach might reveal varying degrees of bias in the way the document is interpreted, it does nothing to help us understand *why* such bias exists. It does nothing to help clarify the assumptions that various groups hold about the nature of men and gender more broadly, or explain how those assumptions align with particular social agendas. Why, for example, do some people apparently believe that testosterone is the biological basis of masculinity? What are the consequences of holding such beliefs? In what contexts, and in what ways, are such beliefs used to refute or justify different perspectives on issues such as sexuality, interpersonal violence, transgender people serving in the military, and so on? Approaching questions such as these requires us to move beyond the "facts" of theory and research in the psychology of men and into how such knowledge is used in societal contexts.

Of course, it's impossible to examine how knowledge is used in society without first having a firm grasp on what that knowledge is. One of the reasons we decided to write this book is that the psychology of men, although a growing field, is still relatively young. There continue to be far fewer books and courses on men and masculinity compared with those on women or gender studies more broadly. In 2013, a series of articles on the status of teaching in the psychology of men appeared in the journal *Psychology of Men and Masculinity*. At that time only 61 courses on the psychology of men could be found in the previous 18 years (O'Neil & Renzulli, 2013). In contrast, only seven years after the founding of Division 35 of APA (Society for the Psychological Study of Women) there were 121 psychology of women courses (Russo, 1982). By 1989 there were 230 courses (Matlin, 1989) and the number has continued to grow.

In considering the relative paucity of courses on the psychology of men, O'Neil and Renzulli (2013) suggest one reason may be that the material is controversial and intensely personal for both students and faculty. We agree. Our approach to this book has been strongly influenced by the first author's experiences teaching the psychology of men for over 15 years to students ranging from first-year undergraduates to seniors, as well as supervising doctoral students in clinical psychology with a focus on men and masculinity.

One theme is perennial: the psychology of men is all around us, and the issues matter; violence, suicide, war, child custody, the list goes on. Yet the very same constant immersion in gender that makes it so compelling also makes it quite slippery to study. This is not only a matter of having to work hard to achieve traditional values of objectivity in social science. It is also a matter of considering how our own theories and research findings, *our knowledge products*, may function in the social world. In other words, it matters how we think and talk about gender, not only because we need to get it "right" in a scientific sense, but also because different ways of thinking and talking about important social issues like gender, race, and class have very real and very powerful consequences for individual and collective lives.

At the same time, students often find it difficult to adopt a more objective and critical perspective on the material, or to let go of easily available stereotypes about sex differences between men and women. And yet, these same students continue to sign up for the courses in growing numbers, and there is no shortage of personal and political motivations for engaging in the material. Over time this productive tension between personal engagement and dispassionate analysis has led Michael to focus more on achieving *breadth and depth with a smaller range of concepts*, and to emphasize how a critical analysis of different perspectives on the psychology of men *can be helpful in the "real world."*

A major theme running through the book is the idea that a wide range of socially significant issues involving men and gender can best be understood by considering the diverse environmental influences on men's thoughts, feelings, and actions, rather than exclusively focusing on assumedly deep-rooted, essential, or universal psychological and biological characteristics of men. In this sense, the title of the book can also be understood as "The Psychology of (Men in Context)." This approach is not about an ideological commitment to nurture over nature. It is meant to underscore and account for the vast between-person and within-person variability that exists in boys and men. For example, although various forms of masculinity emphasize emotional stoicism and excessive self-reliance, many men will express emotional vulnerability and seek help under the right circumstances. Conversely, there are countless situations where men may apparently resist or subvert traditional masculinity while at the same time reinforcing those very same notions. Consider this kind of statement, not uncommon on college campuses in the U.S.: "No homo bro, but that shirt looks really good on you." Is this a progressive rejection of homophobia, a homophobic slur, or both? A thoroughgoing psychology of men must be able to account for blends, contradictions, inconsistencies, and the contextual variations that shape and constrain men's thoughts, feelings, and actions.

What Is Masculinity?

It is impossible to study the psychology of men without encountering the term "masculinity." It can often show up several times in a single paragraph, if not a single sentence, and this book is no exception. You might assume that such a widely used term has a precise and unanimously agreed-upon definition, and you would be semi-correct; most theorists, researchers, and therapists can agree that masculinity has something to do with what it means to be a man. But beyond that, masculinity tends to be just as slippery for professionals to define as it is for everyday people trying to figure out how to follow its mandates. Is masculinity a personality trait? A set of beliefs? A social role? A set of brain structures? A set of norms or expectations for how men should behave? Or something else?

Perhaps not surprisingly, psychologists vary in how they define masculinity although there is also a considerable amount of overlap in their definitions. Throughout the book we consider some specific theories and areas of research that have carved out definitions of masculinity as well as ways to measure it. For now, consider a few different ways psychologists might think about defining masculinity.

Masculinity is:

1. *A social role*—ways of acting, thinking, and feeling that society considers appropriate for men. For example: men should be interested in, knowledgeable about, and good at sports.
2. *A set of social norms*—ways of acting, thinking, and feeling that individuals in society consider common or "normal" for men. For example: most men don't wear facial makeup.
3. *A stereotype*—a widely held, fixed, and oversimplified idea about how men are. For example: men don't like asking for directions.
4. *An ideology*—a collection of beliefs and values regarding men that is constructed and reinforced through a wide range of cultural practices. For example: the ideology that men should be the ones who make important decisions and control the finances of their families is supported by giving the check to the man at the end of a meal, bureaucratic categories such as "head of household," men being portrayed as decisive big money financiers in the media, and so on.
5. *A discourse*—ways of talking about the nature of men that portrays individuals and groups in different ways (e.g., as a pro-feminist, as someone sympathetic to men, as an open-minded liberal when it comes to gender issues, and so on). For example: the statement "No homo, but you look hot in that shirt bro" establishes the speaker as heterosexual while also expressing appreciation for the way his friend looks.
6. *A gendered behavioral repertoire*—ways of establishing oneself as appropriately male in the eyes of one's social environment. For example: a teenage boy laughs at sexist or homophobic jokes even though they make him uncomfortable in order to avoid being shamed by his friends.
7. *The biological essence of manhood*—the genetic legacy of evolution leaving distinctly masculine brain structures, thought processes, etc.

Several things are worth noting about these different ways of defining masculinity. First, there is considerable overlap between them. Ideologies, roles, and norms are all based on the idea that there are ideas about how men should be that are "out there" in society and somehow end up "in here" when they come to affect our actions as individuals. Thus, there seems to be a common metaphor running through each of the concepts.

Second, these differing definitions of masculinity partly result from the separate and historically changing terminologies preferred by various disciplines in psychology and other social sciences. For instance, "gendered behavioral repertoire" uses distinctly psychological jargon. "Ideology" marks a more sociological concept. The concept of "role," moreover, has been employed in the study of gender in both psychology and sociology but has recently been critiqued and supplanted by more of a focus on discourse and social norms.

Third, the differences between these concepts are not only matters of historical variations in academic jargon. In fact, there seem to be some potentially meaningful differences between these ways of defining masculinity. A role, for example, suggests a relatively fixed way of thinking, feeling, and acting (e.g., a role in a movie or play). An ideology, in contrast, seems to suggest more of a system of beliefs or attitudes held by an individual or a group. Also, ideologies are not cold scientific beliefs. They place strong value (e.g., "good"/"bad") on things. The ideology that men are inherently more rational (good) than emotional (bad) is only one of myriad examples.

Finally, they each construct masculinity in ways that make particular parts of gender more or less visible to us and, as a result, open up different ways of looking at men's gendered behavior. Imagine, for example, that you were curious about why some men can become virtually obsessed with the game of golf, sometimes to the point of engaging in repeated angry outbursts, tossing their clubs in the water, or hurling anti-feminine epithets at their friends ("Nice putt, Nancy! Put your dress back on!!"). From the perspective of social norms, you might consider the degree to which such actions are considered acceptable, or even expected, in the context of competitive sport. Those same actions viewed from the perspective of a gendered behavioral repertoire might lead you to consider the way they establish the actor as appropriately masculine in a context of disappointment in one's failure to perform up to expectation. And from the perspective of gender ideologies your focus would shift to the various ways athletic performance is portrayed as normative and expected for men in society and supported by entrenched practices (e.g., referring to males' professional sports in gender neutral ways, while marking the same sports as gendered for women (e.g., the National Basketball Association versus the Women's National Basketball Association)). Now imagine that you were interested in developing ways to teach young boys to tolerate frustration and to accept and value themselves regardless of their athletic ability. How might your approach differ depending on which framework you adopted?

Is Masculinity Good or Bad?

Over the last three decades there has been a considerable amount of empirical research linking masculinity to a wide range of mental, physical, and interpersonal problems in living (recall the publication of the APA Guidelines for working with boys and men that began this chapter). Perhaps not surprisingly, the idea that masculinity is a problem has been met with a wide variety of reactions from psychologists, therapists, the media, and others. Some people consider a critical analysis of masculinity, de facto, to be a criticism of men. From this perspective, men who take a critical stance toward masculinity are suffering from some kind of gender-based self-loathing, or they have been brainwashed by angry feminists, or both. Another perspective acknowledges the existence of problematic forms of masculinity but argues that psychologists have under-studied masculinity's more positive forms. The argument here is that the key to enhancing men's well-being (and, by extension, the well-being of people of all genders) is not only to get rid of harmful ideas about masculinity (e.g., that to be a good man is to dominate women), but also to replace them with positive, pro-social meanings of manhood (e.g., to be a good man is to be honest and emotionally forthright).

Our perspective on the question of whether masculinity is good, bad, or both, is … "well, it's complicated." To start with one has to distinguish between the content of masculinity (e.g., what particular meanings of manhood are being promoted at any place or point in time) and the function of masculinity (e.g., what are the historical and current consequences of encouraging men to "be masculine" in the first place?). For example, if we could magically wave a wand and start teaching young boys that "be a man son!" means "be in touch with your feelings!" perhaps that would be a sort of progress. On the other hand, it's also more of the same; we would still be policing boys' conformity to gender norms and ideologies.

Second, the question of whether there are positive forms of masculinity cannot be answered solely with empirical research. Researchers may find, for example, that men who are more honest and emotionally forthright have better relationships, and are less likely to endorse sexist beliefs about women, but are those qualities productively referred to as masculinity? Or, are they simply positive qualities of humanity in general? Our concern with the social impact of different ways of talking about men and masculinity is a theme that recurs throughout the book. In short, we believe that psychologists are not only in the business of "discovering" things about men and masculinity, but also "creating" them. Thus, it matters not only what we study but also how we talk about it.

We return to the question of positive versions of masculinity in Chapter 11. For now, we feel compelled to make one thing very clear: neither of us consider ourselves even remotely "anti-male." We both care about men's well-being as we care about the well-being of people of all genders. And we have both spent a considerable amount of time trying to understand men's experiences, to help them in therapy, and so on. Nonetheless, we continue to believe that *taking a critical stance toward the effects of masculinity in men's lives is not the same as criticizing men*; the point is not that men are bad. The point is that masculinity can have detrimental and sometimes deadly effects when it is produced and consumed rigidly and uncritically.

Overview of the Book

The book is divided into four parts. This introduction, along with a history of the psychology of men (Chapter 2) form Part One and provide some social and historical context to the subsequent parts. Part Two presents five major paradigms or approaches to understanding the psychology of men. The biological paradigm (Chapter 3) interprets men's thoughts, feelings, and behaviors as resulting from (not surprisingly!) a range of biological processes and mechanisms. In this chapter we provide the basic tenets of an evolutionary psychological perspective on men. We also consider the scientific evidence regarding the role of testosterone in men's behavior, and the question of whether there is compelling evidence of biologically based sex differences in psychological characteristics.

The social learning paradigm (Chapter 4) considers the way our social environments teach us about the meanings of men and masculinity. The chapter provides a basic primer on the nature of social learning, alongside empirical evidence that such processes are involved in how boys and men come to be gendered beings.

Students often confuse a social learning paradigm with the social constructionist perspective which is explored in Chapter 5. Although both perspectives eschew biological determinism in favor of an environmental/social lens on men and masculinity, they differ considerably in their focus. Social learning is about how our environments *shape* our understanding of men and masculinity. Social construction is about how *we create meanings of men and masculinity and, in doing so, shape our environments*. Accordingly, in this chapter we present research that focuses on the way language practices create meanings of masculinity, and the various ways masculine gender roles and norms are constructed, reinforced, contested, and subverted in human interactions through language, dress, and a wide range of social institutions.

By the time students have been exposed to the social learning and social construction of masculinity they are typically beginning to see these processes play out in their day-to-day lives. Inevitably, the question arises: why is this all going on?! Chapter 6 provides a feminist perspective on the psychology of men and is focused on exploring the roles of power and patriarchal culture as more distal social forces that give rise to and maintain masculine gender roles, norms, and ideologies. A central theme of the chapter is the notion that the social learning and social construction of masculinity serve to reinforce the oppression of women, although this is rarely a conscious or deliberate process at a psychological level. Instead, most boys and men enact gender because it is the path of least resistance.

Moreover, there are social consequences (e.g., policing of masculinity) for failing to do so. From this perspective, a psychology of men and masculinity becomes a psychology of how concepts of gender serve to distribute power in society.

Chapter 7 presents an intersectional perspective on the psychology of men. Not all men share the same definitions of masculinity, nor the resources to enact it in ways valued by the dominant culture. Young African-American boys, for example, are statistically disadvantaged when it comes to finances, education, healthcare, and so on. Yet they are exposed to many of the same messages about what it means to be a man (e.g., be big, strong, and important). Thus, many of the challenges faced by African-American youth, such as gang involvement, can be understood as rational attempts to enact masculinity without the same resources as White, wealthy, young men. More generally, the chapter focuses on research demonstrating the variable ways masculinity is socially learned and constructed among men of different racial, ethnic, and socioeconomic backgrounds. A central theme of the chapter is the notion that both universals and particulars exist across men of different races, ethnicities, classes, and sexual orientations.

Part Three of the book considers the application of each of the paradigms introduced in Part Two to issues of societal concern. Chapter 8 focuses on the psychology of men in relationships. These include parenting relationships, intimate relationships, and relationships with friends. Here we consider relationships as a dynamic system in which men both learn masculinity from the top down and construct masculinity from the bottom up. For instance, masculinities affect what kinds of friendships men make and how willing men are to form close friendships. Those friendships, be they intimate, distant, or teasing, in turn shape what men think of as masculinity. Throughout this chapter, we underscore that men are not "doomed" to form particular kinds of relationships because of masculinity by highlighting research that shows the many ways that men's relationships defy stereotypes of themselves as independent and non-relational.

Chapter 9 focuses on violence and aggression. The overwhelming majority of violent crime is committed by men, and the overwhelming majority of men are not violent. In what sense, then, is a psychology of men and masculinity implicated in societal violence? To answer this we consider the ways aggression and dominance have been identified as recurrent themes in each of the perspectives covered in Part Two. For example, dominance and aggression play central roles in the social learning and social construction of masculinity, and, from a feminist perspective, they can also be understood as overt forms of oppression and control. We pay particular attention to the way questions about men's violence and its causes and cures are discussed in the media.

Chapter 10 focuses on men's mental and physical health, including theory and research linking certain gender ideologies to depression, suicide, substance abuse, coronary disease, and men's relative lack of health-promotion and help-seeking behaviors. We draw heavily from empirical research, and also from case studies, clinical anecdotes, and real-world examples. The chapter also includes consideration of how the theories and perspectives covered in Part Two are leveraged in current debates about men's well-being.

Part Four includes two concluding chapters. Research on the psychology of men and masculinity comes from a wide range of philosophical and methodological frameworks. Chapter 11 gives readers the opportunity to dig deeper into questions of ontology (what exactly is "masculinity"?), epistemology (what counts as valid knowledge about men and masculinity?), and additional considerations in the philosophy of science. For more curious and ambitious readers this chapter could potentially be read first in order to provide a broader perspective on the issues covered in the previous chapters. Alternatively, it may serve as a sort of capstone for the previous sections.

The final chapter attempts to address the perennial question, "what can I do about all of this?" We begin by providing readers with an opportunity to assess their own beliefs and assumptions, and values regarding men and masculinity. This is followed by specific cognitive, behavioral, and interpersonal strategies that can be used to make changes in how one views themselves and/or men in their lives. The second part of the chapter considers resources that can help people to stand up and oppose sexist, homophobic, and other oppressive social forces in their lives.

Throughout the book you will find sections entitled, "For Consideration." Our goal here is to give you an opportunity to consider the personal and societal relevance of various theories and research findings in the psychology of men. There are no right answers to these questions and we encourage you to approach them as food for thought rather than a test. You may even want to discuss them with friends or family members, as many of our students have done over the years.

Finally, when reflecting on these issues, we hope that you see the psychology of men in your own personal context. Our own experiences are part and parcel of working in this field. They are also part of the reason we are so captivated by studying the psychology of men. We hope the same is true for you.

References

American Psychological Association (APA) (2007). Guidelines for psychological practice with girls and women. *American Psychologist, 62*(9), 949–979.
American Psychological Association (APA) (2012). Guidelines for psychological practice with lesbian, gay, and bisexual clients. *American Psychologist, 67*(1), 10–42.

American Psychological Association (APA) (2017). *Multicultural guidelines: an ecological approach to context, identity, and intersectionality.* Retrieved from: www.apa.org/about/policy/multicultural-guidelines.pdf.

American Psychological Association (APA) (2018). *APA guidelines for psychological practice with boys and men.* Retrieved from: www.apa.org/about/policy/psychological-practice-boys-men-guidelines.pdf.

American Psychological Association (APA) (2019). A closer look at the APA guidelines for psychological practice with boys and men [news release]. Retrieved from: www.apa.org/news/apa/2019/boys-men-look.

Bruce, T. (2019, January 10). 'Traditional masculinity' is harmful, could lead to homophobia and sexual harassment, Psychological Association says [television broadcast]. *Fox and Friends.* Retrieved from: https://video.foxnews.com/v/5987884895001/#sp=show-clips.

Coleman, P. A. (2019, January 14). The APA says traditional masculinity hurts boys. Of course it does. *Fatherly.* Retrieved from: www.fatherly.com/love-money/apa-traditional-masculinity-hurts-boys-men.

Dreher, R. (2019, January 7). Manhood as mental disorder. *American Conservative.* Retrieved from: www.theamericanconservative.com/dreher/manhood-as-mental-disorder.

Grohol, J. M. (2019, January 24). Men can take it: reactions to the APA guidelines on men and boys. *Psych Central.* Retrieved from: https://psychcentral.com/blog/men-can-take-it-reactions-to-apas-guidelines-on-boys-men.

Levant, R. F. & Wong, Y. (2017). *The psychology of men and masculinities.* Washington, DC: American Psychological Association.

Matlin, M. W. (1989). Teaching psychology of women: a survey of instructors. *Psychology of Women Quarterly, 13*(3), 245–261.

O'Neil, J. M. & Renzulli, S. (2013). Introduction to the special section: teaching the psychology of men—a call to action. *Psychology of Men & Masculinity, 14*(3), 221–229.

Pruet, J. (2019, January 8). New American Psychological Association guidelines declare 'traditional masculinity' harmful to boys and men. *The Blaze.* Retrieved from: www.theblaze.com/news/masculinity-harmful-to-men.

Russo, N. F. (1982). Psychology of women: analysis of the faculty and courses of an emerging field. *Psychology of Women Quarterly, 7*(1), 18–31.

2

HISTORY OF THE PSYCHOLOGY OF MEN AND MASCULINITIES

*M*uscles are in a most intimate and peculiar sense the organs of the will. *They have built all the roads, cities, and machines in the world, written all the books, spoken all the words, and, in fact, done everything that man has accomplished with matter. If they are undeveloped or grow relaxed and flabby, the dreadful chasm between good intentions and their execution is liable to appear and widen.*

(G. Stanley Hall, 1905, p. 131)

*I*t has a name almost as distasteful as the practice itself. It is manspreading, *the lay-it-all-out sitting style that more than a few men see as their inalienable underground right. Now passengers ... have a new ally: the Metropolitan Transportation Authority. Taking on manspreading for the first time, the authority is set to unveil public service ads that encourage men to share a little less of themselves in the city's ever-crowded subways cars ... Women have theories about why some men sit this way. Some believe it is just a matter of comfort and may not even be intentional. Others consider it an assertion of power, or worse.*

(Emma G. Fitzsimmons, *New York Times*, 2014)

For Consideration

After finishing the chapter, try rereading the two quotes at the beginning. In what ways are "men" or "man" discussed similarly or differently in the scene from 2014 compared with G. Stanley Hall's writing in 1905?

Introduction

From "manspreading" on the subway to "mansplaining" at the dive bar, from men's rights movements to men's health specialists: men and masculinity are subject to extensive focus in the modern world. In psychology, scholarship on masculinity has exploded since the late 1980s. This explosion has produced research on a diverse landscape of topics: the factors that influence men's violence (Kilmartin & McDermott, 2016; Moore & Stuart, 2005), the reasons why men are reluctant to go to the doctor (Addis & Hoffman, 2017; Addis & Mahalik, 2003; Good & Wood, 1995; Hammer, Vogel, & Heimerdinger-Edwards, 2013), and the ways that boys police other boys' masculinity (Adams, Anderson, & McCormack, 2010; Reigeluth & Addis, 2016) are just a few of the examples.

In a sense, men have always been in psychology. After all, research conducted *by* male scholars dominated psychology historically. Nevertheless, research *on* men—as a distinct category of human beings—is relatively new. In this chapter, we will see the crucial intellectual developments that have, over the last century and a half, led men to become increasingly visible subjects of interest to psychology. In addition, we will see how psychology has radically transformed how it thinks about masculinity. Until the 1970s, psychology viewed masculinity as something *healthy* for men. But since the 1970s, one of the few uniting ideas in the psychology of men and masculinity—a field riddled with different perspectives—has been the notion that traditional masculinity can be *harmful* for men and the people around them (Addis, Mansfield, & Syzdek, 2010; Levant, 1996).

It's not just psychology that has changed. As a society, we have also changed the way we view men and masculinity. In fact, our whole vocabulary has shifted. We didn't used to have a language to talk about men's *gender*, social *roles* (see Chapter 4), *social construction* (see Chapter 5), or *patriarchy* (see Chapter 6). And even where the language was the same, the ideas could be radically different. While Americans at the turn of the last century did use words like "manhood" and "manliness," like social scientists at the time, they thought that maleness was the natural and healthy expression of men's biological makeup.

This change in popular discourse is illustrated by an 1899 letter that Theodore Roosevelt wrote to G. Stanley Hall, the founder of the then newly formed American Psychological Association (APA). Roosevelt expressed his concerns to Hall that, as modernity swept across the United States, manliness was slowly eroding away. Roosevelt lamented:

O*ver-sentimentality, over-softness, in fact, washiness and mushiness are the great dangers of this age and of this people ... I feel we cannot too strongly insist upon the need of the rough, manly virtues. A nation that* *cannot fight is not worth its salt, no matter how cultivated and refined it might be.*

(Roosevelt, 1899)

There are several historical lessons we can draw from Roosevelt's words. First, they show how Roosevelt defined masculinity: something "rough" and not at all "mushy." But, more deeply, they also reflect the male-centric perspective dominant at the time. For instance, notice how Roosevelt points to "the people" but does not mention "men" specifically. A contemporary reader would not have batted an eye at the use of words such as "man," "mankind," and "humanity" as synonyms; until the late 20th century, the word "man" was used generically for all human beings (Miller & Swift, 1976). The same things that, from Roosevelt's perspective, made for good men, also made for a good citizenry.

As you can see, there have been dramatic shifts in the ways society has portrayed men and masculinity over the last hundred years. While maleness used to be widely interchangeable with humanness, masculinity is now portrayed as a distinct gender expression. While manhood was once almost universally taken as a virtue, it is now critiqued and problematized. These changes don't merely reflect whimsical changes in popular opinion. They should instead be considered alongside broader changes in economics, politics, family structures, and social scientific research on men and masculinity.

This chapter will provide historical context to help make sense out of the present day psychology of men and masculinity. We begin by discussing historiography—that is, the way that history is written. We then review key historical developments in psychology, such as psychoanalysis, sex differences research, MF scales, Bem's androgyny studies, as well as broader social movements like second-wave feminism and the men's liberation movement. We'll see how these movements, as well as Bem's research, marked a major turning point for the field and ushered in what scholars call the "new psychology of men." We conclude the chapter by examining some backlash to men's liberation, tracing the development of the psychology of men and masculinity as a distinct subfield within psychology, and by considering some new directions in which the field has moved over the last 20 years.

History (in Context)

Many students of science might question the value of examining the history of their field, let alone its *historiography*. After all, isn't the point of science exactly to overturn past misconceptions? Why should we care about the past or about how it is written?

Science, psychology included, is commonly looked at as promising slow and steady progress towards capital "T" Truth. In historiographic terms, this kind of scientific progress narrative is called **presentist** history. Presentism is also sometimes referred to as "heroic" historiography, because such narratives tend to center on individual scientists who get depicted as pushing the envelope forward through their intellectual prowess or creativity. You are probably familiar with this style of writing history, since it is the default for most textbooks in psychology. For example, David Myers' blockbuster introductory textbook (2010) focuses on particular figures, like B. F. Skinner, as instrumental agents in generating intellectual traditions like behaviorism (another classic example is Boring, 1929).

In the specialized field of *history of psychology*, however, presentism has fallen largely out of favor. Instead, the field favors what might be called a **contextualist** historiography. This approach examines things like the political, economic, cultural, and broader intellectual context of psychology. Instead of focusing on *great men*, these historians highlight more marginalized voices in psychology—women psychologists or racial minority psychologists, for example. Most importantly, these historians are less interested in using history to celebrate the apparent progress of psychology, and more interested in using history to critically unpack some of psychology's bedrock assumptions—such as the ideas that psychologists can be objective and separate from the phenomena that they study, or that those phenomena (masculinity included) are *universal*—unchanging across time and space (Furumoto, 1989). Critical, contextualist history shows that much of what psychology studies actually changes in fairly radical ways over time. But this dynamism can be very hard to appreciate without taking a bird's-eye view.

A metaphor is instructive here. Consider the Himalayas. To someone without knowledge of geology, mountain ranges like the Himalayas seem completely permanent and unchanging across time. People of past eras must have struggled to understand how they were formed. Divine intervention would have seemed like the only plausible explanation.

Now imagine that we had a videotape of the Himalayas that condensed the last 50 million years into ten minutes. The human lifespan is so short that any single person, indeed, any single culture will only see but one frame of the entire videotape. As far as we are concerned, the video is for all intents and purposes paused. But imagine, for the sake of argument, that you could press play on this video of the Himalayas, and then speed it up so that a hundred thousand years were condensed into a single second. All of a sudden, the Himalayas wouldn't seem so unchanging. In fact they might look more like a fluid—rippling, bending, and melting as millennia of geologic forces unfold in the blink of an eye. It is likely that if geologists of past centuries magically had access to such a video they would have discovered the importance of erosion, glaciation, and plate tectonics to mountain formation far sooner. But, in the "pause view" to which we are limited, those dynamic forces are much harder to see.

The psychology of men and masculinity might be very much like the Himalayas. Masculinity may, to the untrained eye, appear to be innate and unchanging. However, examining the psychology of men and masculinity through a historical lens can offer a unique and valuable perspective on the phenomenon of masculinity that would be unavailable in the still frame.

In the story we tell below about the psychology of men and masculinity, we do employ some presentist tropes. But we also have contextualist concerns about the *intermeshing of society and psychology*. As scholarly concepts of masculinity have emerged and shifted, so too has the public's grasp of these concepts—and vice versa. In other words, it is not only psychologists that have had a stake in psychological research and practice on men and masculinity. For example, Stanley Milgram's studies of obedience triggered a wave of concerns that the American male of the 1960s was too deferent to authority, ripe for subservience to a fascist or communist government should one emerge in the United States (Nicholson, 2011). In other words, Milgram's research was not just a contribution to the psychology of social influence. His research was used in newspaper op-eds and speeches calling for men to reject complacency and act instead as "free standing individuals" (Nicholson, 2011, p. 262). Findings of psychological research get discussed outside of psychology, and potentially can alter the very phenomena that psychology studies, a theme we return to in Chapters 6 and 11. And when psychological research on men and masculinity gets taken up in public discourse, psychology changes the very face of masculinity.

Everywhere and Nowhere: A Psychology (of Men) at the Turn of the 20th Century

In the year 1899, when Theodore Roosevelt wrote the letter to G. Stanley Hall quoted above, psychology was a relatively new social science. For context, in 1899 the APA—then just 125 members strong—celebrated the organization's seventh birthday (Benjamin, 1988), and the first psychological research laboratory, founded by Wilhelm Wundt, was only 20 years old (Benjamin, 1988).

Psychology in 1899 reflected the gender politics of the society in which it was embedded. The field was dominated almost exclusively by men, with many obstacles placed in front of aspiring female psychologists. In 1895, at Harvard University, Mary Whiton Calkins (who would go on to become the APA's first woman president in 1905) defended her doctoral dissertation in psychology. A highly esteemed psychologist visiting from Germany, Hugo Münsterberg, called her "one of the strongest professors of psychology in this country" (Münsterberg, 1894). But although she had completed all the requirements, Harvard denied her the degree and insisted that she could only receive a degree from Radcliffe College, Harvard's all-women affiliate (Furumoto, 1980).

For much of the early years of psychology, men were paradoxically both at the center of research and at its periphery. In one sense, men were everywhere. Research was overwhelmingly carried out by men, research subjects were predominantly male, and, inevitably, men's ideas dominated the field (Morawski, 1985; Shields, 1975). In another sense, men *as men*, men as a unique category of people, were absent from the picture. American psychologists strove to document the psychology of Black Americans (Morawski, 2004; Patrick & Sims, 1934; Richards, 2003), homosexuals (Hegarty, 2003; Herek, 2010), criminals (Schuessler & Cressey, 1950) and women (Shields, 1975; Terman, Johnson, Kuznets, & McNemar, 1946; Woolley, 1910), but men were never studied as a group that might have its own unique psychology. Instead men tended to appear only as the norm to which these other groups were compared.

Psychoanalysis and Masculine Sexual Identity

Ten years after Roosevelt's letter arrived in G. Stanley Hall's mailbox, Hall received another letter, one that would profoundly shape how subsequent generations of American psychologists would understand masculinity. The letter he received was from Sigmund Freud—then a somewhat obscure Austrian neurologist—accepting an invitation to present a series of lectures at Clark University. Freud's Clark lectures would introduce the American psychiatric and psychological communities to Freud's intellectual brainchild: psychoanalysis.

Before delving into Freud's take on masculinity, let's get some background on the psychoanalytic perspective he was writing from. *Psychoanalysis* was developed by Freud and his mentor, Josef Breuer, as an approach to treating patients whose symptoms could not be explained by any physical problems (Freud & Breuer, 2004). Freud understood these psychiatric symptoms as the result of repressed, deep-seated psychological conflicts. For example, imagine a young boy whose father has for years yelled at him for being "pathetic" or "unmanly" because he's reluctant to play sports. This verbal abuse might cause the boy to develop feelings of anger or even hatred towards his father. But these feelings would conflict with other aspects of the boy's experience—his attachment to his father, his fear of what might happen were he to disobey his father, or his identification with his father as a role model. Freud argued that our minds manage these kinds of internal conflicts through defense mechanisms such as repression, projection, and sublimation. For some people, Freud thought, these defense mechanisms can become dysfunctional and cause severe psychological distress. He argued that those individuals might be helped through psychoanalysis to develop insight into these conflicts.

Freud soon developed his ideas from a clinical approach into a full-blown theory of human personality, one in which sexual identity played a central role. Freud posed the highly provocative hypothesis that human sexuality was present from birth; that the germ for later adult expressions of sexuality lay in the child's desire for reconnection with the mother. This desire inevitably gets upended by realizing that the father stands in the way of the boy's desire. Freud explained, "It is the fate of all of us, perhaps, to direct our first sexual impulse towards our mother and our first hatred and our first murderous wish against our father" (Freud, 1955, p. 262). Freud believed that defense mechanisms were needed to quash an internal conflict between desire for the mother and fear of the father's retaliation (which he called the fear of castration). He held that only by repressing this *Oedipal complex* could the boy come to identify with the father and begin to acquire a truly male identity.

The boy's *fear of castration* at the hands of the father is particularly central to Freud's theory of sexual identity. Therefore, his distinction between male and female sexual development necessarily hinged on biological "facts": boys have a penis to lose, whereas girls do not. In other words, Freud thought that boys naturally develop a male sexual identity because they possess male genitalia, and women naturally develop a female sexual identity because they have female genitalia. Freud believed that, unlike boys, girls experience penis envy, which sets the stage for later female sexual development.

There are several key takeaways from Freud's thinking. First, it is illustrative of his social context. Like many of his contemporaries, Freud's thinking was androcentric: he took the male experience as a stand-in for the experience of all human beings. For example, his theory of the Oedipus complex centered on the development of sexuality in boys. In contrast, he wrote that female sexual development was "a dark continent for psychology" (Freud, 1926/1959, p. 212), although his hunch was that the process was analogous to the process he observed in boys. Freud's concept of sexual identity is also important because it laid the groundwork for later research on masculinity and femininity with putatively "objective" psychological tests. But before turning to those tests of masculinity, we set the stage with a brief overview of research that compared women with men: studies of sex differences.

Sex Differences

The increasing influence of evolutionary theorizing in early 20th-century psychology brought questions of sex differences to the fore. From an evolutionary perspective, there was a clear rationale for comparing men and women. In the 19th century, biologists documented impressive instances of sexual dimorphism in the animal kingdom, such as the nearly threefold difference in size between female and male Hawaiian garden spiders. These cases of sexual dimorphism were not easily explained by Darwin's theory of natural selection (1859). Darwin's critics therefore challenged him to explain why seemingly useless sexual differentiation, such as the male peacock's impressively ornamented plumage, might emerge (Argyll, 1867). Darwin's solution to this seeming puzzle? The theory of *sexual selection*: that sexual dimorphic features function to increase an individual's chances of reproductive success (see Chapter 3 as well).

This evolutionary logic, when applied to describing human society in the early 20th century, suggested that personality and behavioral differences between men and women were "natural," that is, calibrated over generations of sexual selection. Simply put, the evolutionary logic is that men and women differ the way they do because, evolutionarily speaking, that is most advantageous to our fitness as a species. But what went unquestioned was whether sex *differences* were a good starting point for studying men and women's sex.

From the turn of the last century to the 1920s, hundreds of studies were carried out investigating differences between men and women. These included, for example, comparisons between men and women's associative thinking, sexual appetite, and motor speed as measured by tapping on a telegraph key (Minton, 1986; Morawski, 1985; Woolley, 1910). What these studies found surprised many observers. Few sex differences were detected. And of those that were found, most were very subtle. Many seemed to slightly favor women (Morawski, 1985). The largest differences that were found tended to be in terms of attitudes or behaviors that were more clearly "sociological" than biological (Woolley, 1910, p. 10), for instance, that women preferred to tie "decorative" knots while men preferred to tie "hard" knots (Acher, 1910). Most strikingly, researchers repeatedly found that the variation *among* men and women far outpaced differences *between* men and women.

Despite inconsistent evidence of meaningful psychological differences between men and women, prominent scholars continued to argue that men were superior in numerous domains. Helen Thompson Woolley, the author of the first study of sex differences in psychology (1903), was unsparing in her criticism of this research. She wrote, "There is perhaps no field aspiring to be scientific where flagrant personal bias, logic martyred in the cause of supporting a prejudice, unfounded assertions, and even sentimental rot and drivel, have run riot to such an extent as here" (Woolley, 1910, p. 340). Whether driven by prejudice or not, the search for sexual differences continued to dominate the field.

In the 1930s, however, some changes began to emerge. In particular, the influx of Freudian notions of sexual identity into American psychology and a growing body of research on men's "sexual inversion" (Burton, 1947; Ellis, 1900) opened powerful new methodological and theoretical tool kits for psychologists interested in men and women. These developments began to usher in the idea that people possessed sex roles that were (1) separable from biological sex, (2) continuous rather than binary, and (3) measurable using simple questionnaires.

Measuring Sex Role Identification: The M–F Scales and Male Inverts

In present-day psychology, we might understand "sexual identity" or "sex role" as more or less synonymous with "gender." However, in the early 20th century, "sexual identity" and "sex role" did not mean what we today mean by "gender." Following after Freud, psychologists in the 1930s thought of *sex role identification* as the individual's acquisition of the traits appropriate for their biological sex. Those traits tended to get defined in terms of what (White, middle-class) men in the 1930s were stereotypically like: "powerful, strenuous, active, steady, strong, self-confident, with preference for machinery, athletics, working for self, and the external/public life" (Morawski, 1985, p. 212). These stereotypical norms were also taken as ideal—the epitome of healthy sexual development. In other words, well-adjusted men were expected to be masculine, and well-adjusted women were expected to be feminine. When these expectations were violated and men failed to develop the male sex role, it indicated that some pathological process was at play. Men who were not like typical men were seen not only as different: they were deficient or *"inverted."*

The question of measuring male inversion, that is, homosexuality, was a timely concern in broader society during the first half of the 20th century. In the military, generals and recruiting officers were wary of inducting homosexual men into their ranks, fearing their presence would prove corrosive to military units' cohesion. Within the mental health system, homosexuality was also a topic of major interest. Until 1973, psychiatry's canonical system of categorizing psychopathology, the *Diagnostic and Statistical Manual of Mental Disorders*, classified homosexuality as a mental disorder. In addition to viewing homosexuality as a disorder in its own right, psychiatrists and psychoanalysts considered it a risk factor for other disorders. Thus, in the military, psychiatry, and elsewhere, there was a growing demand for identifying homosexuals. Institutions needed an effective, objective way of measuring sexual orientation, a way that was both predictive and covert—because of the stigma, the expectation was that few men would openly report homosexuality. The emerging field of psychological assessment promised just such a solution to this conundrum.

Lewis Terman and *Catherine Cox Miles'* Attitude-Interest Analysis Test (AIST; 1936) was the first scale to measure sex-related attributes. They conceptualized sex characteristics as a single variable moving along a continuum of *masculinity–femininity (M–F)*. To measure masculinity-femininity, they had subjects complete multiple-choice items across seven subtests. For example, Terman and Miles counted as masculine a response of "no" to questions such as "Do you like to have people tell you their troubles?" (Morawski, 1985, p. 205). Terman and Miles' scale was followed up by similar M–F self-report scales. Within a few years, the projective M–F Scale of the Vocational Interest Blank (VIB; Strong, 1936), the M–F Scale on the Minnesota Multiphasic Personality Inventory (MMPI; Hathaway & McKinley, 1943), and the Rorschach inkblot test (Hegarty, 2003; Rorschach, 1921) were all being used to differentiate individuals along a spectrum of masculinity to femininity.

While piloting the scale, Terman and Miles noted the case of a gifted child who scored high on femininity and who also happened to manifest *"sexual inversion"*—as homosexuality was often labeled in psychology and psychiatry in the early to mid-20th century (Morawski, 1985). Why "inversion?" Homosexuality was viewed as an "inversion" precisely because homosexuality was thought to map onto a reversal of appropriate sex role attributes. Masculinity and attraction to women were seen as synonymous. In other words, heterosexual males were thought to be masculine, and homosexual males were thought to be feminine. This assumption was so taken for granted that Terman and Miles touted the fact that the M–F scale could discriminate between homosexuals and non-homosexuals as evidence of the scale's validity (Minton, 1986). Terman and Miles were not outliers in viewing sex role identification as inseparable from sexual orientation: the MMPI's M–F scale was also validated on a sample of homosexuals (Shields & Dicicco, 2011). Thus, instruments such as the AIST, VIB, and MMPI's M–F scales were applied to detecting "latent homosexuals" in prisons (Burton, 1947; Walker, 1941), in hospitals (Minton, 1986), and in the military (Doidge & Holtzman, 1960); although additional research showed that these scales actually were quite poor in detecting homosexuality (Burton, 1947; Doidge & Holtzman, 1960).

The application of the MMPI, VIB, and AIST scales to screening for homosexuality underscores two key historical points. First, it shows that psychology historically defined masculinity as a set of characteristics that were the *natural and expected product of development*. Second, the use of the M–F scale to measure male inversion shows that psychology historically defined masculinity *in terms of what masculinity is (supposedly) not*, since the use of M–F scales for measuring homosexuality relies on the assumption that homosexuality is *opposite* to masculinity. Third, even though psychologists such as Terman and Miles were trying to discover *objective* facts about masculinity and femininity, the dominant values of the society they lived in and beliefs about what is normal and abnormal shaped both the nature of their research and the way that research was put to use.

From Sex Roles to Gender Roles

In the 1960s and 1970s, cracks in the M–F paradigm became increasingly apparent. In particular, there was growing skepticism over whether sex role identification was a one-dimensional construct: a continuum with masculinity anchored at one end and femininity at the other. In a landmark review of key M–F scales such as the AIST and MMPI, Anne Constantinople (1973) argued that psychometric research had failed to produce convincing evidence that masculinity and femininity were two sides to the same coin. Constantinople proposed that psychologists would actually be better off measuring masculinity and femininity as *separate* constructs, to leave room for the possibility that there might also be people who show high masculinity *and* high femininity (or individuals who do score low on both). *Sandra Bem* (1974; 1975) would soon take up this call in her research on androgyny and the development of the *Bem Sex Role Inventory* (BSRI).

Just as Constantinople (1973) had recommended, the BSRI was constructed with separate scales for masculinity and for femininity. In this regard alone, Bem's scale represented a theoretical shift from the earlier M–F scales, which had conceived of masculinity–femininity as a single construct. But Bem's new scale also came with a distinctly feminist political message. In her writing, Bem made her views explicit, declaring that the "system of sex role differentiation … serves only to prevent both men and women from developing as full and complete human beings" (1975, p. 634). Her research found that individuals scoring high on *both* masculinity and femininity tended to show the most adaptability to situational demands (1975). This was a profound shift from the thinking that underlay research with the M–F scales. Bem did not view men's strict adherence to masculinity as healthy—she viewed these sex roles, in fact, as *unhealthy* when exercised rigidly. Instead, Bem advocated a flexible mixture of masculinity and femininity: *androgyny.*

Even before Bem's landmark research, *second-wave feminism* had been making inroads within academic psychology and the broader culture, something we discuss in more detail in Chapter 6. For now, we'll focus on just one book. *Simone De Beauvoir's* (1960/1949) *The Second Sex* is widely considered second-wave feminism's founding document. Her book contains a number of critiques aimed at earlier psychological scholarship on women and femininity. For instance, De Beauvoir argued that while Freud built a detailed account of male sexual development (including concepts like the Oedipal complex), he uncritically "adapted" (De Beauvoir, 1960, p. 66) this model to account for women's sexual development. More generally, De Beauvoir argued, social science had taken the male experience as the starting point. Women were defined as an Other—in contrast to the supposedly universal male. She posited that this fundamental asymmetry in scholarship on masculinity and femininity paralleled and maintained a larger system of economic, political, and social inequality between men and women.

In psychology, feminist scholars' attention to power relations between men and women made them question not just earlier generations' research on sex differences and the unequal representation of women in academic and professional psychology—it also caused them to rethink the very way that sex roles had been conceptualized. In particular, they critiqued the idea that sex roles either directly or indirectly resulted from genitalia or biological sex. As De Beauvoir wrote, "one is not born, but rather becomes a woman" (De Beauvoir, 1960, p. 301). De Beauvoir and those inspired by her work made a sharp distinction between biological sex and gender. For her, gender (unlike biological sex) did not emerge from *within*. Instead gender came from *without*—imposed *on* the individual *by* society. These socialized and constructed gender roles, she argued, helped fuel inequality between men and women.

There are several takeaway points from second wave feminism's contribution to psychology. First, feminists argued that gender roles imposed by society were distinct from biological sex and they disputed the idea that an individual's gender emerged naturally from their biology. Second, feminism overturned the idea that masculinity was healthy for men and that femininity was healthy for women. Third, asymmetrical power relations between men and women became a key concept for understanding gender more broadly. Fourth, and finally, through the 1960s and 1970s feminist scholars became increasingly less interested in thinking of gender as a set of individual-level traits—instead, their attention was drawn to what gender *does*, how men behaving like men and women behaving like women kept the patriarchy in place.

At first, these ideas were not applied to men's experience. But, after several decades of research, a social movement related to feminism—the men's liberation movement—brought these notions into psychological research on men.

Men's Liberation

As we saw in the previous section, feminists offered a significant and subversive reconceptualization of women's gender. Beginning in the early 1970s, feminism also provoked a growing concern with men's gender. This concern consolidated into the men's liberation movement—a name that evoked similar progressive social movements such as women's liberation and black liberation. Men's liberation activists read books such as Warren

Farrell's *The Liberated Man* (1974), which documented masculinity as an overly rigid and limiting social role. These authors and their followers viewed overturning traditional standards of masculinity as part and parcel of women's liberation (Messner, 1998).

One particularly notable leader of the men's liberation movement was Chicago-based psychologist *Jack Sawyer*. By the time he was getting involved in men's liberation, Sawyer had already established himself as a prominent psychologist. He had worked for the United States Army and taught at the University of Chicago, where he received both Rockefeller and National Science Foundation fellowships (Sawyer, 2001). And although he originally specialized in clinical and industrial psychology, Sawyer became increasingly interested in the application of psychology to contemporary social issues such as racism and sexism over the course of the 1960s. In 1970, he led a workshop on "The Male Liberation Movement," the first of its kind, and later that year became the first person to publish on "men's liberation" in a scholarly or popular outlet.

Sawyer (1974) sought to enlist men in women's struggle for liberation and equality and to dispute the notion that this battle would necessarily be "a battle *against* men as oppressors. The choice about whether men are the enemy is up to men themselves" (emphasis added, p. 171). Just as Sawyer highlighted inequities between the sexes, he also saw inequality in relations *between* men. Sawyer argued that "part of the price most men pay for being dominant in one situation is subscribing to a system in which they themselves are subordinated in another situation" (p. 171). For Sawyer, the systems of power that kept gay, working-class, and other assumedly non-masculine men subordinate to straight, wealthy, and masculine men could only be understood in connection with men's domination of women. Therefore, men's participation in women's liberation was necessary for achieving men's liberation.

Even as men's liberation gained increasing political visibility, research on masculinity was a largely invisible topic within the psychology of gender for much of the 1970s and 1980s. Indeed, in social science more broadly, the field of gender studies was often taken to be synonymous with "women's studies" (Brooks & Elder, 2016). Although critiques of the male sex role as contradictory and problematic appeared as early as 1959 (Hartley, 1959), it was not until the work of Joseph Pleck (1981) and Robert Brannon (1976) that research critical of traditional masculinity became more widespread within psychology. Pleck and Brannon, like Bem before them, insisted that the gender roles into which men were socialized were unhealthy, both for individual men and for society as a whole.

Joseph Pleck's biography is an illustrative case study in the emergence of the men's liberation movement and the birth of the "new psychology of men" (Levant, 1996). By the late 1960s, the American New Left was in full force, mobilized against the backdrop of the rapidly escalating protest movement against the Vietnam War, the civil rights movement, and second-wave feminism. Nowhere were these movements so prominent as among college students. The counterculture, with its intellectual currents of feminism and social reform, were in full force in Cambridge, Massachusetts by the late 1960s, when Pleck began his undergraduate studies at Harvard University. The year he received his bachelor's degree, 1968, saw the first published use of the word "sexism" (Shapiro, 1985).

Pleck reflected the growing concern for social justice within academia. As a senior, he assisted on a project exploring the racial dynamics of bussing integration (Blum, 1968). He began focusing on masculinity in 1971, when Harvard's psychology department hosted Jack Sawyer as a visiting scholar. Sawyer and Pleck began collaborating, and together organized a "Male Liberation Festival" event on campus (Paoletti, 2015). Their collaboration eventually resulted in an edited volume, *Men and Masculinity* (1974), which was the first significant scholarly publication focused on the social science of men and masculinity. This publication was soon followed up by Brannon's (1976) analysis of the male sex role and Pleck's **The Myth of Masculinity** (Pleck 1981), which laid out the groundwork for the gender role strain paradigm and the new psychology of men (Messner, 1998).

The perspective that Pleck, Sawyer and others associated with the men's liberation movement brought to academic psychology constituted a radical break with the past. In the same way that feminist psychologists had critiqued traditional femininity, so the men's liberation movement saw masculinity not as an essential psychological characteristic of all healthy males, but as a highly problematic, rigid, and harmful social role imposed on men by patriarchal society that privileged men over women. It is this last notion—the idea that gender was fundamentally interconnected with patriarchy, power, and women's subordination to men—that would soon sow the seeds for the disintegration of the men's liberation movement.

Backlash

Since the late 1970s, the men's liberation movement has fractured into three offshoots: the mythopoetic men's movement, the pro-feminist men's movement, and the anti-feminist men's rights movement (Connell, 2005). All three movements share in common a belief that masculinity is in crisis. But they diverge in the solutions they put forward as well as the causes they attribute to this crisis. Because the pro-feminist men's movement will be discussed in relation to feminist frameworks within the psychology of men and masculinity in Chapter 6, we limit detailed discussion here to the mythopoetic men's movements and the men's rights movement.

The **mythopoetic men's movement** grew out of concern about masculinity as a source of patients' distress. Therapists coming from a men's liberation perspective aspired to move their clients towards a more androgynous gender role. Members of the mythopoetic men's movement, in contrast, urge a connection with a "deep masculine," taking inspiration from folklore, poetry, and particularly the writings of Robert Bly. These mythopoetic therapists and affiliated activists see masculinity as having been deformed from its former ideal by modern social upheaval. For example, they worry that the absence of traditional coming of age rituals and the evaporation of blue collar jobs is eroding classical masculine virtues (Kimmel & Kaufman, 1994). People in the mythopoetic men's movement reject the notion favored by pro-feminists that masculinity should be deconstructed, instead viewing the "deep masculine" as a valuable resource (Connell, 2005) that can be tapped into, often by reconnecting with men in all-male settings.

The *men's rights movement* also departs in substantial ways from the earlier men's liberation movement. But their disagreement with feminist critiques goes much further than the mythopoetic men's movement does. For example, while pro-feminists are likely to view the negative facets of masculinity as the direct or indirect result of men's participation in a patriarchal society, men's rights activists view masculinity per se as unproblematic, and instead cast blame on *feminists* for undermining men's position within society. Presently organized through online forums such as Reddit and 4Chan, men's rights activists organize around topics such as prejudice against fathers in divorce cases, unfair treatment of male victims of domestic violence, and, above all, what they deem to be feminist hypocrisy. They dispute outright the idea of male privilege, arguing instead that women hold the real power. Although the men's rights movement differs from the mythopoetic men's movement and has sharp political differences with the men's liberation movement, there is one key similarity that unites these movements: a collective awareness of men *as men*.

For Consideration

What patterns do you see reoccurring throughout the history of the psychology of men and masculinity?

The New Psychology of Men

The bulk of present-day researchers in the psychology of men and masculinity trace their heritage to the men's liberation movement and, specifically, Pleck (1995) and Brannon's (1976) scholarship (Wong, Steinfeldt, Speight, & Hickman, 2010). They extended Pleck's (1995) gender role strain paradigm by developing scales that measure constructs like gender role stress (Eisler & Skidmore, 1987), male gender role conflict (O'Neil, Helms, Gable, David, & Wrightsman, 1986), masculine ideology (Thompson & Pleck, 1986), and conformity to masculine norms (Mahalik et al.,

2003), to name just a few. With these tools in hand, *the new psychology of men* has produced a wealth of knowledge on the correlates of male gender role socialization in terms of mental health outcomes, relationships, violent behavior, and a whole host of other variables.

As psychological research on men and masculinity accelerated during the late 1980s and early 1990s the field began to consolidate professionally. In 1995, the APA approved the creation of its 51st division, The Society for the Psychological Study of Men and Masculinity. And the psychology of men and masculinity has continued to grow in the 21st century. APA Division 51 launched its own journal in 2000, *Psychology of Men & Masculinity*. Psychologists of men and masculinity also publish in a variety of other gender and health-related journals in psychology and in affiliated disciplines. Professional conferences—such as APA's annual convention, the National Conference on Men and Masculinity, and the World Conference on Men's Health and Gender—consistently feature research and speakers from the psychology of men and masculinity (Brooks & Elder, 2016; Cochran, 2010).

Researchers in the new psychology of men inherited much from the men's liberation movement and, in turn, second wave feminism. And from its outset, the field has been aware of these roots. For instance, in its mission statement, Division 51 acknowledged "its historical debt to feminist-inspired scholarship on gender" (The Society for the Psychological Study of Men and Masculinity, 1995). The new psychology of men, for the most part, adopted the feminist distinction between biological sex and socially constructed or socially learned gender. And like men's liberation activists and scholars, researchers and practitioners in the new psychology of men were committed to helping free men from the constraints of traditional masculine gender roles and describing in detail the myriad harmful effects of masculinity. Moreover, like Bem's research, the new psychology of men has had a strong emphasis on objective psychological measurement and empirical research. The field has also departed from its feminist heritage in several ways. In particular, relatively little research has attended to men's privileges. In other words, while feminism asserts that men are both benefited and hurt by masculine gender roles, the new psychology of men has tended to focus primarily on the latter, on men's pain. In the process, the new psychology of men has taken an analysis of patriarchy out of central consideration.

What does the field look like today? The relationship of masculine gender role socialization to mental health, violence, and relationships have remained the dominant topics in journals such as *Psychology of Men & Masculinity* (Wong et al., 2010). Psychologists of men and masculinity have also expanded the field to study such diverse areas as fatherhood, men's body image, media depictions of men, and men's sexuality. Moreover, in recent years the field has witnessed an influx of more critical methodologies and theoretical frameworks. These new directions within the psychology of men and masculinity are discussed below.

For Consideration

In the present day, many psychological researchers study men specifically, while many other researchers study women specifically. What benefits and disadvantages are there to studying men and women separately?

Emerging Directions in the Psychology of Men and Masculinity

In the 1990s and early 2000s, the psychology of men and masculinity was dominated by quantitative, correlational research on the relationship between masculinity and various negative outcomes (Whorley & Addis, 2006). Today, studies examining the relationships of masculine norm adherence to other variables of interest continue to have a prominent seat at the methodological table. However, the field has also witnessed an increasing methodological diversity. Experimental research has become increasingly common. In addition, researchers attend more actively to the ways masculinity intersects with race, sexuality, and socio-economic status. Qualitative studies also appear with greater frequency in prominent journals like the *Psychology of Men & Masculinity*. Finally, some scholars have begun reconsidering the new psychology of men's negative view of masculinity, and have advocated a positive conceptualization.

Experimental Approaches

If we take the theory that masculinity is a learned set of behaviors seriously (see Chapter 4), this suggests the possibility that masculinity can be changed. Experimental manipulations of masculinity promise to do exactly that—to show how gender varies not only across men and women, and not only between men, but also varies within individual men, from situation to situation. What happens, for example, when you threaten masculinity? This is the question that researchers in the *precarious manhood* paradigm have asked (Vandello & Bosson, 2008). Across numerous laboratory studies, these researchers have shown that threatening men's masculinity can lead male research participants to enact various stereotypically masculine behaviors. For example, Vandello, Bosson, Cohen, Burnaford, and Weaver (2008) randomly assigned men to either engage in an ostensibly feminine task, braiding hair, or a gender-neutral but mechanically equivalent task, "rope strengthening." They hypothesized that men asked to braid hair would view this as a potential threat to their masculinity and would try to compensate by engaging in stereotypically masculine behavior. Bosson and colleagues found support for this hypothesis: when given the choice between solving a puzzle or punching a punching bag, men who had been in the hair-braiding condition were more likely than control subjects to want to participate in the stereotypically male punching activity. While precarious manhood research is only one experimental approach to the psychology of men and masculinity at present, it is one of the most prominent experimental paradigms within the field.

Multiple Masculinities

Within sociology, gender studies, anthropology, and increasingly psychology, scholarship has given greater visibility to *multiple masculinities* in recent years. This approach starts with the simple observation that not all men are alike. The idea is that men vary not only quantitatively, in the degree to which they endorse traditional masculine gender norms, and not only qualitatively, in terms of to which gender norms they ascribe. Men also vary in terms of a multiplicity of other identities: race, sexuality, class, and others. In other words, the ways masculinity enters the lives of gay, White, middle-class, American men should not be assumed to be identical to the ways it enters the lives of working-class, brown-skinned men in Central America. Multiple masculinities scholars argue that masculinity, considered on its own, is a total abstraction: nobody experiences being male in some pure "unadulterated" form. For example, the authors of this chapter, both White, middle-class, Jewish American men, have never experienced what it is like to be *just* men—we have only ever experienced our maleness in the simultaneous context of our Whiteness, Jewishness, Americanness, and middle-class background. As an approach to empirical research, the multiple masculinities perspective brings a valuable nuance to the social science of men and masculinity. We revisit these topics in detail in Chapter 7.

Multiple Masculinities and History

The multiple masculinities perspective can be used not only to inform empirical research, but also historiography—to help us think critically about dominant narratives. From a multiple masculinities perspective, the picture we've painted—that men's gender was once invisible and is now visible—is quite incomplete. It specifically ignores the experiences of certain groups of men, generally non-White, non-heterosexual, and non-middle class, whose masculinity *was* visible historically. For example, Bederman's (2008) history of race and gender in the United States of the early 20th century shows that Black men at the turn of the century were very much gendered. Specifically, Bederman shows that Black men were often caricatured in popular media as *hypermasculine*, and that this *hypermasculinization* was integral to racist rhetoric. Bederman's analysis reveals that the idea that men only became gendered with the advent of men's studies is not true for racial minorities.

This added complexity to the history of the field invites us to critically examine whether masculinity *really* has become visible for all men. Just as hypermasculinity in the early 20th century was typified by Black men, we might ask whether the contemporary idea of "traditional masculinity" represents all men, or rather particular socio-economic, racial, or political classes? Which men might still be invisible? For example, Wetherell and Edley (1999) have argued that traditional masculinity norms do not seem to capture the attributes of many men at the highest levels of power, such as Tony Blair or Barack Obama.

Discourse Analytic Approaches

Another development in the psychology of men and masculinity is the growth in qualitative research. For instance, methodologies such as thematic analysis, narrative analysis, *discourse analysis*, and interpretive phenomenological analysis (IPA) have become regular fixtures in psychological research on men (Wetherell & Edley, 2014). To illustrate in greater detail what these approaches look like with an example, let's take a closer look at discourse analysis.

Discourse analytic scholars study spoken and written language, using data that ranges from research interviews or focus groups, to popular media or academic texts such as journal articles or textbooks. Discourse analysis, philosophically, makes some big breaks with mainstream psychology. For example, instead of viewing language as a window into the mind, discourse analysis highlights the functional context of language. In other words, people use language in order to achieve particular ends (Wetherell & Potter, 1988). In the psychology of men and masculinity, discourse analysis focuses on both the discourses *of* men and discourses *about* men and masculinity. For example, Edley and Wetherell (1997) have used discourse analysis to examine the notion of the "new man," the idea that contemporary men profoundly reject traditional masculinity norms such as stoicism and dominance in favor of greater emotional openness and nurturing fathering.

In their research, Edley and Wetherell (1997) conducted interviews with a group of boys at an English boarding school. This group explicitly rejected the hypermasculine behavior of the popular, athletic "lads." At the same time, they also enacted traditional masculine norms in subtle ways (p. 209). For instance, these boys positioned themselves as, in a way, *stronger* than the lads: stronger intellectually rather than physically (p. 211). Similarly, the boys contrasted their own *emotional restraint* with the lads' quickness to violence. Through their careful, close reading of the schoolboys' talk, Edley and Wetherell show that these new, supposedly progressive forms of masculinity can also re-appropriate older tropes of traditional masculinity like strength and stoicism. We explore discourse analysis more fully in Chapter 5.

Positive Masculinity

Against the critical view of traditional masculinity typical of most present-day research in the psychology of men and masculinity, several scholars have argued the field needs to consider, "the many beneficial features of traditional masculinity" (Kiselica & Englar-Carlson, 2010, p. 277). These researchers argue that the field's critical bent leaves clinicians neglecting valuable strengths that (supposedly) go hand in hand with traditional masculinity: courage, self-reliance, relationships centered around activity, tension-reducing humor, a focus on group participation, and showing love through generous action. To be clear, scholars and clinicians within the positive masculinity framework eschew the notion that these positive aspects of masculinity come from some "deep masculine" essence or from biological hardwiring. Instead, they view their approach as a pragmatic way of getting men's buy-in to change the way they enact masculinity. We return to this idea again throughout the book, and offer a critique in Chapter 11.

Summary and Conclusion

A historical review shows that the psychology of men and masculinity has undergone dramatic upheavals over the past century. Traditional masculinity was once idealized and taken as the default for human behavior. Masculinity was thought of as essential to men. If men did not show masculine traits, this was considered a problem, if not downright pathological.

But this view of traditional masculinity as a healthy standard was upended by second wave feminism and its male-focused offspring, the male liberation movement. Specifically, these movements asserted that masculinity is not essential to men, but socially learned and constructed, and that masculinity is often *unhealthy* for men and broader society. These assumptions lay the bedrock for the new psychology of men, which, since the late 1990s, blossomed into a distinct subfield. In the chapters that follow, we will dive headfirst into this field.

References

Acher, R. A. (1910). Spontaneous constructions and primitive activities of children analogous to those of primitive man. *The American Journal of Psychology*, *21*, 114–150.

Adams, A., Anderson, E., & McCormack, M. (2010). Establishing and challenging masculinity: the influence of gendered discourses in organized sport. *Journal of Language and Social Psychology*, *29*, 278–300.

Addis, M. E. & Hoffman, E. (2017). Men's depression and help-seeking through the lenses of gender. In R. F. Levant & J. Y. Wong (Eds.), *The psychology of men and masculinities* (pp. 171–196). Washington, DC: American Psychological Association.

Addis, M. E. & Mahalik, J. R. (2003). Men, masculinity, and the contexts of help seeking. *American Psychologist*, *58*, 5–14.

Addis, M. E., Mansfield, A. K., & Syzdek, M. R. (2010). Is "masculinity" a problem?: framing the effects of gendered social learning in men. *Psychology of Men & Masculinity*, *11*(2), 77–90.

Argyll, G. D. C. (1867). *The reign of law* (4th ed.). London, England: Alexander Strahan.

Bederman, G. (2008). *Manliness and civilization: a cultural history of gender and race in the United States, 1880–1917*. Chicago, IL: University of Chicago Press.

Bem, S. L. (1974). The measurement of psychological androgyny. *Journal of Consulting and Clinical Psychology*, *42*(2), 155–162.

Bem, S. L. & Lewis, S. A. (1975). Sex role adaptability: one consequence of psychological androgyny. *Journal of Personality and Social Psychology*, *31*(4), 634–643.

Benjamin, Jr., L. T. (1988). *A history of psychology: original sources and contemporary research*. Malden, MA: Blackwell Publishing.

Blum, J. D. (1968, February 19). Effect of integrated bussing programs studied with soc. rel. 120 group method. *The Harvard Crimson*. Retrieved September 1, 2017, from: www.thecrimson.com/article/1968/2/19/effect-of-integrated-bussing-programs-studied.

Boring, E. G. (1929). *History of experimental psychology*. London, England: Century/Random House UK.

Brannon, R. (1976). The male sex role: our culture's blueprint of man-hood, and what it's done for us lately. In D. S. David & R. Brannon (Eds.), *The forty-nine percent majority: the male sex role* (pp. 1–45). Reading, MA: Addison Wesley Publishing Company.

Brooks, G. R. & Elder, W. B. (2016). History and future of the psychology of men and masculinities. In Y. J. Wong & S. R. Wester (Eds.), *APA handbook of men and masculinities* (pp. 3–21). Washington, DC: American Psychological Association.

Burton, A. (1947). The use of the masculinity-femininity of the MMPI as an aid in the diagnosis of sexual inversion. *Journal of Psychology*, *24*, 161–164.

Butler, J. (1986). Sex and gender in Simone De Beauvoir's Second Sex. *Yale French Studies*, *72*, 35–49.

Cochran, S. V. (2010). Emergence and development of the psychology of men and masculinity. In J. C. Chrisler & D. R. McCreary (Eds.), *Handbook of gender research in psychology* (pp. 43–58). New York, NY: Springer.

Connell, R. W. (2005). *Masculinities*. Berkeley, CA: University of California Press.

Constantinople, A. (1973). Masculinity-femininity: an exception to a famous dictum? *Psychological Bulletin, 80*(5), 389–407.

Darwin, C. (1859). *On the origin of species by means of natural selection.* London: John Murray.

De Beauvoir, S. (1960). *The second sex* (H. M. Parshley, trans.). London, England: Jonathan Cape (original work published 1949).

Doidge, W. T. & Holtzman, W. H. (1960). Implications of homosexuality among air force trainees. *Journal of Consulting Psychology, 24*(1), 913.

Edley, N. & Wetherell, M. (1997). Jockeying for position: the construction of masculine identities. *Discourse & Society, 8*, 203–217.

Eisler, R. M. & Skidmore, J. R. (1987). Masculine gender role stress: scale development and component factors in the appraisal of stressful situations. *Behavior Modification, 11*(2), 123–136.

Ellis, H. (1900). *Studies in the psychology of sex: sexual inversion* (Vol. 2). London, England: The University Press Limited.

Fitzsimmons, E. G. (2014, December 21). Dude, close your legs: M.T.A. fights a spreading scourge. *New York Times*, p. A1.

Freud, S. (1955). *The interpretation of dreams* (J. Strachey, trans.). New York, NY: Basic Books (original work published 1900).

Freud, S. (1959). The question of lay analysis. In J. Strachey (Ed.), *The standard edition of the complete psychological works of Sigmund Freud* (Vol. 20, pp. 177–250). London, England: Hogarth Press (original work published 1926).

Freud, S. & Breuer, J. (2004). *Studies on hysteria.* New York, NY: Penguin (original work published in 1895).

Furumoto, L. (1980). Mary Whiton Calkins (1863–1930). *Psychology of Women Quarterly, 5*(1), 55–68.

Furumoto, L. (1989). The new history of psychology. In I. S. Cohen (Ed.), *The G. Stanley Hall lecture series* (Vol. 9, pp. 9–34). Washington, DC: American Psychological Association.

Good, G. E. & Wood, P. K. (1995). Male gender role conflict, depression, and help seeking: do college men face double jeopardy? *Journal of Counseling & Development, 74*(1), 70–75.

Hall, G. S. (1904). *Adolescence: its psychology; and its relation to physiology, anthropology, sex, crime, religion, and education.* London, England: Sydney Appleton.

Hammer, J. H., Vogel, D. L., & Heimerdinger-Edwards, S. R. (2013). Men's help seeking: examination of differences across community size, education, and income. *Psychology of Men & Masculinity, 14*, 65–75.

Hartley, R. E. (1959). Sex-role pressures and the socialization of the male child. *Psychological Reports, 5*(3), 457–468.

Hathaway, S. R. & McKinley, J. C. (1940). A multiphasic personality schedule (Minnesota): I. construction of the schedule. *The Journal of Psychology, 10*(2), 249–254.

Hegarty, P. (2003). Homosexual signs and heterosexual silences: Rorschach studies of male homosexuality from 1921 to 1967. *Journal of the History of Sexuality, 12*, 400–423.

Herek, G. M. (2010). Sexual orientation differences as deficits: science and stigma in the history of American psychology. *Perspectives on Psychological Science, 5*, 693–699.

Kimmel, M. & Kaufman, M. (1994). Weekend warriors: the new men's movement. In H. Brod & M. Kaufmann (Eds.), *Theorizing masculinities* (pp. 259–288). Thousand Oaks, CA: Sage.

Kilmartin, C. & McDermott, R. C. (2016). Violence and masculinities. In Y. J. Wong & S. R. Wester (Eds.), *APA handbook of men and masculinities* (pp. 615–636). Washington, DC: American Psychological Association.

Kiselica, M. S. & Englar-Carlson, M. (2010). Identifying, affirming, and building upon male strengths: the positive psychology/positive masculinity model of psychotherapy with boys and men. *Psychotherapy: theory, Research, Practice, Training, 47*, 276–287.

Levant, R. F. (1996). The new psychology of men. *Professional Psychology: Research and Practice, 27*, 259–287.

Mahalik, J. R., Locke, B. D., Ludlow, L. H., Diemer, M. A., Scott, R. P., Gottfried, M., & Freitas, G. (2003). Development of the conformity to masculine norms inventory. *Psychology of Men & Masculinity, 4*(1), 3–25.

Messner, M. A. (1998). The limits of "the male sex role": an analysis of the men's liberation and men's rights movements' discourse. *Gender & Society, 12*, 255–276.

Miller, C. & Swift, K. (1976). *Words and women: new language in new times.* Garden City, NJ: Doubleday.

Minton, H. L. (1986). Femininity in men and masculinity in women: American psychiatry and psychology portray homosexuality in the 1930s. *Journal of Homosexuality, 13*(1), 1–21.

Moore, T. M. & Stuart, G. L. (2005). A review of the literature on masculinity and partner violence. *Psychology of Men & Masculinity, 6*, 46–61.

Morawski, J. G. (1985). The measurement of masculinity and femininity: engendering categorical realities. *Journal of Personality, 53*, 196–223.

Morawski, J. G. (2004). White experimenters, White blood and other White conditions: locating the psychologist's race. In M. Fine, L. Weis, L. Pruitt, & A. Burns (Eds.), *Off white: readings on power, privilege and resistance* (2nd ed., pp. 215–234). New York, NY: Routledge.

Münsterberg, H. (1894). *Letter from Hugo Münsterberg to the President and Fellows of Harvard College*, October 23. Cambridge, MA: Harvard University Archives.

Myers, D. G. (2010). *Psychology* (9th ed.). New York, NY: Worth Publishers.

Nicholson, I. (2011). "Shocking" masculinity: Stanley Milgram,"Obedience to Authority," and the "Crisis of Manhood" in Cold War America. *Isis, 102*, 238–268.

O'Neil, J. M., Helms, B. J., Gable, R. K., David, L., & Wrightsman, L. S. (1986). Gender-Role Conflict Scale: college men's fear of femininity. *Sex Roles, 14*(5), 335–350.

Paoletti, J. B. (2015). *Sex and unisex: fashion, feminism, and the sexual revolution.* Bloomington, IN: Indiana University Press.

Patrick, J. R. & Sims, V. M. (1934). Personality differences between negro and white college students, north and south. *The Journal of Abnormal and Social Psychology, 29*, 181–201.

Pleck, J. H. (1981). *The myth of masculinity.* Cambride, MA: MIT Press.

Pleck, J. H. (1995). The gender role strain paradigm: an update. In R. F. Levant & W. S. Pollack (Eds.), *A new psychology of men* (pp. 11–32). New York, NY: Basic Books.

Pleck, J. H. & Sawyer, J. (1974). *Men and masculinity*. Englewood Cliffs, NJ: Prentice-Hall.

Reigeluth, C. S., & Addis, M. E. (2016). Adolescent boys' experiences with policing of masculinity: forms, functions, and consequences. *Psychology of Men & Masculinity, 17,* 74–83.

Richards, G. (2003). *Race, racism and psychology: towards a reflexive history.* New York, NY: Routledge.

Roosevelt, T. (1899, November 29). *Theodore Roosevelt to G. Stanley Hall* [personal correspondence] (Subseries 3, Box 1-3-2). Dr. G. Stanley Hall Papers, Archives and Special Collections, Clark University, Worcester, MA.

Rorschach, H. (1921). *Psychodiagnostik.* Leipzig, Germany: Ernst Bircher.

Sawyer, J. (1974). On male liberation. In J. Pleck & J. Sawyer (Eds.), *Men and masculinity* (pp. 170–172). Englewood Cliffs, NJ: Prentice-Hall.

Sawyer, J. (2001). Jack Sawyer. In *Contemporary Authors Online*. Detroit, MI: Author. Retrieved from: http://libraries.state.ma.us/login?gwurl=http://go.galegroup.com/ps/i.do?p=LitRC&sw=w&u=mlin_c_clarkunv&v=2.1&it=r&id=GALE%7CH1000087354&asid=0a4ac6e997e4ba2797111d4cda3a4ba9.

Schuessler, K. F. & Cressey, D. R. (1950). Personality characteristics of criminals. *American Journal of Sociology, 55,* 476–484.

Shapiro, F. R. (1985). Historical notes on the vocabulary of the women's movement. *American Speech, 60*(1), 3–16.

Shields, S. (1975). Functionalism, Darwinism, and the psychology of women. *American Psychologist, 30,* 739–754.

Shields, S. A. & Dicicco, E. C. (2011). The social psychology of sex and gender: from gender differences to doing gender. *Psychology of Women Quarterly, 35*(3), 491–499.

Terman, L. M., Johnson, W. B., Kuznets, G., & McNemar, O. W. (1946). Psychological sex differences. In L. Carmichael (Ed.), *Handbook of child psychology* (pp. 954–1000). New York, NY: Wiley & Sons.

Terman, L. M. & Miles, C. C. (1936). *Sex and personality: studies in masculinity and femininity.* New York, NY: McGraw-Hill.

The Society for the Psychological Study of Men and Masculinity (1995). Mission statement. Retrieved October 22, 2017, from: http://division51.net/about/governance/mission-statement.

Thompson, Jr, E. H. & Pleck, J. H. (1986). The structure of male role norms. *American Behavioral Scientist, 29*(5), 531–543.

Thompson, H. B. (1903). *The mental traits of sex.* Chicago, IL: University of Chicago Press.

Vandello, J. A., Bosson, J. K., Cohen, D., Burnaford, R. M., & Weaver, J. R. (2008). Precarious manhood. *Journal of Personality and Social Psychology, 95,* 1325–1339.

Walker, E. L. (1941). The Terman-Miles "MF" test and the prison classification program. *The Pedagogical Seminary and Journal of Genetic Psychology, 59,* 27–40.

Wetherell, M. & Edley, N. (1999). Negotiating hegemonic masculinity: imaginary positions and psycho-discursive practices. *Feminism & Psychology, 9*(3), 335–356.

Wetherell, M. & Edley, N. (2014). A discursive psychological framework for analyzing men and masculinities. *Psychology of Men & Masculinity, 15,* 355–364.

Wetherell, M. & Potter, J. (1988). Discourse analysis and the identification of interpretative repertoires. In C. Antaki (Ed.), *Analysing lay explanation: a case book* (pp. 168–183). London, England: Sage.

Whorley, M. R. & Addis, M. E. (2006). Ten years of psychological research on men and masculinity in the United States: dominant methodological trends. *Sex Roles, 55,* 649–658.

Wong, Y. J., Steinfeldt, J. A., Speight, Q. L., & Hickman, S. J. (2010). Content analysis of *Psychology of Men & Masculinity* (2000–2008). *Psychology of Men & Masculinity, 11,* 170–181.

Woolley, H. T. (1910). A review of the recent literature on the psychology of sex. *Psychological Bulletin, 7,* 335–342.

PART TWO
Ways of Seeing

3

WILL MEN ALWAYS BE MEN?

Biological Perspectives

"Boys will be boys."
"It's all in the genes."
"Men are just wired this way."
"Denying men's and women's fundamental differences is ignoring
    thousands of years of evolution that have made us this way."
"We're all cavemen when you get right down to it."

How often have you heard statements like the ones above? If you talk to people about gender, the odds are good that you will come across these or similar ideas. The notion that biology and evolution exert a powerful role in determining men's thoughts, feelings, and actions regularly features in dialogues and debates about men and masculinity. Likewise, documentary films, popular media, and academic research are all outlets for a biological perspective on gender.

But what exactly does it mean to say that biological processes are central to a psychology of men and masculinity? Does it automatically negate the influence of social and environmental factors? As individuals are we ultimately passive recipients of our genetic legacy, destined to act in the interests of our DNA? Alternatively, perhaps the role of biology in a psychology of men is not an either/or proposition. "It's obviously both!" is by far the most common reaction we hear from students when the question of nature versus nurture arises. But if the contributions of both are so influential and so obvious, why as a society are we perpetually stuck on the question of which is primary?

This chapter addresses these and other questions about the role of biology in a psychology of men. We begin by posing the question, "what does it mean precisely to say that some aspect of men's psychology is 'biological?'" We then provide a brief primer on evolutionary psychological reasoning. Next, we review available scientific evidence in the two areas of research most commonly referenced when considering biological influences on men and masculinity: (1) the potential existence of important psychological sex differences between men and women that may be rooted in our evolutionary history and (2) the role of hormones (especially testosterone) in men's behavior. Finally, we explore the various ways a biological perspective on men and masculinity travels in broader society, outside the hallowed halls of the academy, to support, refute, challenge, or reinforce different perspectives on social issues of concern such as violence, mental health, and children's education.

The Various Meanings of "It's Biological"

What exactly are we saying when we claim that some aspect of men's behavior "is biological?" It's hard to imagine any aspect of human behavior that does not involve biology in some way or another; we could not eat, breathe, think, feel, imagine, sing, go out on a date, or study the psychology of men and masculinity without our bodies, and our bodies are nothing if not biological entities. Still, one gets the feeling that attributing gender to biology suggests much more than the mere existence of brains and bodies. For example, the phrase, "it's biological" can be used to suggest that:

- The behaviors under question are caused by biological processes and nothing more.
- The behaviors under question are much more strongly influenced by biological causes than social or environmental causes.
- The behaviors under question will be highly resistant to any efforts to change them.
- The behaviors under question exist because they are "natural" (i.e., they are designed to be this way).
- The behaviors under question *should* be this way; it would be unhealthy, abnormal, or immoral for things to be different.
- The behaviors under question evolved over thousands of years and have now become "hardwired" to the degree that they are relatively automatic and cannot be affected by conscious attempts at control.

In fact, none of these ways of thinking about behavior are consistent with a modern scientific understanding of biology and evolution. And yet, they are increasingly common ideas in the public sphere. The argument for separating young boys and girls in school is nowadays buttressed by the assertion that their brains are fundamentally different. Despite increasing evidence that football and other violent sports place men and boys at risk for brain injury and lifelong disability, if not death, we hear that such sports should not be regulated because males are "inherently aggressive" and "need an outlet." When people of different genders have trouble communicating or forming intimate relationships, their challenges are attributed to "fundamental differences that are evolutionarily hardwired."

But if we know that biological processes are inexorably linked to human activity and, at the same time, that claims like the ones above are inaccurate or highly exaggerated, where is the middle ground? Put another way, how can we think about the role of biology in a psychology of men and masculinity in a way that is consistent with modern scientific reasoning and empirical data? An analogy is helpful here. Consider the question of what makes an automobile move the way it does. Although it may seem like somewhat of a stretch, the search for an explanation of a car's behavior shares many similarities with the search for explanations of human behavior. Both possess an underlying machinery that allows them to take action. For both, that underlying machinery is highly sensitive to the environments surrounding it. And in both automobiles and human beings, the form and function of their behaviors change over the lifetime of the individual and with cultural-historical shifts that alter the meaning of driving, raising a family, and so on.

Let's take the analogy a step further. First, it seems clear in both cases that some sort of underlying apparatus is essential. Without an engine to turn combustible fuel into energy, our hypothetical automobile is going nowhere. But the machinery alone is not sufficient. Cars do not begin to do their thing until someone puts a key in the ignition, turns it on, sets the car in gear, presses the accelerator, and begins to drive. Thus, what makes a car move is not only its engine, wheels, and tires, but also an agentic driver with a sense of purpose; in other words, a reason to move. But that's not the whole picture either. What determines the car's speed and direction? This obviously depends on the driver's intentions—where they want to go. We might even take it a step further and ask what determines where a driver wants to go? And now we're in the realm of cultural and personal history. In 1950s America 17-year-old drivers and their cars may have been headed to a popular dance called a "Sock Hop," whereas in 2019 you would be hard pressed to find such an event anywhere in the country. Our goal in stretching this analogy out is to show that if we want to truly grasp what makes a car behave the way it does, we need to consider how highly interwoven and mutually dependent are the engine, the driver, and the social-cultural environment.

The same is true for human behavior. Some sort of vehicle is certainly necessary for humans to do all the things we do, and a body provides exactly that. The fact that virtually any human activity can be linked to the brain or nervous system is exactly what leads us to sometimes conclude that "it's all biological" when attempting to account for some aspect of human behavior. But all that machinery serves little purpose without some sort of goal-directed activity. At any point in time the options for different activities to emerge are vast. At this very moment, as we sit at the local café writing this chapter, endless options are available. Michael could break into song (much to the chagrin of those around us). Ethan could toss his cup of coffee up in the air. Michael could curl up for a nap on the table. Or we could, among other options, continue writing. Fortunately, we appear to be continuing to write and causing little disturbance around us. But is that because our brains decided this is the best option? Certainly our brains helped contemplate the alternatives and execute the decision, but they did so in constant communication with the environment based on what they have learned through centuries of evolution and the years of our individual lives.

The machinery of the brain and nervous system are highly tuned to our social environments; who and what surrounds us, the social norms governing the situation, the sorts of behaviors possible, and the effects they are likely to produce. Just like a car, we can't go anywhere or do anything of much importance without this machinery. But the singular contraption alone cannot explain the tremendous diversity of human activity, especially when it comes to pervasive, complex, and nuanced social processes like gender. As Stanford biologist and neurologist Robert Sapolsky (2017) says in the book *Behave: The Biology of Humans at Our Best and Our Worst*, it "actually makes no sense to distinguish between aspects of a behavior that are 'biological' and those that would be described as, say, 'psychological' or 'cultural.' Utterly intertwined" (p. 5).

An Evolutionary Psychology Primer

How then can we think about the role of biology in a psychology of men and masculinity? If it's not "everything" then what exactly is it? In fact, there is a tremendous amount of scientific research that has examined the role of biological factors in men's thoughts, feelings, and actions. To appreciate what this kind of research means, and doesn't mean, we first review the logic of evolutionary psychology. Charles Darwin is often credited with developing the theory of evolution, although the idea had been brewing for some time when he came on the scene. Still, Darwin was the first to propose natural selection as the mechanism responsible for the vast array of adaptations across numerous species of living organisms.

Variation is the first concept essential to an evolutionary perspective. Across individuals, within a species, and across species, various adaptations come and go. Some of these are *phenotypic* or observable characteristics and others are *genotypic* (located in our genes). For example, the presence of a Y chromosome in most individuals identified as male is a genotypic variation that has developed over the course of mammalian history. Facial hair, a penis, and testes are examples of phenotypic variations. An adaptation is a variation that solves a particular environmental problem. For example, it has been suggested that a preference for promiscuity in men is an evolutionarily driven adaptation because it allows individual males to enhance the likelihood of reproducing their DNA through multiple offspring. There are, of course, other explanations for promiscuity, but the emphasis on adaptations that solve reproductive dilemmas is central to an evolutionary perspective.

Transmission is the second essential concept in evolutionary theory. Through the processes of sexual reproduction and cellular replication, genotypes and the phenotypes they encode are passed down from one reproductive generation to the next. In effect, organisms "inherit" characteristics possessed by individuals who preceded and ultimately gave rise to them through generations of reproduction. Crucially, the process of transmission is imperfect due to *mutation*— the alteration of genotypes at a molecular level. The result is that random variation in how genes reproduce themselves affects the process of transmission. Although the term mutation may make it sound like a somewhat nefarious process, taken as a whole, mutations are definitely for the good; without them, all individuals in a species would be carbon-copy replications of previous reproductive generations. (Heck, we'd still be single-celled!) It's easy to see how such a homogenous state of affairs would work against variation, the first requirement for evolution to work its magic.

What determines which mutations are passed down through reproduction from generation to generation? This question cuts in many ways right to the heart of evolutionary logic. The short answer is that those adaptations that survive and are passed down are the ones that "work." We have eyes because they allowed those before us to see, ears because they allowed them to hear, genitals because they allowed them to reproduce, and large brains because they allowed them to think, solve problems, remember, tell stories, and much more. But what if we dig a bit deeper and ask *why* it's a good thing to see, hear, reproduce, and tell stories? In other words, on what basis can we claim that an adaptation "works?" Consider men's purported higher levels of aggression on average than women. On the one hand, aggression might be a useful adaptation if it leads to increased resources. On the other hand, aggression that's too frequent or poorly focused can quickly put an end to life, and it's hard to see how that would be adaptive from an evolutionary perspective.

Darwin proposed that there are two environmental processes that select which adaptations provide benefits to organisms and thus continue to be passed down through reproduction. In *natural selection*, adaptations that enhance the likelihood of survival are more likely to remain present in the gene pool over time. The tendency to avoid predators, for example, is advantageous to survival. Those individuals within a species who possess the abilities to correctly identify predators and to take action to avoid them are more likely to survive and to transmit those abilities to their off-spring. Over time and across multiple individuals within a population, the adaptation (e.g., we might call it a "fight/flight" response) becomes more common in the genome.

Of course, survival is only part of the picture. If an organism lives a long and healthy life but fails to reproduce, the adaptations it has inherited from previous generations are effectively lost to the wind. Thus, *sexual selection* is the second process that acts on adaptations to determine which are more likely to be passed down and which are more likely to fall out of the gene pool. As a result of sexual selection, any adaptation which enhances an organism's likelihood of reproducing their own genetic material should become more common in the overall population. Consider one potentially obvious example: finding sexual activity pleasurable. Not everyone finds sex pleasurable all the time, and the degree to which we do depends on a wide range of factors. Nonetheless, it appears that most of us are "hardwired" to find the behaviors associated with reproduction appealing. In effect, we "like sex" because the millions/billions of human organisms that came before us who liked sex survived, reproduced, and passed on that tendency to us. In contrast, the mutation/adaptation of "not liking sex" was less likely to lead to having sex, less likely to lead to reproduction, and therefore less likely to be passed down over time.

Natural and sexual selection are really the starting points for considering the evolution of psychological processes. Evolutionary psychologists attempt to understand how psychological processes (i.e., thoughts, feelings, behaviors, belief systems, etc.) may have evolved in ways that benefited the reproductive success of our genetic ancestors, *even though they may or may not be providing survival or reproductive advantages in every individual's current life*. A central assumption in this perspective is that although human cultures may have changed dramatically in the last 10,000 years, our brains and central nervous systems are still quite similar to those found in our nearest hominid ancestors. In effect, we possess hunter-gatherer brains from the Pleistocene era, plopped down in the middle of a new millennium with the internet, global warming, artificial intelligence, and on-line dating all thrown into the mix. In short, if an evolutionary psychologist wants to understand the psychology of men and masculinity in the 21st century, there are three fundamental questions:

1. What survival and reproductive challenges did our earlier male Pleistocene ancestors face?
2. What adaptations did men develop to respond effectively to those challenges?
3. Currently, how are men's thoughts, feelings, and behaviors affected by the intersection between those historical adaptations and the challenges posed by the modern-day world?

One thing is for certain. Around the world, evolution appears to have produced roughly two common and somewhat different phenotypes for the purposes of sexual pairing and reproduction in vertebrates: males and females. We say "appears" and "roughly" because it turns out that not all individuals fit neatly into the dichotomy of male/female; certainly not psychologically speaking, as many individuals experience themselves as somewhere in between male/female, or as non-binary (i.e., not identifying with the dichotomy whatsoever). The same is true physically, as many people are born with ambiguous sexual characteristics that do not obviously point to the conventional distinction male/female. Still, in broad and biological terms, there does seem to be a fair degree of universality in the existence of human males and females. Regardless, evolutionary psychology is less interested in the existence of two *physically* different phenotypes than in the possibility of *sexually dimorphic minds or brains*. In other words, is it possible that men are in some ways fundamentally different than women in how they think, feel, and make decisions on a day-to-day basis? And moreover, are these inherent differences the direct result of evolutionary pressures on our hominid ancestors?

Consider the question of what makes people vigilant about fidelity in romantic relationships. Are we more likely to be jealous if we suspect that our partner is sexually involved with another person? Or does it trouble us more if we suspect a strong emotional connection with a third party? Researcher David Buss and his colleagues (Buss, Larsen, Westen, & Semmelroth, 1992) explored this question from an evolutionary psychology perspective, focusing specifically on male/female differences in **sexual strategies** that were hypothesized to be the result of sexual selection in our evolutionary past. They began with the observation that the human species engages in internal fertilization. In other words, the actual pairing of sperm and egg and subsequent development toward a viable fetus takes place within the female's body. Therefore, at a purely physical level, there is no publicly observable evidence to determine without question which male contributed the sperm. This **paternity uncertainty** raises the possibility that males may be duped into contributing resources toward the development of offspring that are not biologically their own. Thus, theoretically, males on average should be particularly attuned to sexual infidelity in their female partners. According to evolutionary reasoning such a sensitivity would have been selected for in our genetic lineage because those who possessed it should have been better at detecting when they had been cuckolded and thus be less likely to invest their resources in offspring who did not carry their genes. In short, sexual jealousy in men is thought to have evolved because it enhanced the likelihood that males would choose to invest in the survival and reproduction of the "right" offspring.

Buss and colleagues (1992) further reasoned that the situation is reversed for females. Because females are always certain that a developing zygote or fetus contains their own genetic material, they should be less concerned with sexual infidelity and more concerned about males falling in love with other females and consequently diverting resources away from their own offspring. Taking it a step further, evolutionary psychologists have suggested that one successful strategy for females is to "trick" non-paternal males into believing they are responsible for a reproductive event (when in fact they're not) in order to garner more resources for their offspring. Empirical support for this prediction comes from several self-report studies in which men and women are asked to choose which of the two types of infidelity would be most upsetting to them. Across a wide range of ages and cultures, women are statistically more likely to choose *emotional* infidelity and men are more likely to choose *sexual* infidelity (Buss et al., 1992, 1999; Buunk, Angleitner, Oubaid, & Buss, 1996; DeSteno & Salovey, 1996; Kennair, Nordeide, Andreassen, Strønen, & Pallesen, 2011; Sagarin, Becker, Guadagno, Wilkinson, & Nicastle, 2012).

Although such results are consistent with evolutionary theory, it is impossible to determine whether they are the result of sexual selection over the course of human history or the learning of socially constructed gender roles in the course of our individual lifetimes. Questions have also been raised about the validity of the forced-choice method. Studies using more naturalistic methods have produced more equivocal results. For example, when people are allowed to rate how much they are bothered by sexual and emotional infidelity (rather than choose which one is worse), men and women reveal smaller differences in their ratings (DeSteno, Bartlett, Braverman, & Salovey, 2002).

For Consideration

How does the evolutionary theory of sex differences in jealousy fit with your personal experiences?

How much of a difference between males and females would persuade you that the theory is correct (e.g., what if 60% of males were more troubled by sexual infidelity and 60% of females were more troubled by emotional infidelity?).

What other types of evidence would persuade you that evolution has produced very different minds in males and females?

Sex Differences: How Large, How Meaningful, How Come?

As you may imagine, evolutionary psychologists place a strong emphasis on evolved psychological differences between the sexes. And they're not alone. For many people, including not only researchers, but also politicians, law makers, educators, health professionals, and even those with no professional investment in thinking about gender one way or the other, it seems patently obvious that men and women are fundamentally different. Biology is often invoked to reinforce this apparent dichotomy. We hear that men's and women's brains are wired differently, that it's all a matter of testosterone versus estrogen, and that men are programmed to divide and conquer while women are programmed to tend and befriend. Many of these claims are based on stereotypes about the genders and many have also been subject to scientific research to determine their accuracy.

For Consideration

What are some of your stereotypes about differences between men and women? Try completing the following sentences without giving it too much thought beforehand. Your most automatic response will tell you what kinds of stereotypes you possess.

Men are more _____ than women.
Women are more _____than men.

How different are males and females in reality? Scientific research should be able to provide the answers, and the methods for obtaining that knowledge are fairly straightforward; simply choose a psychological or biological characteristic, gather a sample of men and women, measure them on that characteristic, and calculate the average difference between the sexes. Simple, right?

As it turns out, not so much. The existence, size, and importance of psychological sex differences are hotly debated topics (e.g., Fine, 2017; Jordan-Young, 2010; Lippa, 2016). As we will see throughout this book, how people think about these issues and which studies they choose to cite (if they do) are often more a function of particular political or moral view points on gender than they are transparent reflections of scientific facts. Nonetheless, it is helpful to dig into the available research. Doing so with clear vision requires the ability keep straight several specific questions and logical approaches to studying sex differences.

When psychologists study group differences on a variable of interest, they typically calculate the average within each group and then compare the groups mathematically to determine whether the difference is statistically significant. **Statistical significance** is a measure of the probability that a statistical result is due to randomness or non-randomness. Put another way, statistical significance speaks to the likelihood that the results are due to chance, not to an actual difference between the groups. Imagine, for example, that we are interested in whether male and female college students differ in their mathematical abilities. Conveniently, we have a well-validated test of math ability that ranges from

0–100, with 100 being a perfect score. We gather a large sample of students from different colleges and universities around the country—say 3,000 males and 3,000 females. Furthermore, we have selected a diverse sample with respect to ethnicity, race, sexual orientation, and socioeconomic status. Based on the size and demographic characteristics of the sample, we are very confident that we can generalize the findings to the overall population of college students.

Imagine the results are as follows: males score an average of 74.1 and females score an average of 51.2. Moreover, scores are tightly bunched around the average in both males and females. The resulting data might look something like that in Figure 3.1.

Based on these data it would seem reasonable to conclude that men and women differ in their mathematical abilities. Because of our large sample size the results are almost certainly not due to chance. Thus, they meet the criteria of statistical significance. In addition, the difference between the averages for the two groups (22.9 points) seems rather large. The graphical representation of the findings also appears to bear this out. The curves representing female and male scores are clearly different.

Now, imagine the results came out somewhat differently. This time, as Figure 3.2 below illustrates, males scored an average of 74.1 and females

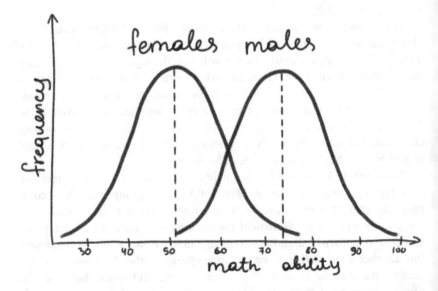

Figure 3.1 Hypothetical data showing a statistically significant and *large* sex difference in math abilities. Research on sex differences in cognitive abilities has failed to find any differences of this magnitude.

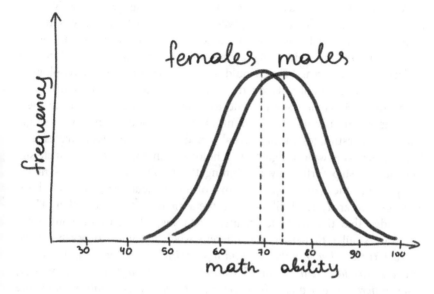

Figure 3.2 Hypothetical data showing a statistically significant but *small* sex difference in math ability. The data show that nearly half of females are higher than the average male and nearly half of males are lower than the average female.

scored an average of 69.8. Once again, the results are statistically significant and are unlikely to be due to chance. Thus, on the one hand the difference may be considered "real" but, on the other hand, it's a pretty small difference. Under such conditions are we justified in concluding that "Men are better at mathematics than women?"

As you might imagine, the answers will vary depending on a person's pre-existing beliefs and assumptions about the degrees of difference between males and females in general. Nonetheless, the two examples point out an important distinction between statistical significance and effect size when it comes to interpreting these kinds of research findings. Whereas statistical significance tells us whether a particular finding is likely to be due to chance, **effect size** tells us how large the difference between groups actually is. And here's the critical take-home message: although the two statistics are related, differences between groups can be statistically significant and also fairly small (depending on the sample size). In other words, just because a difference exists doesn't mean that difference is particularly large or meaningful. This crucial distinction between the probability of a research finding and the actual size of that finding is often minimized or even disregarded in social debates about biologically driven differences between men and women. "Is there a difference?" is not the same question as "How big is the difference?"

Although there is clearly a lot of political baggage that weighs on questions of sex differences in psychological characteristics, let's nevertheless imagine that we were all able to put our pre-existing biases aside and look as objectively as possible at the immense volume of research in this area. What would we find? Fortunately, psychological researcher Janet Shibley Hyde did exactly this in a classic study published in 2005 (Hyde, 2005). Hyde used the technique of *meta-analysis* to combine the results of a large number of previous studies into single quantitative estimates of the actual sex differences between males and females across a wide range of psychological characteristics. In fact, she took it one step further by combining the results of 46 previous meta-analyses on the same topic (a sort of meta-meta-analysis). Based on a systematic analysis of all of these meta-analyses taken together, Hyde concluded that the available scientific data suggest men and women are far more similar than they are different when it comes to psychological characteristics. *The number of findings indicating no significant sex differences was far greater than those indicating sex differences. Moreover, when differences did occur the effect sizes tended to be small or moderate at most.* Ten years later the same findings were replicated by different authors using similar techniques to combine the results of multiple studies (Zell, Krizan, & Teeter, 2015).

The meta-analyses described above suggest that males and females are far more similar psychologically than they are different. But does it mean there are *no* differences? If so, what do we make of individual research studies that *do* find differences? The first step to making sense of the data is to recognize that the existence of difference does not de facto mean that the difference reflects a difference of kind as opposed to a difference of degree. For example, on average, men have broader shoulders than women. However, both men and women have shoulders! Moreover, many women have shoulders that are broader than the average man's. Thus, the statistically significant difference in shoulder width does not reflect a fundamentally different body type—it is simply a matter of difference in average size—a group difference for which there is also tremendous variation within each sex. As philosopher and psychologist Cordelia Fine (2017) points out:

> *When mosaics of mostly small average differences are carelessly squished into uni-dimensional generic claims—men are like this, women are more that—the natural inference is that we are talking about universal characteristics that are "central, deep, stable, inherent—in a word, 'essential'."*
>
> (p. 107, emphasis in original)

Despite Fine's warning, as humans we seem to be biased toward searching for and exaggerating the implications of group differences (Haslam,

Bastian, & Bissett, 2004; Haslam, Rothschild, & Ernst, 2000). Psychological researchers are no less prone to this than others. Consider a recent study by Kucharska (2017) entitled, "Sex Differences in the Appraisal of Traumatic Events and Psychopathology." This research focused on differences between women and men in whether they consider traumatic events psychologically distressing or harmful. A hundred and ninety men and 277 women between the ages of 18–29 were asked about the frequency with which they experienced different types of traumatic events, and also how negatively the events affected them. The findings are presented as indicating that, "For all types of trauma, women reported a stronger negative appraisal of the event than men" (p. 575). However, digging deeper into the actual findings, it appears that the reported sex differences are actually fairly small and appeared for only some of the variables studied. For example, negative appraisal was measured on a seven-point scale (1 = extremely positive impact, 7 = extremely negative). Across all types of trauma, the average for women was 5.71 and for men it was 4.11. Thus, on average, both men and women rated traumatic events as having a negative impact although women rated them slightly more negatively. Although the result was statistically significant because of the relatively large sample size, the actual size of the difference was fairly small. Although the author is careful not to overinterpret the findings, there is no avoiding the fact that the entire rationale for the research rests on the importance of studying (and finding) sex differences between women and men. As we will see later in this chapter, the bias toward interpreting differences rather than similarities is even more pronounced when scientific research finds its way into the popular media.

For Consideration

How different are men and women from your perspective? What did you learn about sex differences growing up and from where did you learn it? Have your ideas about the degree of similarity or difference between men and women changed over time?

There is one final issue worth considering. When we do find differences in psychological characteristics between women and men, it is tempting to quickly conclude that such differences are the result of biological processes. However, social processes such as those explored in Chapter 4 can also produce differences. And, in many ways, the very process of gender socialization in men is driven by an emphasis on difference (e.g., boys are taught *not to act like girls*). Thus, the potential role of gender socialization cannot be ruled out even when the differences studied are biological in nature. Studying men's and women's brains, for example, does reveal some differences, and also many similarities. In such cases it is all too easy to conclude that the differences reflect fundamental "types" that are "hardwired" through evolution. But this interpretation is not well supported by modern biological science.

It is now well known that experience affects brain structure and function. In other words, gender socialization may also produce sex differences in brain structure and function. Nature is not competing with nurture—they are so highly intertwined as to be virtually inseparable (Jordan-Young, 2010; Sapolsky, 2017).

What About Testosterone?

No other hormone has achieved nearly the level of fame, and often infamy, as testosterone. Testosterone, we are told, is the chemical agent at the heart of masculinity, the biological basis of aggression in males, an effective treatment for depression in men, and even a hormone "under attack" when traditional notions of manhood are called into question. Testosterone even played a role in the 2016 United States presidential election when then candidate Donald Trump had his blood testosterone levels tested and the results reported on *The Dr. Oz Show*. Mr. Trump reportedly raised his eyebrows and smiled when his "T" levels were described as "good" (Crupain, 2016). Likewise, a quick Google search for information on testosterone and masculinity reveals statements such as the following:

> *Testosterone levels in men are declining worldwide alongside sperm counts. The hormone that makes men men is disappearing from the human world. As a result, men are becoming more feminine and choosing the paths of weakness, homosexuality, and cuckoldry ... You cannot accept masculine truths if your biology lacks a healthy level of testosterone, the chemical building block of masculinity.*
>
> (Valizadeh, 2017)

Alpha males are the product of high levels of testosterone, which increases aggression. This, contrary to popular opinion, is a useful trait: it makes people brave, reactive and better in battle (Gill, 2016).

The bottom line is that in popular discourse, testosterone has become the hands-down winner for a poster child of the biological basis to masculinity.

As you might imagine by this point, the story emerging from scientific research regarding testosterone and men's psychology is considerably more nuanced. To understand how testosterone and masculinity are (and are not) linked it is helpful to begin by asking what exactly testosterone is. Testosterone is one of many androgen hormones circulating in the bodies of people of all genders, although blood levels are typically higher on average in males. As a hormone, its effects on biological and behavioral processes typically occur within a matter of a few hours to a few days. Blood levels of testosterone are also highly influenced by social-environmental conditions; put an organism into a position of dominance relative to its peers and its testosterone levels will rise.

The influence of environmental conditions on testosterone levels raises a crucial point about the logic of inferring psychological characteristics from biological processes: a correlation between a biological and a psychological variable does not necessarily mean that the former causes the latter. It could be the other way around. Or, it could be that a third, a fourth, or a fifth variable is responsible for the two co-occurring. Imagine, for example, that blood levels of testosterone and sexual arousal are associated to a degree that achieves statistical significance. One possible explanation is that rising testosterone causes increased sexual arousal. Another possibility is that increasing arousal results in rising levels of testosterone. And a third possibility is that something else (e.g., close physical contact with an attractive other) causes both blood levels of testosterone and sexual arousal to increase. In order to demonstrate that testosterone or any other hormone plays a clear unidirectional causal role in men's behavior, we would have to demonstrate scientifically that (a) increases in testosterone reliably precede increases in the behavior of interest and (b) experimentally manipulating levels of testosterone reliably produces changes in the behavior regardless of any intervening environmental conditions. As it turns out, researchers have tried to find exactly this sort of evidence and have consistently come up empty-handed (Sapolsky, 2017).

Consider the question of whether testosterone causes males to be more aggressive, competitive, or dominant in their interactions with others. Although there is no evidence that testosterone independently causes males to behave in these ways, it is still possible to examine whether individual differences in blood testosterone levels predict individual differences in aggression or dominance. After reviewing the available research, Sapolsky (2017) concludes, "Among birds, fish, mammals, and especially other primates, the answer is generally no" (p. 101). He goes on to say, "Aggression is typically more about social learning than about testosterone, and differing levels of testosterone generally can't explain why some individuals are more aggressive than others" (p. 102).

As it turns out, testosterone has a lot to do *with* behavior but it's not clear that it simply does things *to* behavior. Testosterone is not a sort of biological homunculus or supercomputer sitting in the control booth and governing men's actions. And it's not the biochemical essence of what it means to be a man. Neither of those metaphors actually make much sense from the perspective of modern biology. Instead, testosterone's effects are much more subtle and context-dependent. And to complicate things further, testosterone can be affected by changes in behavior as much as it can affect them.

Sapolsky (2017) considers what we know from contemporary research on the role of testosterone in human social behavior. Testosterone makes people less empathic (Chapman et al., 2006; Hermans, Putman, & Van Honk, 2006), less anxious and fearful (Tsai & Sapolsky, 1996), more willing to take risks, more impulsive, and more confident (Boissy & Bouissou, 1994). In short, "Testosterone makes people cocky, egocentric, and narcissistic" (Sapolsky, 2017, p. 103). Crucially, these effects are highly context-dependent and may produce behaviors entirely at odds with each other depending on the situation.

Behavioral endocrinologist John Wingfield and colleagues (1990) proposed the **challenge hypothesis**, which suggests that testosterone increases certain thoughts and behaviors only when the environment indicates a challenge to dominance is at hand. In other words, testosterone increases confidence and risk-taking and decreases anxiety when we receive signals indicating a competitive environment. Critically, when testosterone rises, it does not automatically increase aggression across the board. Instead, it increases whatever behaviors are necessary to maintain status in a particular environment, regardless of whether the behaviors are aggressive. Experimental studies have shown that people can become more generous and collaborative when their testosterone levels rise if behaving this way leads to greater rewards in a laboratory setting (Eisenegger, Naef, Snozzi, Heinrichs, & Fehr, 2010).

What all this suggests is that when it comes to the psychology of men and masculinity, testosterone is anything but an independent orchestrator of stereotypically masculine behavior. Rather, its hormonal effects increase our sensitivity to certain social-environmental messages, and the behavioral effects that result can vary widely depending on the context. Or, as Fine (2017) says, "Rather than being a king who issues orders, T [testosterone] is just another voice in a group decision-making process" (p. 139). Sapolsky (2017) sums it up with the following:

> *Testosterone makes us more willing to do what it takes to attain and maintain status. And the key point is what it takes. Engineer social circumstances right, and boosting testosterone levels during a challenge would make people compete like crazy to do the most acts of random kindness. In our world riddled with male violence, the problem isn't that testosterone can increase levels of aggression. The problem is the frequency with which we reward aggression.*

(p. 107)

Fine (2017) puts it this way:

*A*lthough we're used to thinking of certain kinds of behaviors as "testoster-one fueled," in many cases it would make more sense to instead think of actions and situations as being "testosterone fueling." Social context modulates T levels (up or down), which influences behavior (presumably via changes in perception, motivation, and cognition), which influences social outcome, which influences T levels and so on.

(p. 141)

The Biology of Men and Masculinity in a Societal Context

So far, we have reviewed the logic of evolutionary psychology, findings from research on sex differences in psychological characteristics, and studies exploring links between testosterone and human behavior. It should be clear by now that there is precious little evidence that biological processes exert powerful influences over men's behavior independent of a social environment. Moreover, the war-like dichotomy "nature *versus* nurture" is highly inaccurate in its metaphorical depiction of a battle between biological, social, and psychological processes. Nonetheless, discourse about the power of biology to dictate men's thoughts, feelings, and actions continues unabated. There are several reasons why.

First, in Western cultures the distinction between mind and body has been at the center of our philosophy of knowledge (also known as epistemology, see Chapter 11) for nearly five centuries. According to the philosopher René Descartes, events in the body are wholly separate from events in the mind although one influences the other. For better or worse, this Cartesian dualism has taken deep roots in our culture and has found its way down into the very lines we draw between academic disciplines; biology (a study of life/bodies) is considered a natural science and psychology (a study of minds) is considered a social science.

Second, the mind/body binary has also cast a loop around the way we talk about the causes of our own and others' behavior. Depression is *either* a biological *or* a psychological disorder. Alcoholism is *either* a disease *or* a matter of personal choice. The list goes on.

Third, we stay wedded to this dichotomy despite its inaccuracy, partly because we are invested in its ability to negotiate blame, responsibility, and compassion. Broadly speaking, human actions that are attributed to biology are often viewed as outside the realm of personal control, whereas those attributed to psychological causes are assumed to be at least partly within an individual's control. This reasoning drives much of the emotion surrounding debates about whether problems involving behavioral excesses (e.g., alcoholism, obesity) are diseases worthy of compassion and treatment for the victim, or personal weaknesses more deserving of blame or moral condemnation. In short, our ability to reason rationally about the interaction between biology and psychology often takes a back seat to our desire to make sense of things from a moral and political standpoint.

Fourth, we also tend to overplay the nature/nurture dichotomy as a means of arguing for or against the status quo when it comes to particular social concerns. For example, it is widely known that men commit the overwhelming majority of violent crime in the United States. The argument that men's violence has a strong evolutionary basis is often invoked to argue against the effectiveness of educational campaigns to reduce violence. Such efforts are running against the grain of nature, so the argument goes. Likewise, denial of any biological influences on men's violence and aggression often emerges as a means of providing blanket support for efforts at environmental change.

Finally, research shows that people tend to hold largely essentialist beliefs about gender, often assuming that the dichotomy male/female has a deeply rooted biological essence that influences a wide range of personality traits, beliefs, and behaviors (Haslam et al., 2000; Haslam, Rothschild, & Ernst, 2002; Martin & Parker, 1995; Smiler & Gelman, 2008). Put this together with the question of biology versus social environment and things get oversimplified real fast. In many cases, the mere mention of biology enhances our perception that whatever is being talked about is more "real." Studies have shown that the public finds neuroscientific explanations of phenomena like sex differences more compelling than psychological ones. Simply adding a picture of a brain in a scientific article enhances readers' perceptions of the article's credibility (McCabe & Castel, 2008; Weisberg, Taylor, & Hopkins, 2015).

In short, our ability to think and talk about biology and gender in a critical, nuanced, and more accurate way is severely limited by our own self-interest, by how optimistic we feel about the possibility for change versus the status quo, by our motivations to attribute blame for particular problems in society, and by a pervasive sense that gender is in many ways a reflection of biological destiny. Nonetheless, it can be quite helpful in making sense of popular discourse on the biology of gender to examine how these social processes play out. Below we consider several examples of just that.

The evolutionary history of sex differences often finds its way onto the scene when questions of gender inequality are under consideration. Why, for example, are women historically underrepresented in STEM fields such as engineering and mathematics? And why do studies show that men are consistently less involved than women in day-to-day aspects of child care? Not surprisingly, the idea that men's and women's brains are of two different "types" that are "designed" for different sorts of activities is often invoked to explain such inequalities. For example, former Harvard University president Larry Summers suggested that innate "taste differences" and discrepancies in "intrinsic aptitude" between men and women account for women's underrepresentation in STEM fields (Summers, 2005). Such a statement leverages evolutionary psychological reasoning to justify the status quo; women presumably are less likely to enter and remain in STEM fields because their brains are not designed to succeed in these fields, and they find such fields inherently less appealing. Of course, the conclusion is refuted by research on sex differences in psychological characteristics (described above), but that does not stop it from being used to make inequalities in STEM seem like an unalterable foregone conclusion.

Biological explanations of men's behavior are also used to argue both for and against the desirability of changing gender roles. In 2011, a large-scale longitudinal study published findings indicating that the transition to fatherhood is associated with lowering levels of testosterone in men (Gettler, McDade, Feranil, & Kuzawa, 2011). Based on what we know about testosterone, it should not have been surprising that the hormone responds to such a monumental event as having a child. But media interpretation of the study's findings took things much further. *The New York Times* (2011) reported it this way:

> "*The real take-home message,*" said Peter Ellison, a professor of human evolutionary biology at Harvard who was not involved in the study, is that "*male parental care is important. It's important enough that it's actually shaped the physiology of men.*" "*Unfortunately,*" Dr. Ellison added, "*I think American males have been brainwashed to believe lower testosterone means that maybe you're a wimp, that it's because you're not really a man. My hope would be that this kind of research has an impact on the American male. It would make them realize that we're meant to be active fathers and participate in the care of our offspring.*"
>
> (Belluck, 2011)

Note how the description of a correlation between two variables (lower testosterone and having a child) is used to support a statement about how things *should* be (i.e., "we're meant to be active fathers and participate in the care of our offspring"). If biology is destiny, then "is" quickly becomes "should"; testosterone is involved in parenting, men have lots of testosterone, therefore men should be involved in parenting.

On the other hand, two days later the website for the National Fatherhood Initiative presented the results of the same study with the headline, "Are Good Dads Wimps?: Fathers and Testosterone" (DiCaro, 2011). Their article went on to praise fathers for their involvement in childcare but the headline nonetheless made the issue clear: testosterone is the biological essence of manhood, manhood is the opposite of wimpiness, so if testosterone levels fall during fatherhood then becoming a father might make a man a wimp. Here we see the metaphor of biology as essence calling into question the plausibility of being both a man and an engaged parent.

The idea that men's and women's brains operate in fundamentally different ways also is invoked to support arguments for gender segregation, particularly in educational contexts. Consider books with titles such as, *Teaching the Male Brain: How Boys Think, Feel, and Learn in School* (James, 2007). Of course the question of whether same-sex school environments produce better educational outcomes is ultimately an empirical one. As you might imagine from the research described above, there is precious little evidence of female and male brain "types." But, until the data become clear, public opinion is no doubt influenced by claims of dramatic differences in learning styles and brain structure and function.

Biological perspectives on men and masculinity also find their way into social debates about the causes of men's violence and aggression. One of the most controversial is the idea that rape has evolved as a viable reproductive strategy in the history of the species (Thornhill & Palmer, 2001). Some men, so the argument goes, are unable to attract a partner for reproduction and therefore turn to force as the only viable strategy. As you might imagine, this is a highly controversial point of view (see Travis, 2003, for a series of critiques). Our point here is that biological perspectives can be used in society not only to explain behavior, but also to make the case, intentionally or unintentionally, that particular behaviors are "natural" in the sense that they are driven by evolution. Of course, all of our behaviors are to some degree influenced by our evolutionary history. However, in many legal systems around the world the premise that particular unlawful actions may have a biological basis can be used to argue for leniency in punishment, if not outright acquittal.

Finally, the biological perspective on men and masculinity often manifests to support the apparent necessity of making exclusively male groups. The mythopoetic movement, for example, comprises men's groups that typically host male-only retreats for the purposes of "rediscovering" men's evolutionary history through activities such as drumming, building spears, and/or telling heroic stories. The argument is that the Industrial Revolution alienated men from their natural, biologically driven relationship to the land and leadership role within families. Several assumptions operate here, including the ideas that (a) men are fundamentally different than women, (b) lack of attention to their deep-rooted differences is harmful to men, and (c) separating themselves from women and enacting their "true" caveman selves is psychologically beneficial.

Summary and Conclusion

Biology is essential for human life, and thus for human behavior. Nothing that we as humans do can happen outside a biological context. But this doesn't mean that biology and biology alone shapes men's behavior. Nor does it mean that evolutionary pressures or testosterone predetermine social inequalities. Contemporary biological research contradicts the elevation of nature over nurture (and vice versa)—clearly both biology and culture are key. Indeed, studies on testosterone's sensitivity to subtle contextual variation illustrates that nature operates *through* nurture.

As we saw in this chapter, research on sex differences is at odds with the position that there are essential, deep, and meaningful psychological differences between men and women—resulting from genes, hormones, or otherwise. In fact, the research finds that in virtually all regards there is much more variation among the sexes than there is between them. In other words, we are dealing with largely overlapping bell curves. And even where significant differences do emerge, in terms of violence perpetration, for example, it is difficult if not impossible to know whether those differences are due to biology or to socialization.

Despite the considerable nuance that a century of research on evolutionary psychology, hormones, and sex differences has achieved, there persists a naïve yet powerful narrative that biology is really all there is to the story of men and masculinities. The argument that an aspect of masculinity is "determined by biology" can be a way to excuse or justify social structures or behaviors. As we'll see in the coming chapters, the implication that masculinity is fixed and unchangeable is sharply contrasted by social learning, social constructionist, feminist, and intersectional perspectives.

References

Belluck, P. (2011, September 12). In study, fatherhood leads to drop in testosterone. *New York Times*. Retrieved from: www.nytimes.com/2011/09/13/health/research/13testosterone.html.

Boissy, A. & Bouissou, M. F. (1994). Effects of androgen treatment on behavioral and physiological responses of heifers to fear-eliciting situations. *Hormones and Behavior*, 28(1), 66–83.

Buss, D. M., Larsen, R. J., Westen, D., & Semmelroth, J. (1992). Sex differences in jealousy: evolution, physiology, and psychology. *Psychological Science*, 3(4), 251–256.

Buss, D. M., Shackelford, T. K., Kirkpatrick, L. A., Choe, J. C., Lim, H. K., Hasegawa, M., Hasegawa, T. & Bennett, K. (1999). Jealousy and the nature of beliefs about infidelity: tests of competing hypotheses about sex differences in the United States, Korea, and Japan. *Personal Relationships*, 6(1), 125–150.

Buunk, B. P., Angleitner, A., Oubaid, V., & Buss, D. M. (1996). Sex differences in jealousy in evolutionary and cultural perspective: tests from the Netherlands, Germany, and the United States. *Psychological Science*, 7(6), 359–363.

Chapman, E., Baron-Cohen, S., Auyeung, B., Knickmeyer, R., Taylor, K., & Hackett, G. (2006). Fetal testosterone and empathy: evidence from the empathy quotient (EQ) and the "reading the mind in the eyes" test. *Social Neuroscience*, 1(2), 135–148.

Crupain, M. (2016, September 15). *The Dr. Oz Show* [television broadcast]. Harpo Studios, New York, NY.

DeSteno, D., Bartlett, M. Y., Braverman, J., & Salovey, P. (2002). Sex differences in jealousy: evolutionary mechanism or artifact of measurement? *Journal of Personality and Social Psychology, 83*(5), 1103–1116.

DeSteno, D. A. & Salovey, P. (1996). Evolutionary origins of sex differences in jealousy? Questioning the "fitness" of the model. *Psychological Science, 7*(6), 367–372.

DiCaro, V. (2011, September 14). Are good dads wimps? Fathers and testosterone [blog post]. Retrieved from: www.fatherhood.org/bid/135306/Are-Good-Dads-Wimps-Fathers-and-Testosterone.

Eisenegger, C., Naef, M., Snozzi, R., Heinrichs, M., & Fehr, E. (2010). Prejudice and truth about the effect of testosterone on human bargaining behaviour. *Nature, 463*(7279), 356–359.

Fine, C. (2017). *Testosterone rex: myths of sex, science, and society.* New York, NY: Norton Press.

Gettler, L. T., McDade, T. W., Feranil, A. B., & Kuzawa, C. W. (2011). Longitudinal evidence that fatherhood decreases testosterone in human males. *Proceedings of the National Academy of Sciences, 108*(39), 16194–16199.

Gill, C. (2016, November 4). It's time we started celebrating masculinity. *The Independent.* Retrieved from: www.independent.co.uk.

Haslam, N., Bastian, B., & Bissett, M. (2004). Essentialist beliefs about personality and their implications. *Personality and Social Psychology Bulletin, 30*(12), 1661–1673.

Haslam, N., Rothschild, L., & Ernst, D. (2000). Essentialist beliefs about social categories. *British Journal of Social Psychology, 39*(1), 113–127.

Haslam, N., Rothschild, L., & Ernst, D. (2002). Are essentialist beliefs associated with prejudice? *British Journal of Social Psychology, 41*(1), 87–100.

Hermans, E. J., Putman, P., & Van Honk, J. (2006). Testosterone administration reduces empathetic behavior: a facial mimicry study. *Psychoneuroendocrinology, 31*(7), 859–866.

Hyde, J. S. (2005). The gender similarities hypothesis. *American Psychologist, 60*(6), 581–592.

James, A. N. (2007). *Teaching the male brain: how boys think, feel, and learn in school.* Thousand Oaks, CA: Corwin.

Jordan-Young, R. M. (2010). *Rainstorm: the flaws in the science of sex differences.* Cambridge, MA: Harvard University Press.

Kennair, L. E. O., Nordeide, J., Andreassen, S., Strønen, J., & Pallesen, S. (2011). Sex differences in jealousy: a study from Norway. *Nordic Psychology, 63*(1), 20–34.

Kucharska, J. (2017). Sex differences in the appraisal of traumatic events and psychopathology. *Psychological Trauma: Theory, Research, Practice, and Policy, 9*(5), 575–582.

Lippa, R. A. (2016). Biological influences on masculinity. In Y. J. Wong & S. R. Wester (Eds.), *APA handbook of men and masculinities* (pp. 187–209). Washington, DC: American Psychological Association.

Martin, C. L. & Parker, S. (1995). Folk theories about sex and race differences. *Personality and Social Psychology Bulletin, 21*(1), 45–57.

McCabe, D. P. & Castel, A. D. (2008). Seeing is believing: the effect of brain images on judgments of scientific reasoning. *Cognition, 107*(1), 343–352.

Sagarin, B. J., Becker, D. V., Guadagno, R. E., Wilkinson, W. W., & Nicastle, L. D. (2012). A reproductive threat-based model of evolved sex differences in jealousy. *Evolutionary Psychology, 10*(3), 487–503.

Sapolsky, R. M. (2017). *Behave: the biology of humans at our best and worst.* New York, NY: Penguin Press.

Smiler, A. P., & Gelman, S. A. (2008). Determinants of gender essentialism in college students. *Sex Roles, 58*(11–12), 864–874.

Summers, L. (2005, January 14). Remarks at NBER conference on diversifying the science and engineering workforce. Retrieved April 5, 2005 from: www.president.harvard.edu/speeches/2005/nber.html.

Thornhill, R. & Palmer, C. T. (2001). *A natural history of rape: biological bases of sexual coercion.* Cambridge, MA: MIT Press.

Travis, C. B. (Ed.) (2003). *Evolution, gender, and rape.* Cambridge, MA: MIT Press.

Tsai, L. W. & Sapolsky, R. M. (1996). Rapid stimulatory effects of testosterone upon myotubule metabolism and sugar transport, as assessed by silicon microphysiometry. *Aggressive Behavior: Official Journal of the International Society for Research on Aggression, 22*(5), 357–364.

Valizadeh, R. (2017, March 9). The decline in testosterone is destroying the basis of masculinity [blog post]. Retrieved from: www.returnofkings.com/116463/the-decline-in-testosterone-is-destroying-the-basis-of-masculinity.

Weisberg, D. S., Taylor, J. C., & Hopkins, E. J. (2015). Deconstructing the seductive allure of neuroscience explanations. *Judgment and Decision Making, 10*(5), 429–441.

Wingfield, J. C., Hegner, R. E., Dufty, Jr, A. M., & Ball, G. F. (1990). The "challenge hypothesis": theoretical implications for patterns of testosterone secretion, mating systems, and breeding strategies. *The American Naturalist, 136*(6), 829–846.

Zell, E., Krizan, Z., & Teeter, S. R. (2015). Evaluating gender similarities and differences using metasynthesis. *American Psychologist, 70*(1), 10–20.

4

TEACHING BOYS AND MEN

Social Learning Perspectives

I know what you guys are thinking in your research. But it was different in my family growing up. My father encouraged us to express our emotions. If something was bothering me and I started crying, he'd say, "That's okay son. You get it all out. Just go behind the barn there until you're done and then come on back."

—"Bob" age 60

This chapter is all about learning. Not in the academic sense, but in a social sense. How do we learn to think, feel, and act in ways that are expected by those around us, such as family members, friends, and authority figures? And how do we learn to avoid doing things that others consider inappropriate? For psychologists, the study of social learning is about trying to understand how social experience affects human behavior in its broadest sense.

As it turns out, encounters with the meaning of gender are some of the earliest and most powerful learning contexts we face. Studies have shown that humans can discriminate between male and female voices and faces as early as six months old (Fagan & Singer, 1979; Miller, 1983). But the lessons don't stop in childhood. Gendered social learning continues throughout life as we accumulate experiences and as the cultural practices around us shift in different directions. For example, when Michael was a young teenager, he rarely if ever saw a boy or man wearing pink clothing. It simply wasn't done, and it wasn't hard to learn that wearing the color pink was a behavior that "boys shouldn't do." However, as Michael approached the later teen years, the "preppy" style of dress came full bore to Southern California and, within the span of a few weeks, boys all around him were wearing pink shirts with rolled-up collars.

Clearly, messages from our social environments about the meanings of gender can change over time. And yet, some messages are very stable. For instance, as we will see in Chapter 6, the meanings of manhood and masculinity can vary across different races, sexualities, or cultures. However, the notion that to be appropriately masculine requires *avoiding anything considered feminine* is remarkably consistent across cultures. Thus, if men's social learning about gender were like literature, it would be fair to say that what's on the current reading list is always a mixture of what's currently hot as well as some timeless classics.

Understanding how gendered social learning works requires consideration of the psychological processes that allow us to be so strongly affected by experience. When young adult men are praised by male friends for drinking large quantities of alcohol, how exactly does that praise alter their future drinking behavior? How do they come to associate drinking with masculinity? And what experiences lead some men to become advocates for gender equality while others continue to act and think in ways that are oppressive to other genders? These are just a handful of the many questions addressed by the study of gendered social learning.

For Consideration

Which individuals or groups in your own history have been particularly influential in your learning about what masculinity is and isn't? What specifically have you learned about the meanings of masculinity?

It takes only a little reflection on our lived experience to realize that the list of things we learn about men and masculinity is a long one. What clothes men should and shouldn't wear, how men should interact with people of other genders, attitudes towards sports, childcare, what is love versus sex, how men should respond to problems in their lives—the list goes on. In fact, there is so much we learn about gender that psychologists have tried to place some boundaries around different aspects of social learning in order to create an simpler, more ordered understanding of the processes involved. With few exceptions, we can boil down the study of men's gendered social learning to two questions: (1) *what* is learned, and (2) *how* is it learned?

Basic Mechanisms of Gendered Social Learning

To appreciate how the psychology of learning views human activity, the first thing you have to do is expand your concept of the term **"behavior."** Most of us think of behaviors as concrete actions and we distinguish these from thoughts, feelings, and biological processes. However, from a learning perspective, behavior is not only brushing your teeth, walking two steps forward, or clicking a mouse. It's also *feeling* the loss of a loved one, *imagining* what might happen tomorrow, or *dreading* that you won't be able to lift an extremely heavy object and will appear weak. Behavior is human activity in the most inclusive sense—it occurs on the outside *and* the inside.

The next thing you need to do is distinguish between the forms of behaviors and their functions. *Form* describes the overt characteristics of a behavior. For example, what do particular actions look and sound like? For how long do they occur? Are they verbal or non-verbal, loud or soft, and so on. *Function* describes the current and historical conditions that give rise to the behavior. In effect, form describes the "what" of behavior and function describes the "why."

Questions Associated With the Form of an Activity

- Who was there?
- What happened?
- How long did it last?
- What came first, then what, then what, etc?
- What exactly was said?
- How did it start?

Questions Associated With the Function of an Activity

- Why did this happen?
- Where did this come from?
- Why now?
- What other activities have similar functions to this one at this time?
- What consequences follow this activity?
- What consequences tended to follow it in the past?
- What future activities are being made more likely as a result of what's happening here?
- What future activities are being made less likely as a result of what's happening here?

From a gendered social learning perspective, we cannot deem particular actions as having something to do with masculinity based simply on their form. Instead, we must consider the possible functions of different actions. Is watching sports on television an example of doing masculinity? It depends on whether such behavior was learned in a gendered context and elicited by gendered cues in the environment. Some men watch sports for pure enjoyment. For others, it's something they learned to do because they were expected to do so as males. And some men watch sports for different reasons depending on the time and place.

What about behaviors with forms that seem obviously gendered? It's certainly tempting to assume that flexing one's muscles in front of other men at the gym, accusing another male of being a woman or gay because he prefers wine coolers over beer, or making homophobic jokes to a male doctor during a digital prostate exam are instances of masculinity operating. But what about the opposite situation, where actions with forms seen as stereotypically non-masculine (e.g., crying) might actually have functions that result from the social learning of masculinity? In fact, one of us had a memorable experience that exemplified this seeming discrepancy between form and function.

Several years ago, Michael attended an all-day men's retreat. Many of the men present were psychologists and the goal was to create an environment where the attendees were relatively free from the demands of masculinity and able to experience what it's like to be emotionally open with each other while putting aside any hints of stereotypically gendered behavior. As the process unfolded, individual men began to share more personal details about their lives. Eventually the first tear was shed and members of the group responded supportively. But then an intriguing process appeared to arise. Many of the people who spoke subsequently appeared to be working very hard to portray themselves as *more* emotionally open than the other guys. The process was not direct and overt—no one said, "You think you can be sad, just watch me!" Still, there did seem to be a competitive crying dynamic emerging in the group process. In other words, although the form of the behavior (crying) appeared to deviate from masculine social learning, the function (competition) was entirely congruent with gendered mandates to be competitive.

In order to study the functions of learned behavior, psychologists have identified several different mechanisms of learning, many of which are found not only in humans but in chimpanzees, dogs, pigeons, and a wide range of other living organisms. The fact that these learning mechanisms are shared by non-humans does not mean that "men are no different than monkeys." As we will see later in this chapter, one thing that distinguishes human learning is the capacity for language (i.e., verbal learning). But there are other ways in which the mechanisms of human and non-human learning are remarkably similar. Learning psychologists often refer to these as *basic* learning mechanisms because, in their purest forms, they are the foundational building blocks for the countless ways that experience affects us over the course of our lives.

Reinforcement is a process in which the consequences that follow particular actions make those actions more likely to occur in the future. The process happens so frequently and in so many different areas of life that we rarely acknowledge it. We smile when we greet people because in the past doing so has been followed by others smiling at us. We drink when we're thirsty because experience has taught us that doing so will be followed by the positive consequence of having our thirst reduced. We read because the behavior of reading is (hopefully) followed by increased understanding, parents' praise, or sheer enjoyment.

Reinforcement plays a role in all areas of life, but it becomes particularly salient in contexts where our social environment has certain standards or expectations to which individuals are held accountable. Gender is one of those contexts. Consider the long list of "dos" and "don'ts" related to gender: men should be tough, in control of their emotions, self-reliant, good at sports, sexually aggressive, financially successful, and so on. In contrast, women should be kind, attractive, empathic, good with children, etc. In reality, of course, people of all genders vary in these characteristics. Nonetheless, society appears to have a strong investment in teaching individuals to aspire to these expectations and social reinforcement plays a central role in the process. Consider how young boys learn to value and pursue athletic ability. Cheers, big smiles, or a brand new shiny basketball are just a handful of the positive consequences that may reinforce behaviors related to athletic interest and performance.

Just as behavior is likely to increase following a positive consequence, actions that are followed by negative consequences tend to decrease over time. Learning psychologists refer to this process as **punishment** and it is fairly common in gendered social learning, particularly when it comes to masculine roles and social norms, many of which specify thoughts, feelings, and actions that are considered inappropriate for boys and men. Consider these statements which can be heard at playgrounds, schoolyards, and athletic events across the U.S.

- "Big boys don't cry."
- "Go ahead and whine for your mamma!"
- "You've got to learn to suck it up and keep your emotions under control."
- "Don't be a pussy/girl/gay, etc."

Such statements serve to punish behaviors such as expressing vulnerable emotions, seeking the comfort of a caregiver, or doing anything that is perceived as feminine or homosexual.

Research has shown that young boys, to a greater degree than young girls, experience a wide range of forms of social punishment for deviating from their assigned gender norms (Chaplin, Cole, & Zahn-Waxler, 2005; Idle, Wood, & Desmarais, 1993). For example, one study found that fathers attend differentially to "submissive" emotions like anxiety and sadness and "disharmonious" emotions such as anger depending on child gender. They are more likely to ignore boys' sadness and anxiety and more likely to attend to boys' anger. The authors conclude that this process has the effect of subtly reinforcing gender stereotypic expressions of emotion (Chaplin et al., 2005). Another study found that school-aged boys experience more intense peer devaluation when breaking gender norms than do girls (Zucker, Wilson-Smith, Kurita, & Stern, 1995). It appears that masculinity is regularly *policed* in the lives of boys and men through delivery of a wide range of aversive consequences for violating gender roles and norms. These aversive consequences can include verbal shaming, ridicule, accusations of homosexuality or femininity, and at times even physical assaults and beatings. For example, a transgender student at Ethan's high school was lit on fire while commuting home for wearing a dress on the city bus.

Negative reinforcement describes a process in which actions increase because they are followed by the removal of something aversive or unpleasant. We put on more clothing when we are cold because in the past that behavior was followed by ridding ourselves of the chills. Likewise, eating is typically followed both by the taste of something good (positive reinforcement) and also by the elimination of hunger (negative reinforcement). *Avoidance* learning is a particular type of negative reinforcement in which our actions are strengthened not by the removal of something aversive, but by keeping away from things we expect to be aversive altogether. Less technically speaking, avoidance learning is all about figuring out what *not* to do in particular situations.

As it turns out, avoidance learning produces some fairly specific and predictable consequences for human functioning and is also quite common in gendered social learning. When we learn to think, feel, and act in particular ways in order to avoid something bad happening, anxiety, fear, and *hypervigilance* (being extra on-guard to potential threats) often come along for the ride, particularly when in situations where avoidance may be necessary or may have been necessary in the past. Such reactions are useful evolutionarily because they help us to prepare for potential real dangers in our environment. For example, it was adaptive for our ancestors to worry about lions if that anxiety and anticipation led them to keep safe by staying away from lions' dens. But what about when we learn to fear and avoid people, things, and situations that do not pose a real or substantial threat? In these cases, anxiety can turn into a chronic problem that restricts our activities and reduces our quality of life. In fact, anxiety disorders are among the most common mental health problems humans experience and include fear of heights, animals, open spaces, public speaking, to name just a few.

A similar type of avoidance-based process is common in gendered social learning for boys and men. Although it is not typically thought of as an anxiety disorder per se, the results can negatively impact quality of life in similar ways.

For Consideration

What are some people, places, or things that young boys are taught to avoid or else they are at risk of social punishment? What forms of punishing consequences are used to shape boys' and men's behavior?

We pose the question above to our students every year and here are some of the answers they come up with:

- Crying
- The color pink
- Gay people
- Sweet alcoholic drinks
- Needing or asking for help
- Expressing physical or emotional pain
- Losing at sports
- Certain types of music (e.g., highly emotional music or music that might be deemed "gay" for any number of reasons)
- Anything considered feminine
- Being "whipped" (i.e., caring too much about a girlfriend or letting her make too many decisions for you)
- Losing control of your emotions
- Being unable to perform physically in sports or sex.

This is just a partial list of the many things masculine roles and norms compel boys and men to avoid. The list of "don'ts" may actually be longer than the list of "dos" when it comes to men's gendered social learning. It's therefore not surprising that many boys and men can experience considerable anxiety and fear when they perceive themselves as at risk of failing at the demands of masculinity. In fact, researchers Joseph Vandello and Jennifer Bosson have coined the term "*precarious manhood*" to describe how masculinity is typically "hard won and easily lost"; it is a precarious state that can easily be taken away when individuals fail to behave in ways that are expected by masculine gender norms (Vandello, Bosson, Cohen, Burnaford, & Weaver, 2008). In one study, the researchers found that when reporting job preference, men concerned about being perceived as feminine avoided stating a desire for flexible work schedules (Vandello, Hettinger, Bosson, & Siddiqi, 2013). If a given individual's gendered learning history is strong enough, he may come to restrict his life in numerous ways in order to avoid the aversive consequences he anticipates will befall him should he fail. As we will see later in this chapter, the psychological experiences of strain, anxiety, fear, and avoidance play a central role in several of the most well-developed theories of masculine social learning.

Modeling is the last basic mechanism of social learning and can be distinguished from reinforcement, punishment, and avoidance by the absence of consequences affecting the learning process. When humans learn through modeling, we learn to do what others do simply by watching and imitating their actions. Research has shown that modeling is extremely common in gendered social learning (Bussey & Bandura, 1984, 1999).

We are more likely to model the actions of those we consider similar to ourselves, and also those we perceive as having status or respect. As you might imagine, this makes modeling more common for young boys when they are around male peers and in same-sex groups. Styles of dress, ways of talking, specific vocabularies, hobbies, and attitudes toward women and other genders are all fair game for modeling. For example, when Ethan was growing up in Northern California most boys wore baggy jeans. Tight-fitting jeans would have been considered overly feminine (or might have elicited homophobic teases). But by the mid-2000s, hipsters began wearing their jeans tight. As fashion began to show images of men wearing skinny jeans, over time they became part of a trendy style. Noticing the men around him had skinnier pants than he did, Ethan learned to model.

Michael was nine years old when his family moved from Oklahoma to Los Angeles. In the span of less than a year, he went from sporting cowboy boots and bolos to donning skateboard shoes, Ocean Pacific shorts, and Hawaiian surfer-style shirts. He also worked hard to abandon his slight Oklahoma "twang" of an accent and replace it with the casually mellow pace of Southern California speech. The specific behaviors associated with masculinity that Michael learned to model were different in Oklahoma versus Southern California. In Oklahoma, demonstrating masculinity was about physical toughness and not backing down from a fight. In California it was more about being "cool" as defined by the largely surfer culture. In retrospect, it's clear that this was also a difference in masculinity based on race, economics, and social class; the young (White) boys in Michael's Californian school came from greater wealth than the boys in Oklahoma and had within their reach a wider range of ways to demonstrate masculinity (e.g., designer clothing or expensive cars) compared with the working-class boys in Oklahoma. Thus, just as reinforcement, punishment, and avoidance are context-dependent, so the way masculinity gets performed and subsequently modeled can vary by class, race, and geographic location.

When Is Social Learning Gendered?

The mechanisms described above come into play in all types of social learning. However, not all social learning is necessarily gendered. The ways we eat, dress, and talk, the music we listen to, how we cope with painful emotions, and our approach to intimate relationships may or may not be influenced by what we have learned about gender. Consider this brief conversation between two male friends:

DEREK: How's it goin', man?
RICO: Not bad, not bad. What's going on?
DEREK: Nothing. Same shit, different day. Except my freakin' dog is sick. Barely could wake her up this morning, wouldn't eat, and we had to take her to the vet.
RICO: Damn. That sucks. They probably charge you the big bucks too. Last time I took mine to the vet I was out at least three hundred. What a racket.
DEREK: Seriously [sighs and shakes head].

What do you notice about this interaction? Ostensibly, it's simply a matter of two men greeting each other with small talk. They quickly establish that there is nothing unusual going on and nothing to be concerned about. However, Derek then reveals that his dog is sick and that, apparently, she almost died. Rico acknowledges Derek's concern ("that sucks") and then shares his own similar experience.

Researchers in the psychology of men would probably point to several things about this exchange that reflect the social learning of masculinity. Both men establish quickly and firmly that they are unbothered by anything. Derek voices vulnerable feelings through anger/frustration ("freakin' dog") rather than pain. And just in case there's any remaining chance that Derek's vulnerable feelings of loss will enter the conversation, Rico shifts the focus to himself and subtly changes the topic from the loss of a loved companion to the financial "racket" of the veterinarian. Each of these conversational moves is congruent with the masculine social norm of *emotional restriction*—avoiding expressions of emotions like sadness, fear, or anxiety. We might then conclude that their approach to the interaction is at least partially a result of gendered social learning. Taking it one step further, we might argue that their conversation is not only a product of past social learning, but that the conversation itself creates a context for further learning, if only by reinforcing messages learned long ago (e.g., "When you're bothered by something emotional play it off as stress or anger, and if another male reveals something to you that upsets him share a story of your own to take the focus away from him").

If we dig down into the question a bit deeper, how can we say with confidence that gender plays a role in Derek and Rico's conversation? It's also possible that the nature of their interaction is a product of their individual personalities and perhaps cultural, ethnic, or socioeconomic norms alongside gender. Of course, it's rarely possible to identify the precise cause(s) of any social behavior because our interactions are the products of multiple historical and contemporary rivers of influence. Nonetheless, we can identify the conditions under which certain social processes such as gender are more or less likely to play a role.

First, gendered social learning is more likely to play a role when gender is present *materially* in the environment. In other words, the fact that both Rico and Derek identify as male, to themselves and to each other, makes it more likely that behaviors previously learned in the context of homosocial (all male) environments will emerge. Behaviorally speaking, their gender serves as a **discriminant stimulus**—an event which signals the presence of a relationship between specific actions and specific consequences. A red blinking light on the road is a discriminant stimulus because it signals that the behavior of driving through an intersection without stopping may well be followed by the consequence of a collision. For Derek, the presence of another male asking the question, "How's it going?" may have signaled that the behavior of stating clearly what he was feeling (e.g., "I love my dog so much and I'm worried about losing her") would be followed by an aversive consequence rather than a positive reinforcer. The manner in which Derek hedges his bet supports this interpretation; he discloses the facts of the situation, but cloaks them in stereotypically masculine language, perhaps in an effort to preempt any negative response from Rico.

The presence of other males in the environment does not by itself mean that the behaviors which occur are the result of gendered social learning. Whether the material presence of gender functions as a discriminant stimulus depends on the learning histories of the people involved. For some men, the company of other males is a strong discriminant stimulus because their presence carries significant meaning in their personal learning histories. For other men, the material presence of gender does not carry the same significance. Individuals also differ in how sensitive they are to the presence of gendered cues in the environment. For some men, the presence of a single male (or female) is enough to reliably elicit talk about sports, athletic prowess, financial success, or other topics that they perceive as appropriately masculine. For others, the environment needs to be much more saturated with cues for their gendered learning history to emerge. The specific composition of groups can also affect the likelihood that gendered behavior will surface. All-male sports teams, for example, provide numerous cues for gender-relevant behavior. Not only because all of the players are male, but also because of the proximity of sports equipment, gyms, weights, older male authorities (coaches), for example.

Gender can be present in the environment in *symbolic* ways as well. Different language, images, and even colors come to connote masculinity and serve to cue masculine repertoires of behavior. Consider the greeting, "How's it goin', man?," which began Derek and Rico's exchange. This is a very common greeting between males in the United States, one that uses a symbolic stimulus ("man") to signal that the current context is gendered and that appropriate behavior should follow. This is typically neither a conscious nor an intentional process. Instead, as a result of past social learning, it is much more automatic. Studies have shown that gendered behavior can be influenced by subtle environmental events that occur below the level of our conscious awareness. For example, one study found that men who were primed with masculine words such as "father" or "suit" through their car radio (as opposed to feminine words like "mother" or "lipstick") actually drove faster (Schmid Mast, Sieverding, Esslen, Graber, & Jäncke, 2008).

For Consideration

What are some examples of objects, events, words, places, etc. that might symbolically cue masculine repertoires of behavior?

The Social Learning of Masculinity: Take-Home Points

As you can see by this point, the social learning of masculinity is a pervasive process; it shows up in a wide range of contexts across the lifespan, and the lessons repeat themselves. These lessons are at times direct and overt (e.g., "Man up and quit being a girl!"). Other times, the messages are subtler, such as when an adult man in his 60s learns not to discuss his personal health concerns with other men because it appears to make them uncomfortable (perhaps he notices that the room gets quiet).

Earlier, we considered several basic mechanisms of learning, including reinforcement, punishment, avoidance, and modeling. Although each of these psychological processes is involved in the social learning of masculinity, it would be a mistake to think they operate in isolation of one another. Instead, multiple consequences are typically involved in developing and maintaining gendered behavior. For example, telling or laughing at misogynist jokes may be the result of both positive reinforcement (approval from one's peers), negative reinforcement (avoiding being shamed or criticized for not going along with others), and modeling (having seen other males engage in this kind of humor). Thus, gendered social learning works less like a machine, with individual gears and levers acting in isolation, and more like an organic system where multiple contexts, cues, and consequences come and go to produce masculinity in situations that have called for it in the past.

If we return to a question posed in the introduction—what is masculinity? —we can now see how it would be answered from a social learning perspective. *Masculinity is repertoires of learned behavior in a gendered social context. More precisely, masculinity can be seen as learned repertoires of behavior that establish an individual as meeting socially defined standards for how males are expected to behave.* Whether or not such behavior emerges in any particular social context depends on both the strength of whichever gendered cues are present and the individuals' unique learning histories. In a metaphorical sense, masculinity can be thought of as operating similar to an allergy. At the biological level, allergies are our bodies' coordinated reaction to perceived environmental threats (i.e., allergens). Whether an allergic response occurs depends on both the amount of allergen present in a situation and our individual sensitivity to the presence of that allergen. Some people will sneeze at the slightest amount of pollen in the air. But pump enough into the room and eventually everyone will begin sneezing. Masculinity works the same way: some people will act it out with barely the slightest provocation, but the greater the strength and frequency of gendered cues in a situation the more individuals tend to "get on board" with what they think is expected.

Meta-Models of the Social Learning of Masculinity

Over the last three decades researchers in the psychology of men have developed several broad paradigms for understanding the social learning of masculinity: gender role strain, gender role conflict, and conformity to masculine norms. There are ongoing debates about whether particular paradigms are best described as emphasizing "social learning," "social construction," or some combination of the two (e.g., Addis & Cohane, 2005; Levant & Richmond, 2016). However, for our purposes, we consider them all under the rubric of social learning because all of them focus on how environmental/societal meanings of masculinity influence the thoughts, feelings, and actions of individuals.

Each of these different paradigms is consistent with the basic mechanisms of social learning we described earlier in this chapter. Some even make periodic mention of reinforcement, punishment, and so on. Nonetheless, it is helpful to recognize that these paradigms evolved not out of basic research in the psychology of learning, but largely out of social and practical concerns in the field of counseling psychology, including social justice, feminism, gender equality, and the desire to influence the process of psychotherapy and counseling to include a focus on men and masculinity. As a result, there is relatively less concern with exploring the mechanisms of *how* gender is learned (the function), and relatively more concern with identifying exactly *what* is learned (the form).

These paradigms also share certain assumptions. They include:

1. Masculinity is socially learned rather than biologically hardwired.
2. Masculinity is often problematic, contradictory, and psychologically restrictive.

3. There are individual differences in the degree to which gendered social learning affects individuals.
4. There are multiple ways masculinity can affect individuals and also multiple different types of masculinities.
5. The social learning of masculinity depends upon and ultimately serves the existence of patriarchy as a social system (see Chapter 6).

Gender Role Strain

As we saw in Chapter 1, the psychology of men first gained traction as a distinct subfield with psychologist Joseph Pleck's (1975, 1981) feminist-inspired research on the male gender role. Pleck (2017) viewed his *gender role strain paradigm* (GRSP) as a radical break from earlier scholarship, which he termed the gender role identity paradigm (GRIP). He argued the GRIP had dominated psychology and other social sciences for over a century and had inaccurately represented the nature of gender. According to Pleck, the GRIP assumed that masculinity and femininity are properties of individuals that reflect the essential nature of what it means to be male or female. From this perspective, optimal human functioning occurs when individuals possess those psychological and physical characteristics that define their appropriate gender (i.e., women possess female bodies and high degrees of femininity while men possess male bodies and high degrees of masculinity). Note that from this perspective, what defines masculinity is neither learned, nor historically variable; it is simply those things that are fundamental to being a man. It's an unquestioned, obvious given.

Pleck's (1981) book, *The Myth of Masculinity*, thoroughly critiqued the GRIP and offered the GRSP in its place. The GRSP posits no essential qualities that define men or masculinity but instead makes the following assumptions:

1. Contemporary gender roles are operationally defined by gender stereotypes and norms.
2. Gender roles are contradictory and inconsistent.
3. The proportion of people who violate gender roles is high.
4. Violation of gender roles leads to social condemnation.
5. Violation of gender roles leads to negative psychological consequences.
6. Actual or imagined violation of gender roles leads individuals to overconform to them.
7. Certain prescribed gender roles are often dysfunctional.
8. Violating gender roles has more severe consequences for males than for females.
9. Each gender experiences gender role strain in its paid and family roles.
10. Historical change causes gender role strain.

In different ways, each of these assumptions portrays masculinity as historically determined, environmentally contingent, and problematic. Rather than being seen as an internal, stable, and essential part of men's personalities, masculinity is now understood as a socially agreed upon set of values, ideologies, and roles that are taught and enforced by our communities.

The publication of *The Myth of Masculinity* provided the concept of **gender ideology** with fertile ground for theoretical development and empirical research. Levant (2011) described masculine ideologies as beliefs about thoughts, actions, and behaviors that are appropriate (and inappropriate) for males. The social learning roots of Levant's approach to ideology are evident in the following quotation:

> *In the current formulation, traditional masculinity ideology is posited to exert social influence through interactions resulting in reinforcement, punishment, and observational learning. Traditional masculinity ideology thus informs, encourages, and constrains boys and men to conform to (or comply with, or obey) the prevailing male role norms ... by adopting certain socially sanctioned (prescribed) masculine behaviors and avoiding certain forbidden (proscribed) behaviors.*
>
> (Levant & Richmond, 2016, p. 25)

Levant and others began systematic programs of research to measure masculinity ideologies and assess their impact on a wide range of indicators of human well-being. Such research is typically carried out with self-report questionnaires that assess differences in the degree to which individuals endorse different aspects of traditional masculine ideologies. These include the Male Role Norms Scale, the Male Role Attitudes Scale, and the Male Role Norms Inventory-Revised (Levant, Hirsch, Celentano, & Cozza, 1992; Levant et al., 2007; Pleck, Sonenstein, & Ku, 1994). Individual items on these measures tend to cluster into particular "sub"-ideologies including, Avoidance of Femininity, Self-Reliance, Dominance, and Restrictive Emotionality.

A recent review of research using these measures concluded that available data support central tenets of the GRSP (Levant & Richmond, 2016). For example, gender norms appear to vary according to cultural context and social location of individuals (e.g., race, class, socio-economic status). Moreover, as Pleck originally hypothesized, endorsement of traditional masculine ideologies is statistically predictive of a wide range of individual and relational problems including relationship violence, alcoholism, lower levels of father involvement in child-rearing, sexual aggressiveness, and negative attitudes toward help-seeking.

Pleck (1995) identified three different types of psychological strain created by traditional masculinity ideologies. **Discrepancy strain** is fostered when a person fails to live up to their own internalized ideals of how men should act, think, and feel. For example, a man who endorses the ideology that "real" men should be financially successful and always provide for their families might experience discrepancy strain if he has difficulty finding a job or must rely on his spouse for financial support. *Dysfunction strain* describes the ways in which various traditional masculine ideologies are inherently unhealthy when they are rigidly enacted by individuals. Emotional restriction, for example, has well-documented negative psychological consequences, but individual men may still enact it on a regular basis for fear of losing their "man card" if they openly express vulnerability. Finally, *trauma strain* refers to the negative consequences of the process of masculine gender socialization itself. Physical fights, humiliation, bullying, and other forms of social rejection are common strategies used in teaching young boys about the demands of masculinity. For some individuals, these early experiences are powerful enough to leave lasting scars that negatively impact relational and psychological well-being into adulthood.

Gender Role Conflict

Gender role conflict (GRC) has been a central organizing construct in research on the psychology of men and masculinity for over three decades. James O'Neil (1982), who coined the term, defines GRC as a psychological state that occurs when men experience internal distress or external conflict with others as a result of rigid or harmful gender roles (O'Neil, 2008, 2015).

The GRC paradigm shares much in common with the GRSP discussed above, although it also differs in significant ways. First, GRC is defined as a psychological *state* resulting from gendered social learning. In theory, this means that the degree of GRC a person experiences might vary by the day, the hour, or even the minute. This makes sense conceptually because of the contextual nature of social learning. Most of what we learn from our social environment is highly contingent; we learn to do and not do some things under some circumstances but not under others. Unfortunately, the measurement of GRC in empirical research has tended not to focus on moment-to-moment psychological states, but instead relies on self-reported general tendencies (e.g., "Affection between men makes me uncomfortable").

The second way the GRC paradigm extends the GRSP is by identifying additional interpersonal and intrapsychic processes that translate "out there" masculine ideologies to "in here" individual experiences. For example, *gender role devaluation* is defined as negative or derogatory criticism of oneself or others. *Restrictions* refer to situations in which gendered social learning leads individuals to attempt to control, hem in, or limit one's own or other people's behavior. Finally, O'Neil (2015) considers *violations* to be the most severe form of GRC, taking place when people psychologically or physically cause pain to themselves or others. Physically attacking gay individuals or bullying young boys who eschew traditionally masculine activities like sports are particularly poignant examples of violations. Devaluation, restriction, and violation can all transpire as part of enacting masculinity or as a result of breaching masculinity norms. Finally, these forms of GRC can come from within, such as when a man teases others or berates himself, or from outside, when he is mocked by others.

Research has suggested that GRC results in four specific patterns of psychological conflict: preoccupation with success, power, and competition; restrictive emotionality; restrictive affectionate behavior between men; and conflict between work and family. As with the GRSP, research has shown that individual differences in the degree to which people experience conflict in these domains statistically predicts a wide range of interpersonal and psychological problems in living. These include depression, anxiety, stress, negative attitudes toward help-seeking, low self-esteem, poor relationship satisfaction, alcohol and substance abuse, and negative attitudes toward sexual and racial minorities (O'Neil, 2015). It is also not surprising that measures of gender role conflict are correlated with measures of traditional masculine ideologies. In other words, people who endorse more traditional beliefs about what it means to be a man are also more likely to experience higher levels of gender role conflict and its associated problems.

Conformity to Masculine Norms

Alongside studies of gender role conflict and gender role strain is an increasing body of research on individual differences in *conformity to masculine social norms*. This research began with Mahalik and colleagues' (2003) development and publication of the Conformity to Masculine Norms Inventory (CMNI). Mahalik and his collaborators took a somewhat different approach to measuring the effects of the social learning of masculinity by focusing directly on the social psychology of norms (Cialdini & Trost, 1998; Sherif, 1936). According to Mahalik et al. (2003), "Conformity to masculine norms is defined as meeting societal expectations for what constitutes masculinity in one's public or private life" (p. 3). Societal expectations are communicated through both *descriptive norms* (what is perceived to be statistically "true," "common," or "normal") and *injunctive norms* (how people are expected to act, think, and feel). For example, the masculine gender norm of self-reliance has both descriptions of how men stereotypically *are* ("men don't like asking for help") and injunctions to act as men are *supposed* to ("men should handle problems on their own").

Mahalik and colleagues (2003) worked with a group of master's and doctoral-level students in counseling psychology from diverse ethnic and racial backgrounds to identify common masculine norms based on both personal experience with U.S. culture and a review of the existing research literature. This resulted in 11 masculine norms included in the final CMNI measure, including, Winning, Emotional Control, Risk-Taking, Violence,

Dominance, Playboy, Self-Reliance, Primacy of Work, Power over Women, Disdain for Homosexuals, and Pursuit of Status. As with GRSP and GRC research, conformity to these norms has been statistically associated with a wide range of problematic outcomes (Addis, Reigeluth, & Schwab, 2016).

For Consideration

What similarities and differences do you see in the forms of masculinity identified in the three paradigms? How are the functions of masculinity similar and/or different across the paradigms?

The Social Learning of Masculinity in Societal Context

As with the previous chapter, we close this one by considering the various ways a social learning perspective has been used in the past and might be used in the future to address a wide range of societal concerns related to men and masculinity. The idea that masculine norms and ideologies are learned from society is a powerful assumption resting at the heart of numerous efforts to change what we teach boys and men about gender. This makes sense because if we assume that masculinity is largely learned then it follows that the messages we receive about what it means to be a man can be changed, or perhaps even eradicated altogether. Efforts to intervene in the social learning of masculinity come in a wide range of forms. It is now relatively commonplace to find TED talks, CNN exposés, and a variety of *media stories* focused on topics such as changing definitions of masculinity, new roles for men in society, or the question of whether masculinity is "dying" (Bennett, 2011; Zimbardo, 2011).

More specific and sustained efforts to alter gendered social learning in men's lives can also be found. For example, over the last three decades, clinical and counseling psychologists have developed new *techniques and clinical approaches* for working with men in therapy (Brooks, 2001; Englar-Carlson & Stevens, 2006; Primack, Addis, Syzdek, & Miller, 2010; Rabinowitz & Cochran, 2002). Many of these efforts are designed to make the process of therapy more palatable to men since it is well documented that men are less likely than women to seek help for problems in their lives, an issue we address in detail in Chapter 10. Others are designed to provide individual men with knowledge and coping skills (e.g., emotion education, challenging thoughts and beliefs about what it means to be a man) that will help them free themselves from the restrictive effects of masculine norms. While these approaches are compelling in principle, there currently is no empirical evidence that the process or outcome of therapy is demonstrably enhanced by focusing specifically on issues related to men and masculinity. In addition, critics note that individual or group therapy reaches only a small portion of men in society, and only those that are willing and able to come to treatment.

Another approach rooted in social learning is to attempt to raise awareness about the psychological and physical costs of some masculine ideologies on a larger societal scale, often through *public health campaigns*. For example, an Australian organization called Spur Projects (n.d.) is dedicated to finding innovative ways to reduce the rates of suicide in men. It encourages young men to "soften the fuck up"; in other words, to publicly express the vulnerable sides of themselves. Much of the language in the campaign seems intentionally congruent with more traditionally masculine norms (e.g., reference to a "wing man"). At the same time, the campaign seeks to deliver and reinforce an alternative message: there is nothing unmanly about having problems in life and seeking help to deal with them.

Theoretically, the presence of these kinds of campaigns provides opportunities for new and different gendered social learning. Similar types of programs exist in other countries. In the United States, the last two decades have witnessed a growing number of media products (e.g., documentary films, websites, educational curricula) that challenge traditional norms in the effort to expose men and boys to messages about the harmful effects of restrictive masculine ideologies, and the benefits of freeing oneself from gender role strain and conflict to whatever degree possible.

Efforts to alter what boys and men learn about masculinity also take place in *educational settings*. For example, many American colleges and universities now have mandatory workshops or classes designed to reduce the incidence of sexual assault. Some of the topics covered include addressing myths about male sexuality (e.g., "men can't control their behavior when they are sexually aroused") and raising awareness about misogyny and the sexual objectification and exploitation of women.

Against these progressive campaigns to deconstruct masculinity's harmful effects, there exists a powerful backlash, and efforts to maintain the status quo abound. Many male-targeted magazines, television shows, organized sports, and musical styles continue to model and reinforce concepts of masculinity that are decidedly anti-feminine, emotionally restrictive, and dominance-oriented. The magazine *Men's Health*, for example, portrays health almost exclusively as a matter of developing muscle mass and having lots of ("good," heterosexual) sex. The United States has also witnessed an increase in anti-feminist men's rights movements that promote an ideology in which men are seen as victims of women's progress in society. Other "pro-male" collectives lament what they perceive as the erosion of traditional masculinity and seek to create learning environments that promote many of the same gender norms others are attempting to deconstruct. At times, the very existence of social learning itself is called into question in order to support a more status-quo/essentialist perspective on men and masculinity (e.g., "boys will be boys"/ "Men are inherently hunters and women are gatherers," etc.).

It is also revealing to observe the various ways a social learning per-spective can be leveraged to *justify, excuse, explain,* or *combat* issues such as violence, aggression, and sexual assault. While these actions are often attributed to an essential masculine nature in men, there are also instances where a social learning perspective is invoked. For example, in the days and weeks following a mass shooting in the United States, we often hear an outpouring of concern about "what we're teaching our kids" by virtue of widespread exposure to guns and violent video games. Similarly, high rates of sexual assault on college campuses are often attributed to the presence of *rape culture,* which promotes the sexual objectification of women and encourages men to adopt numerous myths about gender and sexuality (e.g., "when women say 'no' they often mean 'yes'").

A social learning perspective can also be leveraged on an individual basis to make sense of and respond more effectively to the gendered pres-sures around us. The first step is to enhance your awareness of when and how gendered social learning is operating in your environment. All people can develop their abilities to identify processes of reinforcement, punish-ment, and modeling as they are occurring in real time. And oftentimes simply commenting on this (to oneself and/or others) can create enough psychological distance in the moment to provide an opportunity for a thoughtful choice. As an analogy, our decisions about what to eat on a daily basis are constrained by the dietary norms and availability of differ-ent foods around us. However, we still have choices within these con-straints; we can eat mindfully, not just mindlessly!

We also have the ability to practice and reinforce alternative gender norms in our communities. We can ask boys and men about their vulner-able emotions and listen to their answers without shaming them. We can model how to confront misogynist and homophobic behavior, and we can lead by example in developing boys' and men's capacity for intimacy and relatedness as opposed to dominance. In short, as agentic human beings we are both the recipients and the orchestrators of gendered social learn-ing. How we approach it is up to us.

Summary and Conclusion

Social learning perspectives focus on the ways individuals are shaped by their environments. Boys and men are exposed to a wide range of masculine roles, norms, ideologies, and discourses that affect their behaviors in the broadest sense of the term. Reinforcement strengthens thoughts, feelings, and actions that are considered appropriately masculine. Punishment weakens behaviors that are considered inappropriate, and avoidance strengthens behaviors that help boys or men to escape from shame, criticism, and physical or emotional injury for violating masculine social norms or ideologies. Along with model-ing, these basic mechanisms of learning become gendered when sex or gender are present materially or symbolically in the social environment. Several meta-models of the social learning of masculinities have been developed including gender role strain, gender role conflict, and conformity to masculine norms. These models tend to focus on the form/content of masculinities (e.g., emotional restriction, anti-femininity, competition) rather than the function/process of gendered social learning (e.g., reinforcement, punishment, avoidance). Research shows that individual differences in exposure to such learning predict a wide range of indicators of human functioning; men who adhere more strongly to traditionally masculine norms and ideologies are at greater risk for depression, substance abuse, relationship conflict, and a host of other social problems. Finally, a social learning perspective is often leveraged societally as a way to explain, justify, or advocate altering a wide range of social issues related to men and masculinity.

References

Addis, M. E. & Cohane, G. H. (2005). Social scientific paradigms of masculinity and their implications for research and practice in men's mental health. *Journal of Clinical Psychology, 61*(6), 633–647.

Addis, M. E., Reigeluth, C. S., & Schwab, J. R. (2016). Social norms, social construction, and the psychology of men and masculinity. In Y. J. Wong & S. R. Wester (Eds), *APA handbook of men and masculinities* (pp. 81–104). Washington, DC: American Psychological Association.

Bennett, W. J. (2011, October 4). Why men are in trouble. *CNN*. Retrieved from: www.cnn.com/2011/10/04/opinion/bennett-men-in-trouble/index.html.

Brooks, G. R. (2001). Masculinity and men's mental health. *Journal of American College Health, 49*(6), 285–297.

Bussey, K. & Bandura, A. (1984). Influence of gender constancy and social power on sex-linked modeling. *Journal of Personality and Social Psychology, 47*(6), 1292–1302.

Bussey, K. & Bandura, A. (1999). Social cognitive theory of gender development and differentiation. *Psychological Review, 106*(4), 676–713.

haplin, T. M., Cole, P. M., & Zahn-Waxler, C. (2005). Parental socialization of emotion expression: gender differences and relations to child adjustment. *Emotion, 5*(1), 80–88.

Cialdini, R. B. & Trost, M. R. (1998). Social influence: social norms, conformity and compliance. In D. T. Gilbert, S. T. Fiske, & G. Lindzey (Eds), *The handbook of social psychology* (pp. 151–192). New York, NY: McGraw-Hill.

Englar-Carlson, M. E. & Stevens, M. A. (2006). *In the room with men: a casebook of therapeutic change.* Washington, DC: American Psychological Association.

Fagan, III, J. F. & Singer, L. T. (1979). The role of simple feature differences in infants' recognition of faces. *Infant Behavior & Development, 2*, 39–45.

Idle, T., Wood, E., & Desmarais, S. (1993). Gender role socialization in toy play situations: mothers and fathers with their sons and daughters. *Sex Roles, 28*(11–12), 679–691.

Levant, R. F. (2011). Research in the psychology of men and masculinity using the gender role strain paradigm as a framework. *American Psychologist, 66*(8), 765–776.

Levant, R. F., Hirsch, L. S., Celentano, E., & Cozza, T. M. (1992). The male role: an investigation of contemporary norms. *Journal of Mental Health Counseling, 14* (3), 325–337.

Levant, R. F. & Richmond, K. (2016). The gender role strain paradigm and masculinity ideologies. In Y. J. Wong & S. R. Wester (Eds), *APA handbook of men and masculinities* (pp. 23–49). Washington, DC: American Psychological Association.

Levant, R. F., Smalley, K. B., Aupont, M., House, A. T., Richmond, K., & Noronha, D. (2007). Initial validation of the male role norms inventory-revised (MRNI-R). *The Journal of Men's Studies, 15*(1), 83–100.

Mahalik, J. R., Locke, B. D., Ludlow, L. H., Diemer, M. A., Scott, R. P., Gottfried, M., & Freitas, G. (2003). Development of the conformity to masculine norms inventory. *Psychology of Men & Masculinity, 4*(1), 3–25.

Miller, C. L. (1983). Developmental changes in male/female voice classification by infants. *Infant Behavior and Development, 6*, 313–330.

O'Neil, J. M. (1982). Gender-role conflict and strain in men's lives. In K. Soloman & N. B. Levy (Eds), *Men in transition* (pp. 5–44). Boston, MA: Springer.

O'Neil, J. M. (2008). Summarizing 25 years of research on men's gender role conflict using the Gender Role Conflict Scale: new research paradigms and clinical implications. *The Counseling Psychologist, 36*(3), 358–445.

O'Neil, J. M. (2015). *Men's gender role conflict: psychological costs, consequences, and an agenda for change.* Washington, DC: American Psychological Association.

Pleck, J. (2017). Forward. In R. F. Levant & Y. J. Wong (Eds), *The psychology of men and masculinities* (pp. xi–xxi). Washington, DC: American Psychological Association.

Pleck, J. H. (1975). Masculinity—femininity. *Sex roles, 1*(2), 161–178.

Pleck, J. H. (1981). *The myth of masculinity.* Cambridge, MA: MIT Press.

Pleck, J. H. (1995). The gender role strain paradigm: an update. In R. F. Levant & W. S. Pollack (Eds), *A new psychology of men* (pp. 11–32). New York, NY: Basic Books.

Pleck, J. H., Sonenstein, F. L., & Ku, L. C. (1994). Attitudes toward male roles among adolescent males: a discriminant validity analysis. *Sex Roles, 30*(7–8), 481–501.

Primack, J. M., Addis, M. E., Syzdek, M., & Miller, I. W. (2010). The men's stress workshop: a gender-sensitive treatment for depressed men. *Cognitive and Behavioral Practice, 17*(1), 77–87.

Rabinowitz, F. E. & Cochran, S. V. (2002). *Deepening psychotherapy with men.* Washington, DC: American Psychological Association.

Schmid Mast, M., Sieverding, M., Esslen, M., Graber, K., & Jäncke, L. (2008). Masculinity causes speeding in young men. *Accident Analysis & Prevention, 40*(2), 840–842.

Sherif, M. (1936). *The psychology of social norms.* Oxford, England: Harper.

Spur Projects (n.d.). Soften the fck up. Retrieved from: http://softenthefckup. wearespur.com.

Thompson Jr, E. H. & Pleck, J. H. (1986). The structure of male role norms. *American Behavioral Scientist, 29*(5), 531–543.

Vandello, J. A., Bosson, J. K., Cohen, D., Burnaford, R. M., & Weaver, J. R. (2008). Precarious manhood. *Journal of Personality and Social Psychology, 95*(6), 1325–1339.

Vandello, J. A., Hettinger, V. E., Bosson, J. K., & Siddiqi, J. (2013). When equal isn't really equal: the masculine dilemma of seeking work flexibility. *Journal of Social Issues, 69*(2), 303–321.

Zimbardo, P. (2011). The demise of guys? [Video file]. Retrieved from: www.ted.com/talks/zimchallenge?language=en.

Zucker, K. J., Wilson-Smith, D. N., Kurita, J. A., & Stern, A. (1995). Children's appraisals of sex-typed behavior in their peers. *Sex Roles, 33*(11–12), 703–725.

5
MAKING MASCULINITIES
Social Constructionist Perspectives

C hapter 4 was all about the vast number of ways we teach boys and men to act, think, feel, and, above all, to establish themselves as appropriately masculine in the eyes of the surrounding culture. Such a learning perspective on the psychology of men is particularly good at highlighting the ways in which the social environment shapes gender. But a learning perspective is less adept at addressing two questions that many social scientists see as central to understanding men and masculinity. First, how exactly are values, ideologies, and gendered social norms created? To say that such things exist in our social environments begs the questions of where exactly they exist, how they got there, and what they're made of.

Second, what about the ability of individuals to resist the mandates of the world around them? Social learning perspectives appear to leave little or no room for free will. Nevertheless, we see many men and boys around us managing to act in ways that run counter to dominant norms and ideologies surrounding masculinity. Men who have sex with men, teenage boys who express grief and sadness rather than anger, adult men who confront others about sexism and misogyny in the workplace—such behavior poses a challenge for psychological accounts of men and masculinity based solely on social learning.

This chapter explores an alternative approach that is often confused with social learning: the social constructionist perspective. While a learning viewpoint focuses on how individuals are shaped by societal meanings of gender, a constructionist perspective asks exactly *how* (and sometimes *why*) such meanings are created in the first place. As it turns out, the social construction of masculinity is extremely context dependent, highly variable across time and space, and often intimately linked to the personal or political motivations of individuals and groups. Before diving into these processes in detail, we look at some examples of what the social construction of masculinity looks like in action.

Social Construction in Action

One of Michael's hobbies is smoking a tobacco pipe. For the past several years, he has been a member of an online forum of pipe smokers from around the world. Conversational threads focus on all different aspects of smoking a pipe from choosing tobacco, to lighting a pipe, to famous people who smoked a pipe. Most of the membership appears to identify as male, although people often use pseudonymous usernames rather than their actual names so it's hard to be sure.

Recently, one member started a thread in which he asked for advice on how to minimize the smell of pipe tobacco in the house. He had tried everything he knew but his wife could still detect the smell and found it offensive. Several forum members offered suggestions, but the original poster indicated that he had tried them all to no avail. Eventually, another member posted a message saying that perhaps it was time for the original poster either to "give up his man card" or to start asserting some power in his marriage. Shortly thereafter, another member started a new thread questioning whether the forum should be a community where gendered insults like the "man card" comment were allowed. Several members then posted stating that this statement was not intended harmfully, and that anyone who was offended should learn to take things less seriously. Over time the thread turned to a discussion of what counts as evidence of being a "real man" and eventually Michael (Maddis) could no longer resist the temptation to contribute. Here is how things went next:

MADDIS: "Real men" are a myth.

SMOKY MOUNTAIN: History is replete with real men. Men who can inspire. Men who can lead. Every single Medal of Honor recipient = real man. That is a fact. Cute thoughts like there are no real men appeal to the lesser.

MADDIS: Hmm. History is replete with PEOPLE who inspire, lead, receive medals, raise families, and so on. Some are men, some are women, and some fall in between. The fact that some are men does not make them more "real" men. What I'm objecting to is the testing of manhood. I'm not sure why thinking this way makes me "lesser."

ZZ: Y'all just need to straighten your skirts and move it on down the road.

What exactly is happening here? On the one hand, there's nothing particularly striking about the interaction—it's simply a group of people (presumably men) having a friendly conversation with some harmless jokes thrown in for extra spice. On the other hand, this brief exchange reveals quite a bit about the social construction of masculinity. Consider the following ideas that are either explicit or implicit in the language:

- A man concerned about accommodating his wife's wishes with regard to one of his hobbies is at risk of losing his masculinity.
- "Real" men are those who do heroic acts.
- Questioning the idea of "real men" makes someone less of a man.
- Potential conflicts between men about the meanings of gender can be softened with anti-feminine humor.

In this example the social construction of men and masculinity is explicit in the language used; the dialogue is literally about men and masculinity. In other contexts, the process is more subtle and may not rely on explicit language for meaning. Several years ago, at a workshop for high school psychology teachers, a participant described a T-shirt that one of her male students wore to class one day. The T-shirt was bright pink with bold print on the front that said:

"My Black One Is on the Floor of Your Girlfriend's Bedroom."

For Consideration

How does the example of the T-shirt serve to construct meanings of masculinity with regard to:
sexuality,
colors,
intimate relationships between women and men, and
relationships between men?

You may have noticed several things about the T-shirt example. First, wearing the shirt seems like a clear act of communication. But what exactly is being expressed, and to whom? One might say that it's "just a joke," and, indeed, it does seem likely that humor is one of the social functions involved. But, digging deeper, you can see that a humorous interpretation depends on a shared set of assumptions between speakers and listeners. The joke would make no sense if it wasn't understood that the color pink is considered feminine and black is considered masculine. The joke's effectiveness also rests on the shared beliefs that being cuckolded by a male friend is emasculating and that sexual conquests affirm one's masculinity. Wearing the T-shirt to school also serves to reinforce the idea that it is sensible and desirable to make public claims about having engaged in these actions, at least among high school peers.

Social and Constructed Aspects of Masculinity

At the risk of stating the obvious, a social constructionist perspective on the psychology of men treats masculinity as both a *social* process and one that is *constructed*. To approach masculinity as a social process is to emphasize interactions between people at a variety of levels of social organization. For example, in conversations between dyads, different meanings of masculinity are often created through language. The online dialogue above regarding the meaning of the phrase "real men" is a good example. Similarly, in the U.S., elementary school teachers often use the phrase "boys and girls!" to capture students' attention. To the casual eye, this statement seems like a rather innocuous synonym for "students" and is hardly worth commenting on. But if we have even a small dose of awareness regarding the social construction of masculinity, we can begin to see how such everyday statements serve to reinforce the notions that (a) gender is a binary (i.e., every child must fit into either "boy" or "girl"), (b) a person's gender identity is an important part of their formal role as a student, and (c) it is standard to separate individuals by gender, even for such mundane purposes as walking outside for recess.

The social nature of constructed masculinities is not limited to verbal interactions between individuals or small groups. It also takes place on a much larger societal level. For example, the tag-line "A Few Good Men" was until 2016 used in U.S. Marine Corps recruiting efforts including radio, television, internet, and print advertising. In four words, it managed to signal that belonging to the Marine Corps confirms one's masculine status as an elite male and to also place a strong boundary around those who are not as well-suited to the corps (i.e., people of other genders or men who are not "good" enough).

As the above examples show, socially constructed masculinities often emerge in explicitly gendered language. But it's not always this way. Some of the most subtle, pervasive, and yet powerful meanings of masculinity are reassembled and reinforced in the mundanity of everyday life. Consider a group of young men at a bar watching a hockey game on television. What actions are considered normal and appropriate for the participants? The list might include watching the game, commenting with authority on various aspects of team strategy and individual skill, drinking alcohol, yelling when a fight breaks out, and cheering loudly and fist bumping when the home team scores. In contrast, it would likely be considered less normal and appropriate to read a poem, admit ignorance about the rules of the game, drink herbal tea, or talk about your personal life. The combination of acceptable/common and unacceptable/uncommon activities among a group of males contributes to context-specific meanings of masculinity that are socially created and socially reinforced.

If Not Socially Constructed, Then What?

The idea that meanings of masculinity are socially constructed can seem rather obvious once you consider it. After all, human beings are intimately involved in defining what it means to be women and men. What then is the purpose of developing an entire paradigm under the rubric of social construction? A bit of historical context is useful here. Many social scientists credit the sociologists Peter Berger and Thomas Luckmann for kindling the widespread adoption of social constructionist perspectives, although the roots of this perspective can be found in a wide range of theoretical perspectives on diverse social phenomena (e.g., Kuhn, 2012; Mannheim, 1952; Schutz, 1967; Wittgenstein, 1953). Berger and Luckmann's (1966) book, *The Social Construction of Reality*, was a reaction against the dominant sociological paradigm of the time which emphasized material and structural determinants of social processes. Contemporaneous sociologists focused primarily on determinants of human activity that were presumed to be relatively concrete and fixed. These included such variables as economics, living conditions, political structures, and so on. Berger and Luckmann's idea, relatively radical for the time, was that social reality is neither fixed nor given. Instead, it is the product of social interactions between people. In other words, human beings socially construct reality.

One crucial point is that, over time, the social origins of our institutions, roles, and norms tend to be forgotten. As a result, we begin to treat such processes as if they are inevitable, unchangeable, and even "natural." For example, most of us now assume that homosexuality refers to a deep-rooted personal identity, if not a biologically driven and essential aspect of one's personality. Most of us are unaware that the term itself is only roughly 150 years old. Prior to its social construction, although there were certainly many people who engaged in sexual behavior with others of the same gender, there was no "gay" or "lesbian" identity available for people to adopt or be labeled with (Foucault, 1990). Thus, "homosexuality" is a socially constructed phenomenon.

When considering this perspective, it is important not to assume that the term socially constructed means imaginary, fake, subjective, easily changed, or choiceful. Our most longstanding social institutions and practices are socially constructed, and also carry with them substantial material consequences for individuals and groups. Capitalism and socialism, for example, are frameworks for economic and political organization that have profound consequences for human lives. And yet they are socially constructed. The same is true for higher education, the legal system in the U.S., styles of dress, the demarcation of "normal" and "abnormal" sexual practices, and so on. In fact, when it comes to human behavior, beyond our most basic bodily functions, it can be hard to find examples of complex and influential processes that are not to a considerable extent social in origin.

At this point you might be wondering, "If most of the things that interest us as psychologists are socially constructed, what is the point of talking about social construction at all?" In his book, *The Social Construction of What?*, philosopher Ian Hacking (1999) tackles exactly this question. He points out that people invoke the phrase "socially constructed" when they want to suggest that "facts" or "realities" which are typically taken for granted as natural or inevitable could actually be otherwise. The idea that men are *inherently* aggressive and competitive, for example, is often attributed to biological evolution. These characteristics are assumed to be hardwired, fixed, and essential to men's makeup. A social constructionist perspective, according to Hacking, would be useful if we wanted to highlight the myriad cultural and historical factors that give rise to this characterization of men, or the many instances in which it appears to be false or lacking in utility. We might, for example, point out that many men are not typically aggressive or competitive, that such behaviors vary considerably depending on social context, and that the idea of a natural aggressive tendency in men itself serves different functions in society such as excusing crimes of passion or justifying a male-only military.

Hacking (1999) also observes that social construction can refer to either a **product** or a **process**. Continuing with the previous example, the widespread idea that men are naturally competitive and aggressive is a social product; it exists in society in many different forms including movies, books, jokes, news articles, and even everyday conversation. But this product (the idea that men are naturally competitive and aggressive) does not appear out of nowhere. It is the ongoing result of countless interwoven social processes that give rise to it, reinforce it, contest it, and morph it. Such social processes are precisely the territory of interest to psychologists taking a social constructionist perspective on men and masculinity.

Approaching the psychology of men from this perspective often involves analyzing and interpreting actions and situations through which meanings of manhood are **formed, sustained, resisted**, and/or **reformulated**. Consider further the idea that "men are naturally aggressive" as a social product, rather than as a proposition that may or may not be true. What are the processes through which such an idea is created in different contexts? Perhaps the current authors might stand on the street corner with huge signs that read "MEN ARE AGGRESSIVE. IT'S THE TRUTH,

TRUST US. WE KNOW BECAUSE WE'RE SCIENTISTS!" Would this performance develop into widespread acceptance of that notion? Probably not—although we might receive some strange looks.

But what if we published an article in a respected news outlet in which we cited, "new biological research linking specific areas of the brain to aggression in men?" What if our names were in bold print followed by all kinds of fancy scholarly degrees? And then what if a major cable news outlet picked up the piece and ran a prime-time segment with the title, "Is there a biological basis to mass shootings?" Perhaps another social scientist critical of our perspective would come on the show and cite alternative evidence. Or maybe a federal prosecutor would come on and express concern about the legal implications of our research. These linkages between science, the media, and issues of human concern have become so common we hardly take notice of them as socially constructive processes. Still, we all know the format and it's not hard to imagine an exchange like the following:

TV HOST: So, Dr. Hoffman, you seem to be saying that men are programmed to be violent? If that's true, it sounds pretty hopeless! I mean, is there anything we can do about it?

PROFESSOR HOFFMAN: Well, that's not really what I'm saying—that things are hopeless—but yes, biology does play a role in men's aggression and we can't deny the scientific facts. For example, our research, which has been published extensively in peer-reviewed journals, shows that the frontal lobe plays a regulatory role in …

CONCERNED PROSECUTOR: —You know that's all fine and good, the science. I'm no expert, and I certainly respect Dr. Hoffman's work, but we have to be thinking about the *real* world here. What's going to happen when we start letting men off for violent acts because, "his brain made him do it?"

TV HOST: Dr. Hoffman, how do you respond to that?

PROFESSOR HOFFMAN: Well, I'm definitely not saying men shouldn't be held responsible for criminal acts. What I'm saying is that there are biological influences on aggressive behavior in men.

TV HOST: Dr. Hoffman, correct me if I'm wrong, but aren't you essentially saying that there is a biological basis to aggression, particularly in men? I mean, based on your research, it cannot be denied. No?

For Consideration

The exchange above is ripe with processes of social construction.

How are "science" and "the real world" positioned in relation to each other?

How are expertise and authority constructed through the language chosen by the participants?

How are specific meanings of biology being constructed by different participants in the dialogue?

How does the context of a brief television news segment influence what can and can't be constructed about men and violence?

Social Construction Versus Social Learning

At this point you might be seeing some similarities between social constructionist and social learning perspectives on men and masculinity. They do share several assumptions, especially the premise that our understanding of manhood is historically changing, socially formed, and varies by context. But they also provide qualitatively different frames around the psychology of men and masculinity. One way to think about this is that each brings different aspects of it into sharper focus. Or, from the perspective of the current chapter, you might say that each paradigm constructs a different understanding of what masculinities are, how they affect people, and how people affect them.

Whereas social learning focuses on the way boys' and men's behavior *is shaped* by masculine social norms, roles, and ideologies, social construction focuses on the *processes through which these same social products are created*. You might be tempted to say that each highlights different parts of a similar process; people create masculinity (social construction) and masculinity in turn influences people (social learning). Yet, as is often the case in social science research, the way researchers frame their studies affects what can and cannot be observed. More radically, the two perspectives actually produce different visions of what masculinity is and how it operates psychologically. For example, social learning researchers tend to focus on a relatively small set of masculine norms and ideologies—often those that are theoretically the most dominant (e.g., hegemonic masculinity). The questions they ask are typically about the *effects* of those norms on individual behavior. How, for example, does the masculine norm of emotional control affect different men's willingness to seek help (Addis & Mahalik, 2003; Wong, Ho, Wang, & Miller, 2017), the way they express sadness or depression (Addis, 2008), or the quality of their intimate relationships (Burn & Ward, 2005)? Note that within this framework, the implicit model of individual responsibility is one of relative passivity; men's actions are assumed to be the consequences of powerful social forces operating from the top-down. The possibility of freedom of choice (e.g., active resistance to or subversion of gender norms) is, at the very least, de-emphasized if not outright ignored.

In contrast, social constructionist perspectives place human *agency* and self-interest directly in focus when analyzing men and masculinity. Agency is the capacity for intentional choice, the ability to willfully bend or shape our environments from the bottom-up in order to accommodate our wishes and desires. Social constructionist researchers also tend to examine a much more diverse array of masculine norms and ideologies; not only those that are common and relatively dominant, but also those that are more marginal, resistant, or subversive.

Is Masculinity a Noun or a Verb?

Grammatically speaking, we typically treat the word masculinity as a noun. As such it has a certain "thingness" to it. We often talk about masculinity as an object that affects people (e.g., "Men with high levels of masculinity are intensely competitive"). Even when the term is used as an adjective, it tends to connote a certain objective quality that a person or process so described possesses. For example, the statement, "That guy is really masculine," presumes that the adjective "masculine" refers to qualities *that the individual possesses* and, thus, we are right back to the notion that masculinity is thing-like: an object, a personality trait, a psychological essence, or otherwise.

In 1987 Candace West and Don Zimmerman published a widely influential article that argued quite the opposite (West & Zimmerman, 1987). The title of the article was "Doing Gender" and it laid out a fairly radical change in how to understand the social construction of gender. In a nutshell, West and Zimmerman proposed that we can better understand gender (e.g., masculinity) as *something that people do* rather than *something that people possess*. In other words, masculinity involves the **performance** of actions which position the actor as a credible member of their socially assigned gender. To say that masculinity is a performance does not imply that it is fake or disingenuous, but rather that it is best understood as a socially interactive and agentic process. In less technical language, masculinity refers to all those actions people engage in to be seen as appropriate representatives of the category "men." In short, a social constructionist perspective conceptualizes masculinity as a verb rather than a noun.

Working from this perspective, it is crucial to note that the performances required to establish oneself as masculine are highly context-dependent. Doing masculinity in the context of a monogamous heterosexual relationship between two people in their 40s trying to figure out how to deal with a broken dishwasher requires different behavioral repertoires than doing masculinity as a 16-year-old in the bleachers at a high school football game. Consequently, psychologists who adopt a social constructionist perspective typically zoom in very closely on the moment-to-moment actions of people doing masculinity. Of particular interest are the situational demands that nudge individuals to make strategic, agentic choices about how to do masculinity in ways that are responsive to the immediate social context and to broader societal norms and ideologies.

Many examples of the strategic construction of masculinities can also be found in the media. For example, over the last three decades, two major hit television comedies in the United States, *Friends* and *Seinfeld*, regularly used humor reliant on male characters' simultaneous reinforcement and rejection of homophobia. In retrospect it's not surprising since many men find themselves in situations where they need to carefully navigate the homophobic demands of hegemonic masculinity alongside emerging, countervailing cultural prohibitions against overt homophobia (McCormack & Anderson, 2014). In one episode of *Seinfeld*, a writer comes to interview two characters, George and Jerry, whom she assumes are a gay couple (Cherones, 1993). The tension builds as the two men engage in a stream of behaviors stereotypically associated with homosexuality (being concerned about whether a piece of fruit has been washed, bickering over whether one doesn't like the other's clothes, etc.). Eventually Jerry realizes what's going on and the two men begin to protest, "We're not gay!!" This quickly gives way to preemptive apologies and disclaimers intended to absolve them from accusations of homophobia ("Not that there's anything wrong with that!" "I have lots of gay friends!" "My father is gay!"). "Not that there's anything wrong with that" quickly became a cultural meme. In a similar vein, Korobov (2004) identified the ways adolescent boys from the Northeast United States use a variety of forms of social inoculation to establish themselves as simultaneously complicit with and resistant to homophobic ideologies. For example, in the context of a focus group one teenage boy stated, "I'm not homophobic" to which another responded, "His aunts are gay." The first quickly followed with, "You're not supposed to say that!"

Stories, Stories, and More Stories: Language, Narrative, and Discourse

You may have noticed that, from a psychological perspective, many of the examples of socially constructing masculinity involve language, particularly everyday informal language. In fact, human talk in its quotidian contexts provides a significant portion of the data taken up in research. In some ways this is nothing new, since psychologists have made use of human language virtually since the inception of the field. However, traditionally, language has been seen as a window into or a reflection of what people think and feel, rather than something of psychological interest in its own right. In contrast, social constructionists approach language, the *speech act*, as a powerful and meaningful social process unto itself. What we say about things is important not because it reveals who we are, but because human talk is the primary avenue through which we construct human experience (Addis, Reigeluth, & Schwab, 2016; Wetherell & Edley, 2014). Moreover, what we say is rarely (if ever) neutral in the way that one might casually observe the weather or note the time. When we talk, we always aim our speech at a particular audience and with some desired end in mind. Through speaking, we construct the world and ourselves as we want them to be, as we think our audience wants them to be, or how we assume our audience thinks we should want them to be. In other words, our talk is ideological. Yet, crucially, it is rarely transparently ideological. As human beings we are sensitive to how our talk is heard, not only by others, but also by ourselves as simultaneous speakers and listeners. As a result, we have developed ways to construct ideological positions through language that are quite flexible, strategic, and sensitive to context.

Wetherell and Edley (2014) describe *discursive psychology* as a social constructionist framework well-suited for approaching the psychology of men and masculinity. Their perspective approaches languages as action-oriented rather than representational. As they present it:

> *Discursive psychology treats masculinity not as an essence to be revealed, but as sets of variable practices that are actively developed and negotiated in relation to other forms of identity in particular cultural contexts. Such practices take many different forms and involve a wide range of activities, such as the disciplining of bodies to match currently ideal physiques, choices of clothes and fashion, leisure pursuits, gendered hierarchies in workplaces, and so on.*
>
> (p. 355)

As the above quote suggests, discourse can involve much more than language. However, when it comes to research, psychologists frequently focus on narratives, conversations, and other speech acts related to men and masculinity. Research has explored the way masculinity is constructed in the U.S. Navy (Barrett, 2001), the space industry (Messerschmidt, 1995), and corporate environments (Baxter & MacLeod, 2005). Several studies have also focused on the way boys and young men construct meanings of masculinity in relationships including with friends (Oransky & Marecek, 2009; Way, 2011) and in intimate relationships (e.g., Korobov & Thorne, 2006). For example, Korobov and Thorne (2006) explored the different ways emerging adult men create both intimacy and distance between themselves when discussing dating relationships and hookup culture.

The Social Constructionist Perspective in "Real" Life

Despite the inescapable presence of social constructions all around us, the social constructionist *perspective* per se does not circulate explicitly as a major player in day-to-day life nearly as often as biological or social learning perspectives. This may be due in large part to the way in which most social constructions depend precisely on the ability to be seen as natural and inevitable (i.e., *not* socially constructed). Thus, as Hacking (1999) argues, one of the primary functions of articulating a social constructionist perspective is to point out that something we take for granted as inevitable or natural could well be different if social conditions were otherwise. Put another way, the social constructionist perspective functions in society to **deconstruct** ideas, symbols, and social practices that are often taken as givens.

Consider societal discourse about men and parenting amidst the increasing visibility of stay-at-home fathers in American society (Rochlen, McKelley, & Whittaker, 2010; Rochlen, Suizzo, McKelley, & Scaringi, 2008). When men actively participate in parenting and do not work outside the home, they often violate traditional western masculine gender norms. As a result, although they may be praised for their progressiveness, they are also potential targets for subtle or overt forms of stigma and the policing of masculinity. Given this broader context, it is useful to consider how masculinity and manhood are constructed in ongoing conversations about stay-at-home fathers. What assumptions about the nature of stay-at-home fathers are taken for granted? What does socially constructed discourse about these men reveal about our beliefs about men's roles in families?

As one example, a quick internet search reveals a website for the National At-Home Dad Network (www.athomedad.org). Under the section "Purpose, Mission, and Core Values," we find the following statement:

We believe a father's masculinity is not diminished by caring for his children. Rather, we believe he is never more of a man than when he is being an involved father. Furthermore, we believe that being an at-home dad is not an abdication of a man's role as provider for his family. In fact, we believe that stepping away from the full-time workforce to raise one's children can be the most valuable and meaningful way a father can provide for his family.

When taking a discursive stance toward these data, we are not concerned with whether the authors are right or wrong about stay-at-home-dads. Nor are we concerned with assessing the authors' "true" beliefs about men and masculinity. In fact, the authors' inner beliefs and intentions are irrelevant. Instead, the text stands on its own and comes into sharp focus: what meanings are being constructed about men, masculinity, and fathering in this brief social product?

As a start, we might ask about gendered norms and ideologies implicit in the blurb—the assumptions about men, masculinity, and parenting, that readers must entertain in order for such discourse to make sense. Consider the first line: "We believe that a father's masculinity is not diminished ...." Such an opening statement presumes that the reader is already familiar with the idea that a man's masculinity *is* diminished by staying at home to raise children. Thus, despite formally rejecting the idea that masculinity and stay-at-home parenting are incompatible, the statement also reinforces that very same notion; its placement at the beginning of a mission statement constructs the premise that men who act as stay-at-home parents inevitably face questions about their masculinity.

Similar ideas are present in statements such as, " ... we believe he is never more of a man than when he is being an involved father." Here we see implicit gendered presuppositions such as (a) it is important for males to "be men," (b) staying at home to raise children may make someone less of a man, but (c) in fact, it actually makes one more of a man. Finally, the gendered notion of men as essential providers for families is reinforced by redefining the meaning of "provider."

The process of social construction also courses through our day-to-day lives when we talk about our inner selves. Psychologists have traditionally described the "self" as a relatively stable, internal, and consistent part of us that contains our wishes, values, and our overall sense of "I" or "me." In everyday life, we tend to proceed as if each of us possesses a "real" self. The real self is often contrasted with what we say and do moment to moment which may or may not line up with "who we *really* are." All of this is so familiar and automatic that it can seem hardly worth commenting on, yet two points are critical to consider from a social constructionist perspective. First, when it comes to "I" and "me," we are not objective scientists neutrally reporting on the facts about ourselves. Rather, the *process* of accounting for our actions in terms of "me" and "not me" is one in which individuals are agentic, strategic, and sensitive to context. Second, and perhaps more radically, the very notion of a "self" can be seen as a constructed social *product*.

Recall the exchange Michael was involved in on the online pipe smoking forum. Several weeks after it concluded, Michael wrote to each of the participants and asked if they would be willing to have their comments reprinted in this book. Each wrote back and agreed. One participant included the following:

Hi Michael,

> *Just FYI, things I say on the forum in those kinds of threads is usually facetious and an attempt to be funny. I fail pretty often! My immediate family is diverse with LGBT and a couple of races presented ... in other words, I'm more socially liberal than "[forum name]" comes across. Anyway, I'm sure there are lots of guys that think the things I post but I just wanted you to know so it doesn't "color" the research for your book.*

Note how the participant creates a concise narrative about his real self versus how his online persona "comes across." Doing so allows him to establish accountability to multiple audiences: the online forum itself, Michael as a participant in that community, Michael as an individual in the context of a backchannel conversation, and the participant himself as both speaker and listener. Again, what is significant here is not the question of which self is "real" or "true." From the constructionist perspective we all construct multiple selves that we deploy strategically, depending on what is at stake in a particular social context. Moreover, our unexpressed *intentions* can have relatively little effect on how others *interpret* constructed selves. In the current example, forum members who read this participant's posts probably don't consider whether he is performing a masculine self that is different from the one he assumes in "real" life. In his comments, he appears simply to be himself. The same could be said of most, if not all human interactions; we rarely pay attention to the multiple selves constructed within and between individuals.

At times a social constructionist perspective can be explicitly taken up as a foil in public debates about the nature of gender. In March 2018, *The National Review* published an article entitled "The Left's Doomed Crusade to Erase Gender Differences," which described Sweden's educational policy of encouraging teachers to promote gender neutrality among young children by actively deconstructing binary gender roles. The author portrays the social constructionist perspective on gender as a naïve attempt to eradicate biologically based differences between boys and girls that will only result in confused and deviant individuals. For example:

Instead of recognizing the differences between boys and girls, however, leftist social engineers seek to confuse boys and girls by having them engage in activities in which they have no interest. Forcing small boys to massage each other's feet—as the Swedish school does—does nothing but promote puzzlement among children. It certainly doesn't teach little boys to become responsible men. It teaches them to become bizarre. And forcing small girls to open windows and scream out of them doesn't teach them to become responsible women. It teaches them to behave like obnoxious brats (Shapiro, 2018).

Finally, it may or may not have occurred to you that this book is an example of socially constructing men and masculinity. Traditional views of science see theory and research as attempts to transcend human self-interest by producing value-free "objective" knowledge. From a social constructionist perspective, academic knowledge is anything but that. Instead, social constructionist approaches sees scholarship about men and masculinity as morally engaged and politically motivated attempts to influence the way others think about human behavior. For example, although this book covers a relatively wide range of perspectives on the psychology of men and masculinity, clearly we are persuaded by the notions that masculinity is non-essential, malleable, and highly intertwined in a wide range of human problems. We're also advocating a view in which critiquing masculinity does not imply condemning men as human beings. We hope to contribute to a societal discourse that positions men as simultaneously *privileged and harmed* by the social construction and social learning of masculinity in the context of patriarchy.

Summary and Conclusion

A social constructionist perspective focuses on the way masculine gender norms, ideologies, and practices are created through human interaction at a variety of levels of social organization. Unlike a social learning perspective, which focuses on the effects of masculinities on individuals, the constructionist paradigm is more concerned with human agency—the widely varying ways in which people actively create, sustain, contest, and reformulate notions of what it means to be a man. An important notion is the model of human beings as invested actors. In other words, we create meanings of masculinity in non-random ways in order to strengthen or propagate our own values, ideologies, and political agendas. From this perspective masculinity is understood not as a noun (i.e., something people possess) but as a verb (i.e., something people do). Crucially, considering the socially constructed and performative nature of masculinity does not render it any less real; it simply shifts our attention from people as relatively passive recipients of gender ideologies (social learning) to the active role and responsibility we all have in creating meanings of gender.

References

Addis, M. E. (2008). Gender and depression in men. *Clinical Psychology: Science and Practice, 15*(3), 153–168.

Addis, M. E. & Mahalik, J. R. (2003). Men, masculinity, and the contexts of help seeking. *American Psychologist, 58*(1), 5–14.

Addis, M. E., Reigeluth, C. S., & Schwab, J. R. (2016). Social norms, social construction, and the psychology of men and masculinity. In Y. J. Wong & S. R. Wester (Eds), *APA handbook of men and masculinities* (pp. 81–104). Washington, DC: American Psychological Association.

Barrett, F. J. (2001). The organizational construction of hegemonic masculinity: the case of the US Navy. In S. M. Whitehead & F. J. Barrett (Eds), *The masculinities reader* (pp. 77–99). Cambridge, UK: Polity.

Baxter, L. F. & MacLeod, A. (2005). Shifting forms of masculinity in changing organizations: the role of testicularity. *Journal of Organizational Change Management, 18*(6), 627–640.

Berger, P. L. & Luckmann, T. (1966). *The social construction of reality: a treatise on the sociology of knowledge*. Garden City, NY: Doubleday.

Burn, S. M. & Ward, A. Z. (2005). Men's conformity to traditional masculinity and relationship satisfaction. *Psychology of Men & Masculinity, 6*(4), 254–263.

Cherones, T. (1993, February 11). The outing [Television broadcast]. *Seinfeld*. Los Angeles, CA: Castle Rock Entertainment.

Foucault, M. (1990). *The history of sexuality. Volume I: an introduction* (R. Hurley, trans.). New York, NY: Vintage Books (original work published in 1976).

Hacking, I. (1999). *The social construction of what?* Cambridge, MA: Harvard University Press.

Korobov, N. (2004). Inoculating against prejudice: a discursive approach to homophobia and sexism in adolescent male talk. *Psychology of Men & Masculinity, 5*(2), 178–189.

Korobov, N. & Thorne, A. (2006). Intimacy and distancing: young men's conversations about romantic relationships. *Journal of Adolescent Research, 21*(1), 27–55.

Kuhn, T. S. (2012). *The structure of scientific revolutions* (4th ed). Chicago, IL: University of Chicago Press (original work published in 1962).

Mannheim, K. (1952). *Essays on the sociology of knowledge* (In P. Kecskemeti, trans.). London, UK: Routledge (original work published in 1928).

McCormack, M. & Anderson, E. (2014). The influence of declining homophobia on men's gender in the United States: an argument for the study of homohysteria. *Sex Roles, 71*(3–4), 109–120.

Messerschmidt, J. W. (1995). Managing to kill: masculinities and the space shuttle Challenger explosion. *Masculinities, 3*(4), 1–22.

National At-Home Dad Network (n.d.). Purpose, mission, and core values. Retrieved from: http://athomedad.org/about/purpose-mission-and-core-values.

Oransky, M. & Marecek, J. (2009). "I'm not going to be a girl" masculinity and emotions in boys' friendships and peer groups. *Journal of Adolescent Research, 24*(2), 218–241.

Rochlen, A. B., McKelley, R. A., & Whittaker, T. A. (2010). Stay-at-home fathers' reasons for entering the role and stigma experiences: a preliminary report. *Psychology of Men & Masculinity, 11*(4), 279–285.

Rochlen, A. B., Suizzo, M. A., McKelley, R. A., & Scaringi, V. (2008). "I'm just providing for my family": a qualitative study of stay-at-home fathers. *Psychology of Men & Masculinity, 9*(4), 193–206.

Schutz, A. (1967). *The phenomenology of the social world* (G. Walsh & F. Lehnert, trans.). Evanston, IL: Northwestern University Press (original work published in 1932).

Shapiro, B. (2018, March 27). The left's doomed crusade to erase gender differences. *National Review*. Retrieved from: www.nationalreview.com/2018/03/gender-differences-children-swedish-pre-school-social-engineering.

Way, N. (2011). *Deep secrets: boys' friendships and the crisis of connection*. Cambridge, MA: Harvard University Press.

West, C. & Zimmerman, D. H. (1987). Doing gender. *Gender & Society, 1*(2), 125–151.

Wetherell, M. & Edley, N. (2014). A discursive psychological framework for analyzing men and masculinities. *Psychology of Men & Masculinity, 15*(4), 355–364.

Wittgenstein, L. (1953). *Philosophical investigations* [Philosophische Untersuchungen]. Oxford, UK: Macmillan.

Wong, Y. J., Ho, M. H. R., Wang, S. Y., & Miller, I. S. (2017). Meta-analyses of the relationship between conformity to masculine norms and mental health-related outcomes. *Journal of Counseling Psychology, 64*(1), 80–93.

6

POWER AND PRIVILEGE

Feminist Perspectives

On a Thursday morning in October, *The New York Times* published an investigation alleging that a celebrated Hollywood producer, Harvey Weinstein, had sexually harassed dozens of aspiring actresses and assistants over the course of several decades. *The Times* revealed lurid scenes of impropriety: Weinstein, naked, demanding a massage from a temp worker in her early 20s; Weinstein grabbing an aspiring actress' breasts, asking whether they were "real"; dozens of one-on-one "professional" meetings in Weinstein's hotel room that quickly turned sexual. One of the movie mogul's employees explained how challenging it was to fend him off: "I was very afraid of him. And I knew how well connected he was. And how if I pissed him off then I could never have a career in that industry" (Nestor, quoted in Farrow, 2017). For decades Weinstein used his wealth to pay off accusations and keep his conduct secret.

In the weeks and months that followed *The Times* story, accusations piled on against Weinstein—and against others. Soon, the misconduct of powerful men, from the comedian Louis C. K. to United States Senator Al Franken, was gaining widespread opprobrium, and public outcry led many of these men to resign or take an early retirement. Under the banner of the Twitter hashtag "MeToo" hundreds of thousands of women acknowledged that they too had been affected by workplace sexual harassment. A movement soon erupted across the English-speaking world.

The #MeToo movement is arguably the most visible form that the feminist movement has taken in recent years. But feminism is about much more than advocacy against sexual harassment and violence. Feminism does not only identify pressing social problems such as sexual harassment. It also offers a worldview that explains problematic behavior such as sexual harassment as part of a much larger system of gender, power, and oppression.

So what is a chapter on feminism doing in a book about the psychology of men? Some readers may wonder, "Isn't feminism all about women's issues? And don't most feminists hate men?" While it is true that the feminist movement has been spearheaded by women, it is not true that feminism is "all about women." As you'll see in this chapter, a feminist perspective on gender—women's gender as well as men's gender—offers key insights into the ways that masculinity relates to men's social power or privilege.

One aspect of feminism that many students—particularly male students—wrestle with is the feminist premise that men have wielded disproportionate power, both historically and in contemporary society. Many of us would like to believe that sexism is a thing of the past. After all, many men regularly experience economic insecurity, social rejection, and personal distress, and the result is that some men feel quite *disempowered* in their day-to-day lives. Indeed, part of what is challenging about understanding feminist theory is the fact that men's power and men's pain are inextricably intertwined: both are the result of patriarchy and gender inequality. Patriarchy, it seems, is a double-edged sword for men (Kauffman, 1999).

It is impossible to do justice to the enormous breadth of feminist thought in a single book, let alone in a single chapter. Our description of feminism therefore papers over some important divisions within a feminist perspective. Feminist movements exist across many different countries and are composed of women and men of all walks of life. There are key theoretical differences distinguishing different feminist perspectives. Notably, there has historically been a large gulf between liberal feminism on the one hand, and radical feminism on the other hand (LeGates, 2001). Liberal feminists aim primarily for women's equality with men and the elimination of gender as an organizing social category, and liberal feminists have tended to view the courts and political processes as a key way of achieving those ends. For example, women's right to vote, reproductive rights, and anti-discrimination laws could all be considered examples of liberal feminist goals. In contrast, radical feminists criticize equity feminism for failing to challenge masculine social norms, question the gender equality advocated by liberals as a distinctly *male* kind of equality, and see attempts to achieve equality as working to make women more like men. Radical feminists focus on more informal ways that gender influences social life, from a macro-economic level to the minutia of heterosexual relations. The reader will forgive us if, for the sake of simplicity, we do not do full justice to these nuances and the variety of feminist thought.

In the pages that follow, we briefly review the history of feminism's different waves: first wave, second wave, and third wave feminisms. We then provide an overview of some key feminist concepts, particularly the concepts of (1) sexism, (2) patriarchy, and (3) privilege, which have arguably had the largest influence on the psychology of men and masculinity. After establishing these concepts, we contrast the feminist approach to masculinity with the approaches we've seen in previous chapters. We want readers to in particular understand the relational and asymmetric frame of feminist approaches. Finally, at the end of the chapter, we look at the ways that feminism has exploded into the public consciousness over the last 50 years. Specifically, we review the ways that feminist analyses of men have been mobilized in pro-feminist community organizing, and also examine varieties of anti-feminist backlash in society.

For Consideration

Examining our perceptions of feminism

Although the biological, social learning, and social constructionist approaches featured in previous chapters are relatively obscure outside of academia, the same cannot be said for feminism and feminists. This is largely because, unlike these other perspectives, feminism is explicitly *political*. Controversy and stereotypes of feminists abound in political discourse and in media, in films, television, and the news.

Try it yourself: First, try writing down a list of five words that come to mind when you think of a feminist. How do you think you came to view feminism this way? Where and from whom did you learn about feminism?

Second, once you have reached the end of the chapter, reread your list of five words and reflect on it. Were there any things about feminism in this chapter that surprised you? Why or why not? What on your list might you change?

The Three Waves of Feminism

Feminism as we know it today is the successor to the women's movements of the late 18th, 19th, and early 20th centuries. Until as recently as the 1880s few democratic societies gave women the vote. In England, up until the 19th century, married women were not allowed to own property, and, after a divorce, custody of children was reserved for fathers (Einhorn, 1986). Women such as Sojourner Truth, Susan B. Anthony, Mary Wollstonecraft, and Ida B. Wells—now seen as representing the *first wave of feminism*—advocated and campaigned for women's civil rights: employment rights, the right to vote, and property rights. They achieved a considerable amount through their organization. In 1921, after years of agitation, American women successfully campaigned for the passage of the

Nineteenth Amendment and earned the right to vote. The first wave of feminism can best be summed up by the push to recognize women as equal citizens under the law.

While it never disappeared, the women's movement gained renewed visibility as the **second wave of feminism** in the mid-20th century, sparked by social upheavals such as the oral contraceptive pill and the entrance *en masse* of women into the labor force during World War Two. Rallying against continued gender inequality, second wave feminists sought to expand on the victories of the first wave. While women did have the vote and property rights, these political victories had failed to upend gender inequality. Rape, domestic violence, and sexual harassment were still poorly recognized by the law (Brownmiller, 1975). Women who sought to end unwanted pregnancies often had to resort to unregulated, illegal abortions. And while women *could* divorce without losing custody of their children, many found themselves trapped in marriages because of a variety of social and economic pressures. Women *could* run for political office, but there were few female politicians. Women *could* pursue any (or almost any) career, but they were not well represented in most well-paying careers, particularly at higher levels.

Although these problems might be fought by changing laws, some second wave feminists argued that only a much broader movement would be capable of advancing women's equality with men. This entailed a radical shift for the feminist movement: activism could not be restricted to political organizing or public life. Hence the famous second wave slogan: "the personal is political" (Hanisch, 1969/2000). In other words, politics does not only occur in the statehouse, the courtroom, or debate hall. All aspects of our daily lives—who does the dishes, who stays home when a child is sick, who is on bottom and on top during sex—are also political. Political precisely in the sense that these daily routines reflect broader power relationships in society between men and women.

Feminist scholars of the second wave charged that women were not held back simply by the law: they were held back, equally if not more importantly, by the *constraints* of the feminine gender role (Freidan, 1963). This argument, albeit applied to men, should now sound familiar to readers. Indeed, many of the central arguments of second wave feminism—for example, the argument that femininity is a *socially imposed role that constrains and hurts women*—were directly transposed from second wave feminism into the emerging field of men's studies and into the psychology of men and masculinity. Feminism's influence is in many ways unsurprising: as noted in Chapter 1, many of the researchers and therapists who developed the new psychology of men and masculinity in the 1970s identified, explicitly, as pro-feminist. Moreover, both feminism and the new psychology of men drew liberally on social learning and social constructionist theories. (However, there were also important—and potentially divisive—differences. While the men's liberation movement tended to emphasize that both women *and men* were hurt by gender, most second wave feminists stressed that men and women were not *equal* victims. Men held advantages and power in many walks of social life—in the government, in the workplace, and in the home—and this dimension had to be reckoned with.)

In contrast to the second wave, **third wave feminism**, which began to take shape in the 1980s and 1990s, is characterized by an *intersectional* approach to critique. The third wave highlighted how gender difference is crisscrossed by the many other ways that human beings differ—along lines of race, class, sexual orientation, disability, as well as age. Accordingly, there could be no *singular* femininity or masculinity, but rather an array of *multiple* femininities and masculinities in which some groups are more dominant and others are less dominant (Connell, 1995/2005). This new perspective triggered a critical reappraisal of the second wave feminist movement: for instance, the Combahee River Collective (1977/2014) argued that second wave feminism had largely been a movement of *White* women, just as the civil rights movement had been a movement of Black *men*. In both instances, *Black women* had been marginalized by the activists supposedly fighting for their interests.

In Chapter 6, we explore this intersectional approach in more detail as we consider the multiplicity of masculinities. For now, we will leave intersectional considerations to the side as we explore in detail the ways that (largely second wave) feminists have conceptualized gender, power, and its effects on men and women.

Putting Gender Into Context: Sexism, Patriarchy, and Power

For many, the word "sexism" evokes an image of an arrogant businessman flirting with his female secretary or a father dressed in a stained white tanktop telling his daughter that "women aren't good at math." In much day-to-day conversation, "sexism" is used to describe *undesirable* attitudes and behaviors—prejudice and discrimination against a group based on that group's gender or sex. Sexism, typically, is something that many of us would like to think *other* people have, but not something that *we* have. Some men, for example, are quite defensive whenever it is suggested that they might themselves be harboring sexist attitudes or be behaving in a sexist way. However, this more commonplace definition of sexism is a bit different from the way that it has been conceptualized in feminist scholarship.

From a feminist framework, sexism is much more than behaving negatively towards someone simply because of their gender. This is not to say that individual instances of bigotry directed at women are unimportant for understanding how gender hierarchies persist. Nevertheless, from a feminist perspective sexism encompasses all the ways that gender serves as an organizing principle to our economy, our politics, even our sense of self. Catharine MacKinnon (1987) offers an excellent summary of the broad scope of sexism:

> *M*en's physiology defines most sports, their needs define auto and health insurance coverage, their socially designed biographies define workplace expectations and successful career paths, their perspectives and concerns define quality in scholarship, their experiences and obsessions define merit, their objectification of life defines art, their military service defines citizenship, their presence defines family, their inability to get along with each other ... defines history, their image defines God, and their genitals define sex.
>
> (p. 36)

Because the term "sexism" has such a strong linguistic baggage, many academic feminists have replaced it with the term "patriarchy" in order to clear up any misunderstanding that sexism refers only narrowly to the negative ways that men behave towards women (hooks, 2004; LeGates, 2001). Etymologically, "patriarchy" derives from the Ancient Greek words "pater," meaning "father," and "arkos," meaning "to rule." Patriarchy, then, literally means "rule by the father." However, in contemporary usage, **patriarchy** refers to *a society-wide arrangement in which men wield disproportionate political, economic, social, and cultural power*. The gender pay gap, teenage boys whistling at girls walking down the sidewalk, the idea that women are more nurturing or caring than men—all of these are pieces of patriarchy.

One way to understand the origins of patriarchy is through an evolutionary lens. While evolutionary psychology has typically been portrayed as anathema to feminist thought, feminist Darwinians argue that there is no inherent incompatibility between the two approaches (Liesen, 2008). For example, Barbara Smuts (1995) traces the origins of patriarchy to differences between the male and female relationships to sex and reproduction. As discussed in Chapter 2, because males do not have to put much energy into reproduction, males that mate with many females will tend to be more successful, all things considered. In contrast, humans' long gestation periods should incentivize females to choose males that will assist in raising offspring. These competing interests set up what Patricia Adair Gowaty (1997) calls "sexual dialectics": the push and pull of competing male and female sexual strategies.

Feminist Darwinians reject the idea that resolution of these sexual dialectics is biologically based or fixed in genetic stone.[1] Smuts (1995) points to other primate species like bonobos, in which male offspring leave the group they were born in to seek out mates, females stay in place and tend to develop stronger homosocial female alliances. With strong female–female alliances in place, female bonobos are able to exercise considerable control over mating, which leads male bonobos to adopt more cooperative, conciliatory reproductive strategies. In early human evolution, however, Smuts writes that the alliances were tipped the other way around. Human males tended to stay put while females left their birth groups. The resulting weaker solidarity among females left males essentially unchecked in their ability to control females through violence and coercion. Smuts hypothesizes that males built upon the power difference established by strong male–male alliances and weak female–female alliances, as they consolidated control of resources and as agriculture and early political systems began to develop in prehistory.

Looking towards contemporary society, it is helpful to begin understanding sexism by understanding the many levels at which it (and gender more broadly) operates (Nakano Glenn, 1999). First, sexism exists at an *individual* level. It is manifest in the misogynistic attitudes or behaviors held not only by men, but also by women and gender minorities. Second, at a more macro level, sexism consists of both informal and institutional *structures* such as the family, law, and the economy. Finally, sexism exists at the *symbolic* level of representation and meaning, in terms of the different values attached to masculinity and femininity. For instance, the association of masculinity with rationality and feminism with emotionality or irrationality is one expression of symbolic sexism. We review each of these levels below.

Individual Sexism

Of all the forms that sexism takes, the individual level is by far the most widely recognized. Individual level sexism, or *misogyny*, is made up of individual (1) behaviors, (2) thoughts, and (3) feelings that contribute to women's inequality. You can probably quickly call to mind numerous instances of this kind of sexism: a man interrupting female co-workers, an uncle's off-color joke about blond women at a family dinner, or derogatory phrases such as "you throw like a girl!" or "pussy!" In addition to these *behaviors*, we might think of sexist *beliefs*, like that in sex "no" means "yes." (Note: we discuss rape and rape myths in detail in Chapter 8, pp. 153–166.) Finally, there are prejudiced *feelings* of anger or resentment that some people feel towards women. Scholars term the most overt forms of individual level sexism *hostile sexism.*

A full overview of the many shapes that hostile sexism takes would probably rival the *Oxford English Dictionary* in volume. Most readers will be quite familiar with misogynistic beliefs that women's role is at home or with attitudes that see women as submissive, manipulative, and overly emotional. We see no need to provide a full index of hostile sexism here. Instead, we focus our discussion on research that has examined the relationship between masculinity and hostile sexism (Schwartz, McDermott, & Martino-Harms, 2016). First, research has consistently demonstrated a strong association between hostile sexist attitudes and conformity to masculine norms. For example, Wade and Brittan-Powell (2000) conducted a survey of 142 college men that found that traditional masculinity ideology predicted 25% to 39% of the variance in hostile sexist attitudes. Other research has shown that men are more likely to endorse hostile attitudes towards women when they feel their masculinity has been threatened (Gallagher & Parrott, 2011). Surveys suggest that, while pernicious, these hostile sexist attitudes are currently becoming less and less prevalent among men (Spence & Hahn, 1997).

But what about other ways that women are treated differently than men? Peter Glick and Susan Fiske (2001) have argued that while hostile sexism is an important part of understanding sexism at the individual level, contemporary sexism is often more ambivalent in nature, and made up of both positive and negative beliefs about women. For example, what are we to make of the chivalrous gentleman opening the car door for his date, the male student who gives unsolicited help to the female professor struggling with a projector, or the charismatic artist who proclaims his love for women's angelic beauty? Following Glick and Fiske's ambivalent sexism theory, we might consider the above scenarios as examples of **benevolent sexism**: behavior and attitudes that at their surface appear positive towards women but nevertheless construe women as *different* and that play on the exact same stereotypes of women as hostile sexism. The only difference is the framing. Where hostile sexism constructs women as *weak*, benevolent sexism constructs women as *tender*. Where hostile sexism views women as unfit for important jobs in the workplace, benevolent sexism underscores women's ability to mother.

Consider a recent speech by the Russian President, Vladimir Putin, to celebrate International Women's Day. In his address to the women of Russia, in which he quoted a poem by Andrey Dementyev, he extolled:

> *O*nly you, women, are able to create a welcoming atmosphere at work and in a family, to undertake day-to-day care of home and children, and to be a moral example for them .... We are conquered by a woman's soul, and her youth, and motherhood, and even her graying, when that time has come.
>
> (Reuters, 2018)

There are several pieces worth highlighting in this excerpt. Notice, first of all, the overall positive tone of Putin's speech. He praises women's ability to "create a welcoming atmosphere" and waxes on women's beauty. He even appears to position men as subordinate to women: they are "conquered" by women. But alongside these seeming compliments are more insidious implications. For instance, when Putin states that "*only* women" can "create a welcoming environment at work and in the family" and "undertake day-to-day care of home and children" he effectively negates men's responsibility to do either of these things. The implication is that men are incapable of caring for children in the same way as women. We should also observe how Putin subtly hints that women might be less valuable when they are "greying," no longer embodying their role as youthful sex objects or as mothers.

While benevolent sexism may seem like a milder form of misogyny, research suggests that it may actually be more powerful than hostile sexism in buttressing patriarchy. For example, Becker and Wright (2011) found that exposure to hostile sexist messaging tends to increase women's motivation to engage in collective action in favor of gender equality. In contrast to the galvanizing effects of overt hostile sexism, Becker and Wright found that benevolent sexist messaging dampened women's intentions to participate in feminist activism. Rather than constructing femininity in a negative light and risking a backlash from women, benevolent sexism encourages women to adhere to the apparently *attractive* characteristics of femininity.

We'll conclude our discussion of individual level sexism by discussing debates about sexism against men. There is some controversy in both popular and academic discourse about whether sexism against men exists alongside sexism against women. This debate, however, is largely semantics. It arises from a conflation of sexism writ-large with hostile attitudes towards a gender group. Few feminist scholars would deny that negative attitudes towards men, also known as misandry, exist. However, it is much more debatable whether men face the same disadvantages as women at both the structural and symbolic levels of gender, as we will see below. The answer about whether sexism against men exists depends, in the end, on how broadly or narrowly you define "sexism."

Symbolic Sexism

Symbolic sexism is one of the most elusive forms that patriarchy takes. It is evident in the cultural ideals attached to masculinity and femininity such as the associations of masculinity with strength or femininity with nurturance. We might think of symbolic sexism as roughly equivalent to an ideology, one that casts itself over how different genders view each other, themselves, and the world.

You might be wondering to yourself what the difference is between symbolic sexism and, say, hostile sexist or benevolent sexist belief systems about men and women. In short, they are deeply interconnected—the difference really comes down to the difference between whether we're looking at an *individual's* beliefs and attitudes or at *collective* representations, ideologies, or discourses. For example, in Chapter 3 we discussed the concept of traditional masculine norms. We might think of measures such as the Conformity to Masculine Norms Inventory (CMNI; Mahalik et al., 2003) as a collective representation of traditional masculinity. This collective representation is part of the larger *symbolic* order of masculinity. However, when individuals fill out the CMNI, their scores on the instrument capture *individual level* attitudes towards gender. This distinction may indeed seem mushy, but focusing on symbolic sexism has some advantages. Focusing on symbolic sexism foregrounds the way that masculinity is constructed in opposition to femininity. It also emphasizes more widespread representations of women as emotional, and men as contrastingly rational. In particular, scholars focusing on symbolic sexism have highlighted the associations between masculinity and reason, as well as science itself: the ways that gender affects whether a particular knowledge claim gets construed as valid or invalid.

Research on implicit cognition has consistently found that people tend to harbor unconscious associations between men and science on the one hand, and women and the humanities on the other hand (Nosek et al., 2007). More generally, scholars in feminist epistemology have asserted that scientific knowledge itself is gendered, that scientific norms of rationality are a distinctly masculine way of knowing the world (Bordo, 1987). This position is a profoundly radical departure from a traditional perspective on science (see Chapter 11 for further exploration of the philosophy of science). Belenky, Clinchy, Goldberger, and Tarule (1986) suggest that masculinity has privileged a particularly detached way of knowing. They argue that this highly critical and logical mode of understanding is only one of many possible ways of knowing the world, and suggest that the feminine position offers a more connected way, one that emphasizes listening and empathy rather than scrutiny and prodding.

Media is another place where symbolic sexism is located and reproduced. An example of symbolic sexism in the media is provided by the sociologist Erving Goffman's (1976) work on the representation of gender in photographic advertisements. Goffman, who looked at over 500 photographs from a wide array of popular newspapers and magazines, found that sexism gets visually inscribed at once subtly and systematically. For instance, women's hands are disproportionately more likely to be shown lightly touching or caressing objects. Where men's touch is portrayed, it tends to be as a more firm or instrumental grasp. The underlying symbolic order communicated is one in which femininity is associated with passive sensuousness and sexuality, while masculinity connotes an active intervening in the world. Goffman notes other differences: men tend to be placed physically above women to a degree that cannot be accounted for by height differences. Women are disproportionately portrayed lying down. These differences too subtly symbolize men as dominant, literally superior, and women as subordinate.

For Consideration

Gender in the Movies: The Bechdel Test

In a 1985 comic strip, the cartoonist Allison Bechdel sketched a scene with two women walking down a street past a cinema. The first woman asks whether the other would like to go see a movie. To which the other responds,

*W*ell ... *I dunno. I have this rule see ... I only go to a movie if it satisfies three basic requirements. One, it has to have at least two women in it who, two, talk to each other about, three, something besides a man.*

(Bechdel, 1986)

First, consider these three requirements, which later became known as the "Bechdel test." Why might these three requirements be important for the representation of women in film?

Second, think to yourself about a few of your favorite movies or movies that you have recently seen. Do they pass the Bechdel test?

Third, pick one of your favorite movies that does *not* pass the Bechdel test. Try re-imagining how the movie might look—its plot, its characters, and its scenes—if it *did* pass the test. What would be different?

Take away: The Bechdel test is useful as a way of making symbolic sexism more visible. Its results show that there is a pervasive pattern whereby women are represented differently (if at all) compared with men. This difference is not innocuous. By always talking about men, women are confined to a romantic, sexual, or caretaking role. Women become the supporting character, while men drive the plot.

Structural Sexism

Of all patriarchal institutions, the *family* has proved the most enduring—the father's authority over the family is, after all, the etymology of patriarchy. It is also important for the reproduction of patriarchy across generations, as the family is the earliest place that children learn about gender (Bussey & Bandura, 1999; Chodorow, 1999). Research suggests that children's gender stereotypes are influenced by their parents: for example, daughters whose parents hold more traditional gender role stereotypes tend to be less confident in their ability to do math (Tiedemann, 2000).

Moreover, as we saw in Chapter 3 (social learning), fathers of young infants and children tend to more rigidly enforce traditional gender roles, particularly for boys (Endendijk et al., 2014; Chaplin, Cole, & Zahn-Waxler, 2005).

The traditional patriarchal family is organized into discrete gender roles: the male as monetary provider, decision-maker, and disciplinarian; the female as child-rearer, homemaker, and nurturer. These disparate roles demarcate a division of labor between men and women. Historically, this meant that men performed the vast bulk of paid labor while women performed most of the work in the home. However, in the second half of the 20th century, this pattern started to shift as more and more women began to take jobs outside the home. National surveys indicate that married women's increasing contributions to household earning have coincided with a large reduction in the amount of time they spend doing housework. Bianchi, Milkie, Sayer, and Robinson (2000) found that the amount of time that American married women spend doing housework declined from around 30 hours per week in 1965 to 17.5 hours per week in 1995, while men went from 5 hours per week in 1965 to 10 hours per week in 1995. One might be tempted to conclude from these data that women have been able to trade increased hours of paid labor for fewer hours of work at home. This is the conclusion reached by some researchers (Gershuny & Sullivan, 2003). However, other studies find that even in couples in which both husbands and wives spend an equal amount of time in employed labor, husbands do only about half as much domestic labor as their wives do (Lincoln, 2008). Many women face what is, in effect, a "second shift" (Hochschild, 1989).

Women's inequality in the workplace is another manifestation of structural sexism. Let's focus in particular on differences between men's and women's earnings. The **gender pay gap** has been repeatedly demonstrated in cross-national surveys. For instance, the Organization for Economic Co-operation and Development (2008) found that in developed countries in North America, Europe, and East Asia women tend to earn anywhere from 37% less than men, in the case of South Korea, to 5% less than men, in the case of Luxembourg. Most of the nations in their survey, such as the United States, United Kingdom, Canada, and Germany, fall in the 19% to 17% range. In the United States, for every dollar a man earns, a woman can be expected to earn about 81 cents. The Bureau of Labor Statistics' (2011) data indicate that women earn around 23% less than men, but that the pay gap has narrowed considerably compared with 1980, when women made around 40% less than men. Women's lower pay appears to generalize across different areas of the economy—particularly in traditionally male-dominated fields like the financial and manufacturing sectors. And the pay gap has consequences that extend beyond the economy. Take violence, for example: correlational studies show that greater pay equity is associated with reduced domestic violence against women (Aizer, 2010). Researchers have suggested that as women's employment opportunities improve, they may be more able to leave abusive relationships (Gelles, 1976).

Claims of unequal pay have not, however, gone without challenge. Some skeptics, while acknowledging that women are paid less than men, argue that this arises not from discrimination but from women and men's different career choices. For example, researchers point to the fact that women tend to pursue jobs with less work hours than men (Mandel & Semyonov, 2014). For example, female students tend to pursue college majors such as economics, business, or computer science at a lower rate than do male students (Speer, 2017). These critiques do appear to have some empirical backing; however, they also raise more questions. Why do women sacrifice pay for flexibility or lower work hours? Why do they eschew economics or business majors? To answer this question, we have to look at the kinds of expectations society places on women in terms of childcare and household labor. These *symbolic* meanings around woman-hood affect *individual* women's psychologies, which in turn contributes to *structural* inequality. This exchange across different levels of analysis is just one example of how different kinds of sexism can be complexly intertwined.

Interacting Levels of Sexism

We have examined the three levels of sexism (Nakano Glenn, 1999) separately. However, these levels of sexism are not so easily isolated from one another: in practice, they form a complex, interweaving knot of individual, structural, and symbolic forces. This can start to sound a bit heady, but let's take a few examples to see how these levels work together *systemically*. For instance, the household division of labor (a structure) is supported by the meanings attached to motherhood and fatherhood (symbols) that individual men and women learn about and reproduce (at the individual level). In trying to understand the persistence of political dominance by males (a *structural* phenomenon), scholars have focused on *individuals'* biases against female politicians stemming from the *symbolic* equation of masculinity with strength and dominance.

These interacting levels can also show up in ways that appear at first glance more banal. For instance, a colleague of one of the authors tells a story about her search for a job in a children's museum. At one of the first museums that she had applied to, the job recruiters had all the applicants introduce themselves in a circle and say why they were interested in working with children. When it came time for one of the male applicants to speak up, he sarcastically quipped, "I actually dislike kids … but I'll pretend if I get paid for it!"—to much laughter across the room. When a few weeks later she went to another group interview at a children's museum, the same question was asked of the group, and she decided that she would try out the joke herself. When she did, however, she was greeted by a very different reaction than the male applicant had: crickets—an awkward silence.

This story might seem innocent enough, but we can also understand it through a feminist lens on gender. Here, femininity is symbolically associated with the care of children, while masculinity is associated with money-making. Our colleague's attempt at the joke clashed with symbolic femininity, while the successful jokester was playing right into masculinity. We see here, then, how the symbolic level of gender supports individual level gender discrimination.

Male Privilege and Barriers to Awareness

Thus far, we have focused primarily on women's disadvantage. But patriarchy does not only disadvantage women. It also confers significant benefits or *privileges* to men. Male privilege can be divided into two broad categories: unearned advantage and conferred dominance (McIntosh, 1988/2001). *Unearned male advantage* refers to rights or privileges that advantage men but do not necessarily lead to the oppression of women. Thus, unearned advantages are privileges that everyone should or could have, even if they are currently only enjoyed by men. For example, men generally can walk down a city street at night without worrying about being sexually harassed. This is an unearned male advantage. Nobody is harmed by the fact that men do not get catcalled. And it is reasonable to say that women should also not have to worry about this. Some school dress codes offer another example of unearned male advantage. These codes often frequently prohibit clothing that is more typically worn by women—strap tops, leggings, tight clothing—while permitting most clothing typically worn by males. This is an unearned advantage, because boys' ability to wear most of what is in their wardrobe at school does not necessarily result in girls being disadvantaged.

Unlike unearned advantage, *conferred male dominance* describes a set of privileges that will invariably undermine or disempower women. To understand what conferred dominance looks like, let's flip the catcalling scenario presented in the previous paragraph. For the most part, men have the privilege of being able to catcall people of the opposite gender without being reprimanded. Whenever men exercise their catcalling privilege, the target of their catcalling will be marginalized. Because catcalling is an inevitably damaging privilege, we'd call it a kind of conferred dominance. Similarly, the overwhelming predominance of men in positions of political power is a form of conferred dominance. Conferred dominance is zero-sum: privileges that inevitably disadvantage women.

While numerous, male privileges are largely invisible to men. In fact, many men, such as those struggling to find steady jobs or romantic partners, may feel quite *disempowered* in their lives. In some cases, as in the men's rights movement, men may even claim that they are *less* privileged than women or that they are actively disadvantaged by feminist reforms. While limited research exists on how men perceive women's claims of gender discrimination, research in the social psychology of race is instructive. Studies of White Americans' perceptions of racial privilege have found skepticism towards minorities' claims of discrimination—on average, in fact, Whites are likely to view claims of discrimination as an *advantage* that minorities have over them (Wilkins & Siy, 2016). For example, in the 2016 United States presidential election, one of Donald Trump's attacks on his political opponent, Hillary Clinton, was that she was unfairly using her gender or "playing the gender card" (Plank, 2016) to her advantage. Studies also find that men with greater adherence to traditional masculinity are more likely to dispute the idea of gender inequality (Wade & Brittan-Powell, 2000).

There are several powerful psychological mechanisms that may make it more difficult for men to see the ways that privilege affects their lives. One of these is the ***self-serving bias*** (Hastorf, Schneider, & Polefka, 1970). In simple terms, the self-serving bias is a tendency for people to explain their own successes in terms of *internal attributes*, such as their own efforts, personality, or talents, and to ignore *external circumstances* that may have contributed to their success. Donald Trump again provides a clear example. Early in the election, Trump explained that he was able to become a billionaire businessman by being "very smart" (*Fox News* Insider, 2011). Were it not for political opposition, he claimed, he would be widely seen as a "super genius" (Cilliza, 2015). Such internal attributions are just what we would expect according to the self-serving bias—we would not expect Trump to focus on external factors that might have explained his success, such as the million-dollar loans he secured from his father at the beginning of his career. The self-serving bias may make it more difficult for men to acknowledge the unearned advantages and conferred dominance that may have helped them into positions of power.

Complementing the self-serving basis, the ***fundamental attribution error*** may make it harder for men to see the ways that women's lives are impeded by systemic sexism. The fundamental attribution error can be thought of as the flip-side to the self-serving bias; it is a tendency to attribute others' failures to an individual's internal dispositions or traits rather than situational factors. For example, we might imagine that our classmate Gary arrived late to class because he is lazy or forgetful, rather than wondering whether external circumstances like a flat tire or taking care of a sick partner might have gotten in the way. The fundamental attribution error also has potential implications for gender relations: for example, in the case of the workplace gender gap, men may be biased to attribute women's lower pay or the relatively lower representation of women in positions of economic or political power to some personality characteristics intrinsic to women. They may be less likely to consider the external, structural impediments that contribute to women's disadvantage in the workplace.

Closely related self-serving biases and the fundamental attribution error are **beliefs in meritocracy**, an ideology that says essentially, "if you work hard, you'll be rewarded with success, and if you are successful, that must mean you worked hard." As historians and sociologists have demonstrated, these meritocratic beliefs are an integral part of liberal democratic ideals and concepts such as "the American Dream" (McNamee & Miller, 2009). Increases in meritocratic beliefs have been linked to increased support for the status quo and greater resistance to policies meant to increase social equality among both men and women (Day & Fiske, 2017). Meritocratic beliefs are also linked to increased self-esteem among high status groups (O'Brien & Major, 2005). As a high-status group, men may face a risk to their self-esteem by acknowledging their privilege.

Considering these psychological barriers to acknowledging privilege might lead one to feel quite pessimistic about the possibility of men giving up their privilege. However, it is crucial to consider that men's privilege has, at its core, at least one opening. That opening is men's pain. As Michael Kauffman (1999) writes, this opening may be growing with the rise of feminism:

> *In societies and eras where men's social power went largely unchallenged, men's power so outweighed men's pain that the existence of this pain could remain buried, effectively denied because it was amply compensated for. When you rule the roost, call the shots, and are closer to God, there isn't a lot of room left for doubt and pain, at least for pain that appears to be linked to the practices of masculinity. But with the rise of modern feminism, the fulcrum between men's power and men's pain has been undergoing a rapid shift .... As women's oppression becomes problematized, many forms of this oppression become problems for men. Individual gender-related experiences of pain and disquietude among men have become increasingly manifest.*
>
> (p. 71)

According to Kauffman, men's pain can serve as a leverage point in getting them involved in the fight for gender equality. The key, however, is making clear the connection between men's privilege and pain. For example, men are pressured to appear stronger, more confident, and more emotionally stoic than women, which ends up oppressing women. At the same time, this dynamic can create immense fear and anxiety for men as they worry they might fail to live up to those pressures. Similarly, men are privileged by, in general, earning more than women. However, a need to prove one's masculinity by being the primary breadwinner can create strong pressure for men and cause them to sacrifice other parts of life, like love and play. Simultaneously holding the two seemingly incompatible truths of men's pain *and* men's privilege may be a challenging task. However, as we will see later in the chapter, it is a challenge that pro-feminist men's groups are trying to meet.

For Consideration

"Unpacking the Invisible Knapsack" of Male Privilege

The author Peggy McIntosh described the experience of being White as one of carrying around an "invisible knapsack" of unacknowledged privileges (McIntosh, 1988/2001). In order to better understand her own privilege and the ways that Whiteness had affected her life, McIntosh developed a list of the ways that being White had benefited or privileged her. This list included items such as:

6. I can turn on the television or open to the front page of the paper and see people of my race widely represented.
7. When I am told about our national heritage or about "civilization," I am shown that people of my color made it what it is. (p. 165)

McIntosh saw this exercise as a way of "working on" (p. 164) herself. In what ways do you think that reflecting on privileges might be helpful for one's personal growth?

Try it yourself: Following the example set by MacIntosh, create your own list of male privileges. What privileges are associated with having a male body? In what particular ways are men actively favored over other genders? And in what specific ways are they able to avoid discrimination that affects other genders?

After creating your list, reflect on the following questions:

1. How does your own gender make male privileges easier or harder to identify?
2. How do these privileges shape men's lives and psychologies?
3. How do they affect the lives of people of other genders?
4. What makes these privileges invisible to those who hold them?

Feminist Theories of Gender: Asymmetric Relations

Thus far in this chapter, we've explored feminist analyses that see gender as fundamentally intertwined with social power. But what does all of this mean for the psychology of men and masculinity? How exactly does a feminist perspective on masculinity differ from a biological approach, a social learning approach, or a social constructionist approach?

Let's start by contrasting the feminist perspective with a biological perspective. Similar to the biological approach to masculinity, feminism highlights the sexual relationship between men and women as important to understanding masculinity and femininity (Smuts, 1995). A feminist perspective sees male control over female sexuality and reproduction as a core component of patriarchal masculinity, while evolutionary psychologists see competition for reproductive access as shaping a "competitive" masculinity. There are also numerous differences between the way gender looks through a feminist lens compared with a biological lens. Feminists broadly criticize biological perspectives for their perceived *essentialism* (see Chapter 2, pp. 16–40) about gender (Bohan, 1993).

The feminist approach also shares some similarities with social learning (Chapter 3) and social constructionism (Chapter 4). As with both of these perspectives, feminist approaches see masculine gender as distinct from male sex. Also, like social learning theory and social constructionism, feminist perspectives insist that masculinity is not a fixed characteristic, and that it can be transformed through historical change and by increasing individuals' awareness of masculinity. Feminist scholars also often employ concepts such as masculine gender roles that are widely used in social learning theory. Similarly, many feminists take a social constructionist perspective by considering masculinity as something that is continually reproduced, both in political and legal institutions and in the small motions of day-to-day life.

Where feminist scholarship most notably distinguishes itself from social learning theory and social constructionism is in its political orientation and its conceptual focus on three related ideas:

1. Gender cannot be understood without understanding the power structures within which it exists.
2. Gender is relational.
3. That the relationship between masculinity and femininity is asymmetrical.

The position that gender is **relational** means that masculinity cannot be understood without understanding how it gets defined against femininity. Masculine norms of strength, rationality, and independence acquire their meaning against the backdrop construction of feminine tenderness and emotionality. A metaphor helps illustrate what it means to think relationally about gender. For instance, it would be hard to make sense out of theatrical dialogue by listening to only one actor. In fact, you probably would not even comprehend the actor you did hear without knowing the full conversational context. Likewise, from a feminist perspective, masculinity is most legible when we look at it as a part of a broader relationship between masculinity and femininity. Another metaphor you might consider here is thinking about masculinity and femininity as two players in a tennis game: it would be downright beguiling to keep your eyes on only one side of the court! But some caveats should be noted here. Gender relations are not exactly like that of a tennis match: they are sometimes competitive, sometimes cooperative. Moreover, the game is not evenly matched: it is as if the men are playing with a larger racket, the women are serving uphill, and the men grew up down the street from the referee. Because of this unevenness, the relationship between masculinity and femininity is far from symmetrical.

An elaboration on the concept of **asymmetry** can be found in Simone de Beauvoir's 1949 book, *The Second Sex*. She wrote that in philosophical terms the masculine is "absolute" while the feminine is "other" (de Beauvoir, 1949). She explained:

> *The terms masculinity and femininity are used symmetrically only as a matter of form, as on legal papers. In actuality, the relation between the two sexes is not quite like that of two electrical poles, for the man represents both the positive and the neutral, as is indicated by the common use of man to designate human beings in general; whereas women represents only the negative, defined by limiting criteria, without reciprocity.*

De Beauvoir argues that femininity is defined as *those things about women that are different from men*. Femininity is the ways that women stick out as a group. However, according to de Beauvoir, masculinity is *not* defined as the way men differ from women. She cites Aristotle, for instance, who wrote that "The female is a female by virtue of a certain lack of qualities." Men become defined as more fully developed humans—human agency, power, and selfhood acquire a distinctly masculine flavor.

In contrast to de Beauvoir (1949), who theorized that womanhood is relationally defined in opposition to manhood, the men's studies scholar Michael Kimmel (1994) has presented a relational view of masculinity as *anti-femininity* (see also Horney, 1926). Drawing on Freud's theory of the Oedipal complex, Kimmel writes that the young boy's development of a masculine identity entails identifying with the father while de-identifying with the mother. Kimmel states that the boy suppresses supposedly feminine traits of warmth and nurturance,

> *because they will reveal his incomplete separation from mother. His life becomes a lifelong project to demonstrate that he possesses none of his mother's traits. Masculine identity is born in the renunciation of the feminine, not in the direct affirmation of the masculine.*

(p. 127)

Because masculinity is relationally defined in opposition to femininity, Kimmel argues that it is more tenuous than femininity. As a result of this precariousness, men devalue not only women but also gay men, whose sexuality "is cast as feminine desire" (p. 130). Homosexuality, if it is perceived as feminine, must also be continually rejected. One consequence of this rejection of femininity and homosexuality is that closeness with other men becomes threatening. While the psychoanalytic view that Kimmel presents may seem at odds with the perspective posed by de Beauvoir (1949), they both share an understanding of masculinity and femininity as concepts that need to be understood in terms of how they relate to one another asymmetrically.

Feminism in Contemporary Society

As this chapter is being written, the #MeToo movement has generated a groundswell of activism against sexual harassment and brought renewed popular attention to feminism. The social media "MeToo" hashtag was initially designed to draw attention to the number of women who have faced sexual harassment in the workplace. While it is as yet uncertain whether the #MeToo movement will generate long-term changes in workplace culture, its high visibility demonstrates the sheer cultural force of feminism. Another recent example is the January 2017 Women's March, the largest protest in the history of the United States, which drew an estimated 3–4 million participants. Clearly, feminism is and will continue to be a major force shaping the 21st century.

Feminism is a highly polarized topic in contemporary society. Public polling on the proportion of individuals identifying as feminist is inconsistent, no doubt because there is widespread disagreement about what the label "feminist" actually means. Opinion polls suggest that the label of "feminist" itself may be more controversial than the kinds of causes championed by feminists. For example, a 2016 poll in the United Kingdom showed that only 7% of Britons identified as a "feminist," while 61% stated that they "believe in gender equality" but do *not* identify as feminist (Survation, 2016).

Why might so many people believe in a central cause of feminism, gender equality, but not identify as "feminist?" Research suggests that stereotypes about feminism may have a large impact on feminist identification (Roy, Weibust, & Miller, 2007). For instance, studies have found that, when compared with non-feminist women, feminist women are frequently perceived less positively in general, and specifically as less attractive and as more hateful towards men (Twenge & Zucker, 1999). Research also suggests that feminist men are stereotyped as less attractive than non-feminist men (Anderson, 2009). These stereotypes are, of course, without merit; moreover, research on women's attitudes towards men shows that feminist women are actually *less* hostile towards men than non-feminist women (Anderson, Kanner, & Elsayegh, 2009).

Below, we address two contemporary men's movements that have arisen in response to feminism: the men's rights movement and the pro-feminist men's movement. While we describe both here, we do not pretend to be indifferent to the debate. As you have probably guessed by now, both of the authors identify squarely with a pro-feminist approach and have strong moral and philosophical objections to anti-feminism. We nevertheless insist that it is important to understand *how* anti-feminism and the men's rights movement have responded to feminist ideas, and not simply dismiss them as ignorant, reactionary, or hateful.

Pro-Feminist Organizing

Feminist approaches to men have affected society not only through social media campaigns and politics, but also through grassroots pro-feminist organizations. For example, the National Organization of Men Against Sexism (NOMAS) is a group dedicated to overcoming the constraints of masculinity as part and parcel of a broader struggle against sexism, homophobia, and racism. The NOMAS lobbies for legislation, organizes regular workshops to educate men about becoming allies to oppressed groups, and has chapters across the United States that hold regular meetings with feminist, LGBTQ, and racial justice groups. Other organizations such as MERGE for Equality offer training workshops to educators, healthcare providers, and community organizers aimed at creating gender equality by transforming the ways that young boys are socialized. What unites these and other organizations as pro-feminist is their priorities: they do not view gender equality as a means to the end of men's well-being—rather, gender equality is an equal end in itself.

These organizations use a feminist perspective to make the costs of gender inequality more concrete. True, "gender equality," "social power," and "patriarchy" can sound fairly abstract, and this academic language is probably unlikely to motivate many men towards action. However, grassroots organizations focus on what patriarchy looks like in practice—particularly the violence of patriarchy. For example, the Men's Resource Center for Change puts men's violence at the center of their campaign for gender equality. Their mission is to "support men to overcome the damaging effects of rigid and stereotyped masculinity, and simultaneously confront men's patterns of personal and societal violence and abuse toward women, children, and other men" (Men's Resource Center, 2018). Their approach does not see men's pain and privilege as incompatible, but rather as two sides to the same patriarchal coin.

Anti-Feminist Backlash

The feminist movement has since its beginning been met by powerful detractors. In contemporary society, the **men's rights movement** has steadfastly opposed feminist activism. Men's rights proponents deny that sexism against women still exists in contemporary society and highlight ways that men are apparently disadvantaged compared with women. At its more extreme edges, men's rights advocates portray feminism as an inauthentic movement that secretly aims to subjugate men. For example, men's rights activists argue that family courts are more likely to grant child custody to women in divorce cases, and reason that these courts therefore oppress men. Men's rights activists also point to the disproportionate rates of violence committed against men and longer criminal sentences for men compared with women convicted of the same crime.

Although potentially compelling, it is important to note that the above claims of anti-male bias dissolve when adequately contextualized. For instance, a bias in family court decisions needs to be understood within the broader context of gender stereotypes that sustain women's disproportionate share of household labor. Likewise, more severe sentencing for men exists in a context in which men are also advantaged by stereotypes that see men as physically powerful. And, asserting that men's greater likelihood of being a victim of violent crime is evidence of sexism or misandry ignores the fact that men are also the perpetrators of the overwhelming majority of violent crime. Still, while charges of an inherent anti-male bias in feminism are misleading, these claims can nevertheless change the way that men behave towards women. For example, researchers have shown that men with high beliefs in meritocracy tend to respond to information about instances of anti-male bias by becoming more discriminatory against women (Wilkins, Wellman, Flavin, & Manrique, 2018). It is no wonder then that men's rights internet forums, whatever legitimate complaints they might raise, also contain numerous instances of misogynistic language (Goldwag, 2012).

Given the currents of misogyny characteristic of the men's rights movement, it is somewhat surprising that the men's rights movement has mobilized some of the very same rhetoric used by feminists (Messner, 1998). For example, the men's rights activists portray divorce courts as *discriminatory* or *oppressive*. Men's rights leaders point to the fact that in the United States, only men are required to sign up for military conscription as a sign of *gender inequality* favoring women. The men's rights movement has also made plentiful use of feminist ideas of oppressive gender roles. For instance, Herb Goldberg argued that "the liberation of the female has freed her almost totally to pursue and indulge in any of what was considered traditionally masculine … the male however is still role-rigid, afraid to give expression to the female component in him" (Goldberg, 1976, pp. 54–55, as cited in Messner, 1998). In the above excerpt, it is quite clear that while Goldberg endorses the idea that gender can be oppressive to both men and women, he implies that gendered oppression of women is a thing of the past, and that the only form of gendered oppression that now remains is oppression against men. You can see that while the men's rights movement borrows from feminist rhetoric, it does so only selectively. It jettisons the idea that power relations between genders are asymmetric, leaving instead a picture of both men and women (but mostly men) as victims of gender.

Summary and Conclusion

In John Carpenter's (1988) film *They Live*, the main character John Nada stumbles across a box of mysterious sunglasses. When he puts the sunglasses on, he looks around and finds that the glasses change the way that ordinary objects look. He gazes up at billboards that, without the glasses, show a picture of a young woman in a red bikini, gracefully reclining at the shoreline of a tropic beach underneath the caption: "Come to the ... Caribbean." When he puts the glasses on and looks up again at the same billboard, however, he sees only bold black letters on a white background: "MARRY AND REPRODUCE." The glasses show him that the real underlying purpose of these seemingly benign billboards, advertisements, and commercials is social control. The postmodernist philosopher Slavoj Zizek cites this film as an exquisite metaphor for the functioning of capitalist ideology (Zizek, 2009), but we might equally see the film as an illustration of patriarchy. Nada realizes that what had previously seemed like a fairly innocent, sexualized, and perhaps even liberating image of a young woman is actually an injunction to conform to a patriarchal sexual order. The workings of power, it seems to Nada, are everywhere.

Like John Nada's glasses, feminism offers a perspective that highlights how power flows through social life in numerous, subtle ways. For most feminists, the idea that men maintain their dominance simply from the top down, by political authority, or violent control, is only part of the picture. The power inequities in gender result, just as importantly, from the ways that masculinity and femininity are symbolized or represented. At the psychological level, benevolent sexism plays just as influential a role as hostile sexism. And at the structural level, women receive lower pay not because business leaders instruct managers to pay them less but rather because of more subtle forms of discrimination in promotion, the imbalance of power when women negotiate for a raise, and beliefs that women will be more focused on family than on career.

While this picture of a patriarchal society may seem gloomy, it is important to remember that feminism is, perhaps first and foremost, political. While not all feminists agree on whether there are essential differences between men and women and whether gender equality can ever be fully achieved, there is a consensus that gender relations do change through history. That means that a core part of feminism is a belief in the capacity for change at all levels of gender—at the psychological, symbolic, and structural levels. For men, this means that masculinity too can be changed, but that change in masculinity will have to come with an increased awareness of male privilege and a relinquishing of conferred dominance. While there are psychological barriers to men's critical awareness of masculinity and of patriarchy, the growth of pro-feminist men's organizations and of the psychology of men and masculinity suggest that the future of masculinity is yet to be written.

Note

1 While patriarchy appears to be much more common than gender egalitarian or matriarchal societies historically, scholars have pointed at some exceptions to this trend. For example, anthropologists Alice Schlegel (1984) and Diane LeBow (1984) have suggested that the Native American Hopi tribe believed in female superiority and vested women with much political and economic decision-making.

References

Aizer, A. (2010). The gender wage gap and domestic violence. *American Economic Review, 100*(4), 1847–1859.

Anderson, K. J., Kanner, M., & Elsayegh, N. (2009). Are feminists man haters? Feminists' and nonfeminists' attitudes toward men. *Psychology of Women Quarterly, 33*(2), 216–224.

Anderson, V. N. (2009). What's in a label? Judgments of feminist men and feminist women. *Psychology of Women Quarterly, 33*, 206–215, doi:10.1111/j.1471-6402.2009.01490.x.

Bechdel, A. (1986). *Dykes to watch out for*. Ithaca, NY: Firebrand Books.

Becker, J. C. & Wright, S. C. (2011). Yet another dark side of chivalry: benevolent sexism undermines and hostile sexism motivates collective action for social change. *Journal of Personality and Social Psychology, 101*(1), 62–77.

Belenky, M. F., Clinchy, B. M., Goldberger, N. R., & Tarule, J. M. (1986). *Women's ways of knowing: the development of self, voice, and mind*. New York, NY: Basic Books.

Bianchi, S. M., Milkie, M. A., Sayer, L. C., & Robinson, J. P. (2000). Is anyone doing the housework? Trends in the gender division of household labor. *Social Forces, 79*(1), 191–228.

Bohan, J. S. (1993). Essentialism, constructionism, and feminist psychology. *Psychology of Women Quarterly, 17*(1), 5–21.

Bordo, S. (1987). *The flight to objectivity: essays on Cartesianism and culture*. Albany, NY: State University of New York Press.

Brownmiller, S. (1975). *Against our will: men, women, and rape*. New York, NY: Simon & Schuster.

Bureau of Labor Statistics (2011). Women's earnings and employment by industry, 2009. *The Economics Daily*. Washington, DC: U.S. Department of Labor. Retrieved from: www.bls.gov/opub/ted/2011/ted_20110216.htm.

Bussey, K. & Bandura, A. (1999). Social cognitive theory of gender development and differentiation. *Psychological Review, 106*(4), 676.

Carpenter, J. (1988). *They live* [Motion picture]. United States, Universal Pictures.

Chaplin, T. M., Cole, P. M., & Zahn-Waxler, C. (2005). Parental socialization of emotion expression: gender differences and relations to child adjustment. *Emotion*, 5(1), 80–88.

Chodorow, N. J. (1999). *The reproduction of mothering: psychoanalysis and the sociology of gender*. Los Angeles, CA: University of California Press.

Cilliza, C. (2015, August 17). Donald Trump on 'Meet the Press,' annotated. Washington, DC: *Washington Post*. Retrieved from: www.washingtonpost.com/news/the-fix/wp/2015/08/17/donald-trump-on-meet-the-press-annotated/?utm_term=.319004e76f48.

Combahee River Collective (1977/2014). A black feminist statement. *Women's Studies Quarterly*, 42(3/4), 271–280.

Connell, R. W. (1995/2005). *Masculinities* (2nd ed.). Los Angeles, CA: University of California Press.

Day, M. V. & Fiske, S. T. (2017). Movin'on up? How perceptions of social mobility affect our willingness to defend the system. *Social Psychological and Personality Science*, 8(3), 267–274.

de Beauvoir, S. (1949). *The second sex*. Retrieved from: www.marxists.org/reference/subject/ethics/de-beauvoir/2nd-sex/index.htm.

Einhorn, J. (1986). Child custody in historical perspective: a study of changing social perceptions of divorce and child custody in Anglo-American law. *Behavioral Sciences & the Law*, 4(2), 119–135.

Endendijk, J. J., Groeneveld, M. G., van der Pol, L. D., van Berkel, S. R., Hallers-Haalboom, E. T., Mesman, J., & Bakermans-Kranenburg, M. J. (2014). Boys don't play with dolls: mothers' and fathers' gender talk during picture book reading. *Parenting*, 14(3–4), 141–161.

Farrow, R. (2017, October 23). From aggressive overtures to sexual assault: Harvey Weinstein's accusers tell their stories. *New Yorker*. Retrieved from: www.newyorker.com/news/news-desk/from-aggressive-overtures-to-sexual-assault-harvey-weinsteins-accusers-tell-their-stories.

Freidan, B. (1963). *The feminine mystique*. New York, NY: Dell.

Gallagher, K. E. & Parrott, D. J. (2011). What accounts for men's hostile attitudes toward women? The influence of hegemonic male role norms and masculine gender role stress. *Violence Against Women*, 17(5), 568–583.

Gelles, R. (1976). Abused wives: why do they stay? *Journal of Marriage and the Family*, 38, 659–668.

Gershuny, J. & Sullivan, O. (2003). Time use, gender, and public policy regimes. *Social Politics: International Studies in Gender, State & Society*, 10(2), 205–228.

Glick, P. & Fiske, S. T. (2001). An ambivalent alliance: hostile and benevolent sexism as complementary justifications for gender inequality. *American Psychologist*, 56(2), 109.

Goffman, E. (1976). *Gender advertisements*. New York, NY: Harper & Row.

Goldwag, A. (2012). Leader's suicide brings attention to men's rights movement. *Southern Poverty Law Center Intelligence Report, 145*. Retrieved from: www.splcenter.org/fighting-hate/intelligence-report/2012/leader's-suicide-brings-attention-men's-rights-movement.

Gowaty, P. A. (1997). Sexual dialectics, sexual selection, and variation in mating behaviors. In P. A. Gowaty (Ed.), *Feminism and evolutionary biology: boundaries, intersections, and frontiers* (pp. 351–384). New York, NY: Chapman & Hall.

Hanisch, C. (1969/2000). The personal is political. In B. A. Crow (Ed.), *Radical feminism: a documentary reader* (pp. 113–116). New York, NY: New York University Press.

Hastorf, A. H., Schneider, D. J., & Polefka, J. (1970). *Person perception*. Oxford, England: Addison-Wesley.

Hochschild, A. (1989). *The second shift: working parents and the revolution at home.* New York, NY: Viking.

hooks, B. (2004). *The will to change: men, masculinity, and love.* New York, NY: Simon and Schuster.

Horney, K. (1926). The flight from womanhood: the masculinity complex in women as viewed by men and by women. *The International Journal of Psychoanalysis, 7,* 324.

Insider, F. N. (2011, March 31). O'Reilly challenges Trump on his views on Obama's birth certificate [Video]. *Fox News.* Retrieved from: www.youtube.com/watch?v=HQFbVWHnzp0.

Kantor, J. & Twohey, M. (2017, October 5). Harvey Weinstein paid off sexual harassment accusers for decades. *New York Times.* Retrieved from: www.nytimes.com/2017/10/05/us/harvey-weinstein-harassment-allegations.html.

Kauffman, M. (1999). Men, feminism, and men's contradictory experiences of power. In J. A. Kuypers (Ed.), *Men and power* (pp. 59–83). Halifax, Canada: Fernwood Books.

Kimmel, M. (1994). Masculinity as homophobia: fear, shame and silence in the construction of gender identity. In H. Brod & M. Kaufman (Eds), *Theorizing masculinities* (pp. 119–141). Thousand Oaks, CA: Sage.

LeBow, D. (1984). Rethinking matriliny among the Hopi. In R. Rohrlich & E. Hoffman Baruch (Eds), *Women in search of utopia: mavericks and mythmakers* (pp. 8–20). New York, NY: Schocken Books.

LeGates, M. (2001). *In their time: a history of feminism in western society.* New York, NY: Routledge.

Liesen, L. T. (2008). The evolution of gendered political behavior: contributions from feminist evolutionists. *Sex Roles, 59*(7–8), 476–481.

Lincoln, A. E. (2008). Gender, productivity, and the marital wage premium. *Journal of Marriage and Family, 70*(3), 806–814.

MacKinnon, C. A. (1987). *Feminism unmodified: discourses on life and law.* Cambridge, MA: Harvard University Press.

Mahalik, J. R., Locke, B. D., Ludlow, L. H., Diemer, M. A., Scott, R. P., Gottfried, M., & Freitas, G. (2003). Development of the conformity to masculine norms inventory. *Psychology of Men & Masculinity, 4*(1), 3–25.

Mandel, H. & Semyonov, M. (2014). Gender pay gap and employment sector: sources of earnings disparities in the United States, 1970–2010. *Demography, 51*(5), 1597–1618.

McIntosh, P. (1988/2001). White privilege: unpacking the invisible knapsack. In P. S. Rothenberg (Ed.), *Race, class, and gender in the United States* (5th ed., pp. 163–168). New York, NY: Worth Publishers (reprinted from *Peace and Freedom*, 1989, 10–12).

McNamee, S. J. & Miller, R. K. (2009). *The meritocracy myth*. Lanham, MD: Rowman & Littlefield.

Men's Resource Center (2018). About. Retrieved from: www.mensresourcecenter. org/about.html.

Messner, M. A. (1998). The limits of "the male sex role": an analysis of the men's liberation and men's rights movements' discourse. *Gender & Society, 12*(3), 255–276.

Nakano Glenn, E. (1999). Social construction and institutionalization of gender and race: an integrative approach. In M. M. Feree, J. Lorber, & B. B. Hess (Eds), *Revisioning gender* (pp. 3–43). Thousand Oaks, CA: Sage.

Nosek, B. A., Smyth, F. L., Hansen, J. J., Devos, T., Lindner, N. M., Ranganath, K. A., Smith, C. T., Olson, K. R., Chugh, D., Greenwald, A. G., & Banaji, M. R. (2007). Pervasiveness and correlates of implicit attitudes and stereotypes. *European Review of Social Psychology, 18*(1), 36–88.

O'Brien, L. T. & Major, B. (2005). System-justifying beliefs and psychological well-being: the roles of group status and identity. *Personality and Social Psychology Bulletin, 31*(12), 1718–1729.

Organization for Economic Cooperation and Development (2008). *OECD employment outlook 2008 – statistical annex*. Paris, France: OECD. Retrieved from: www. oecd.org/els/emp/40846335.pdf.

Plank, L. (2016, May 25). Men shouldn't be afraid of women, but Donald Trump should. *Vox*. Retrieved from: www.vox.com/2016/5/25/11705018/donald-trump-women.

Reuters (2018, March 8). Putin recites poetry on International Women's Day [Video File]. *Reuters*. Retrieved from: www.reuters.com/video/2018/03/08/putin-recites-poetry-on-international-wo?videoId=407231007.

Roy, R. E., Weibust, K. S., & Miller, C. T. (2007). Effects of stereotypes about feminists on feminist self-identification. *Psychology of Women Quarterly, 31*(2), 146–156.

Schlegel, A. (1984). Hopi gender ideology of female superiority. *Quarterly Journal of Ideology, 8*, 44–52.

Schwartz, J. P., McDermott, R. C., & Martino-Harms, J. W. (2016). Men's sexism: causes, correlates, and trends in research. In Y. J. Wong & S. R. Wester (Eds), *APA handbook of men and masculinities* (pp. 483–501). Washington, DC: American Psychological Association.

Serota, M. (2018, January 11). Dan Harmon confesses to sexually harassing community writer Megan Ganz on his podcast. *Spin*. Retrieved from: www.spin.com/2018/01/dan-harmon-sexually-harassment-community-writer-megan-ganz-podcast.

Sherif, C. W. (1979/1998). Bias in psychology. *Feminism & Psychology, 8*(1), 58–75.

Smuts, B. (1995). The evolutionary origins of patriarchy. *Human Nature, 6*, 1–32.

Speer, J. D. (2017). The gender gap in college major: revisiting the role of pre-college factors. *Labour Economics, 44*, 69–88.

Spence, J. T. & Hahn, E. D. (1997). The attitudes toward women scale and attitude change in college students. *Psychology of Women Quarterly, 21*(1), 17–34.

Survation (2016). *Gender issues poll.* Fawcett Society. Retrieved from: http://surva tion.com/wp-content/uploads/2016/01/Fawcett-Tables-MF-s5611.pdf.

Tiedemann, J. (2000). Parents' gender stereotypes and teachers' beliefs as predictors of children's concept of their mathematical ability in elementary school. *Journal of Educational Psychology, 92*(1), 144–151.

Twenge, J. M. & Zucker, A. N. (1999). What is a feminist? Evaluations and stereotypes in closed-and open-ended responses. *Psychology of Women Quarterly, 23*(3), 591–605.

Wade, J. C. & Brittan-Powell, C. (2000). Male reference group identity dependence: support for construct validity. *Sex Roles, 43*(5–6), 323–340.

Wilkins, C. L. & Siy, J. O. (2016). Playing the race card: Whites believe claiming discrimination is an advantage they don't have. Talk presented at the 17th Annual Meeting of the Society for Personality and Social Psychology, San Diego, CA.

Wilkins, C. L., Wellman, J. D., Flavin, E. L., & Manrique, J. A. (2018). When men perceive anti-male bias: status-legitimizing beliefs increase discrimination against women. *Psychology of Men & Masculinity, 19*(2), 282–290.

Zizek, S. (2009). Denial: the liberal utopia [Blog Post]. Retrieved from: www. lacan.com/essays/?page_id=397.

7

MEN AND MASCULINITIES AT THE CROSSROADS

Intersectional Perspectives

In the previous six chapters we have talked about masculinity in the singular, as if it were largely homogenous, monolithic like the looming object from *2001: A Space Odyssey*. Or maybe, slightly more complexly, it might seem like masculinity is a kind of spectrum: some men are more masculine, maybe some are less masculine, but, in the end, there is *one* spectrum.

If this is the impression you have taken away from previous chapters, it is an understandable one. Indeed, a conceptualization of masculinity as *one thing* is implied by the very tools scientists have used to study it. Questionnaires and scales like the Conformity to Masculine Norms Inventory (CMNI) or the Gender Role Conflict Scale (GRCS) register masculinity as a set of numerical scores across a fixed number of dimensions. Regardless of what the men filling out those scales think masculinity means, regardless of their race, cultural background, age, or sexuality, their gender is reduced to the same set of norms. In so doing, these measures suggest that masculinity is something that varies across men only in degree, and not in kind.

Of course, it can be useful to presuppose that masculinity consists of a set of norms like emotional control, competitiveness, primacy of work, and so on, and then ask men how much they conform to those norms. This conceptualization has allowed psychologists to study relationships between masculinity and a panoply of other constructs and behaviors, like psychological distress, help-seeking, or aggression. Such analyses would likely not be possible without a healthy dose of reductionism. Yet, however useful a singular or homogenizing approach to masculinity might be, this conceptualization betrays a *much* more complicated reality.

For starters, you may have already noticed that the traditional masculinity that we have traced in the preceding chapters does not seem to line up very well with some of the men that you may know. What about male friends, family, and colleagues who *are* emotionally vulnerable? Or who explicitly reject machismo, homophobia, and anti-femininity? Isn't the picture of masculinity we've painted, well, a bit stereotypical? What about the immensely diverse ways that men act, think, and feel?

Variations in masculinity partly reflect the *internal* politics of gender, as powerful men legitimize their dominance by casting other men as subordinate, effete, or less masculine. But this variability also reflects divisions *external* to gender, divisions along lines of race, class, sexual orientation, disability, religion, as well as many other dimensions of human difference. After all, people occupy multiple statuses at once, and masculinity is quite often not the most salient identity. The same forces of racism, homophobia, ableism, and classism that divide society at large also fragment masculinities into multiple groups of Black men, gay men, disabled men, working-class men, and so on. And, even within these groups, there will be heterogeneity. For example, there is no homogenous "gay community." In the United States, gay men vary by race, class, education, political orientation, and so on. Any identity category, when you look at its edges up close, turns out to be inescapably fuzzy.

In this chapter, we will examine differences between masculinities. To do so, we will draw on two related theoretical toolkits. The first, historically developed from within men's studies, is R. W. Connell's (2005) theory of *multiple masculinities*. This theory highlights relations between multiple, dominant (hegemonic), subordinate, marginalized, and complicit masculinities. The second, a loose strand of theoretical approaches that developed out of Black feminism, is *intersectionality* (Crenshaw, 1989), an approach to social analysis that focuses on the ways that multiple axes of identity, such as gender, race, or class, function simultaneously to affect individual and group experiences. Taken together, these theoretical lenses offer a systematic way to understand the blurred multiplicity of masculinities. After outlining these two theories, we will take a tour through a few different kinds of masculinities and demonstrate the ways that multiple masculinities and intersectionality can be used to develop a more nuanced picture of men's gendered lives. Finally, we'll discuss some of the ways that the multiple masculinities and intersectional approaches get used (or, more typically, *don't* get used) in public conversations about men.

Hegemonic, Complicit, and Subordinate Masculinities

While traditional masculinity may be a powerful force, not all men, and, in fact, not even most men enact a traditional masculinity much of the time. As we saw in the chapter on social learning, even men who want to conform to traditional masculine norms are often unable to because those norms are typically unrealistic and frequently contradictory. Most men simply do not have the kind of physical strength of an Arnold Schwarzenegger, earn money like Bill Gates, or enact a prolific heterosexuality like the Marquis de Sade.

The fact that traditional masculinity does not actually characterize most men served as the jumping off point for Australian gender theorist Raewyn Connell's (2005; see also Connell & Messerschmidt, 2005) research on hegemonic masculinity and the multiplicity of masculinity. She questioned how "traditional" masculinity can be dominant if so few men actually enact this form of masculinity. To understand how Connell answered this question, we need to take a quick detour and consider the intellectual context in which the theory of multiple masculinities was developed. In particular, Connell's analysis owed much to second wave feminism (see Chapter 6). Like earlier feminists, Connell argued that viewing masculinity as a set of traits, roles, or norms failed to adequately consider social structures or power. But Connell carried the feminist line of reasoning a little bit further by arguing that social role theories not only neglect power imbalances *between* men and women, but also power hierarchies *among* men. In particular, Connell was interested in how these internal hierarchies between masculinities form, persist, and change.

Connell looked to Antonio Gramsci's concept of **hegemony** to explain how traditional masculinity maintains power over others without resorting to direct and brutal subjugation. Gramsci used the concept of hegemony to explain a puzzle in Marx's theory of class struggle. If the proletariat (farmers and workers) really is so dominated by upper classes, why do they so rarely rise up in violent revolt? Why is it that the working class seems to go along with their oppression? Gramsci argued that their acquiescence can be explained by hegemony: the supremacy of an ideology that makes unequal class relations seem natural and therefore uncontestable.

Connell thought the same principles could explain how the patriarchy is sustained without running into continual resistance by women or subordinate groups of men. According to Connell, in any place and time, there will be one **hegemonic masculinity** that gets prized over other forms. Crucially, hegemonic masculinity is shaped *in opposition to* femininity and subordinate masculinities (such as gay masculinities or Black masculinities). In other words, hegemonic masculinities are defined less by what they are and more by what they are not. Edley and Wetherell (1997) documented this process of *definition against* in their ethnographic work in an English all-boys high school. They found that this school was dominated by a group of "rugby lads" (jocks, in American vernacular). These boys occupied a position of hegemonic masculinity, which they maintained through physical intimidation, popular mandate through elections to student government, and through institutional practices that emphasized athletic achievement above academics.

Hegemonic masculinities are frequently supported by much larger groups of men who enact what Connell termed **complicit masculinities**. In their ethnographic work, Edley and Wetherell found that a complicit masculinity characterized a second group of schoolboys who, intriguingly, defined their masculinity explicitly in opposition to that of the "macho" rugby lads (Edley & Wetherell, 1997). For instance, these other boys portrayed themselves as being quick-witted and genteel in opposition to the lads' supposed brutality and violence. A couple of these boys castigated the lads for their aggression:

KEITH: I think for some of us it would take a bit of working up before [getting violent], but for them they're always ready to give some [aggression].

NEIL: It's like a show of weakness I think that you have to resort to that [violence] so that's probably what stops me from having a go at one of them (p. 212).

This excerpt beautifully documents how definition against works. Us: peaceful, deliberate. Them: violent, trigger happy. Despite Neil and Keith's apparent rejection of the lads' hegemonic masculinity, Edley and Wetherell find they actually enact hegemonic masculinity in subtle ways. For instance, Neil's use of the word "weakness" plays on exactly the same idealization of strength that supports the lads' hegemony, only with a slight twist: Neil and Keith claim they are strong precisely because they do *not* fight. Similarly, the claim that the lads "have to resort" to violence positions Keith and Neil, implicitly, as *more* in control and thus more masculine than the lads. Edley and Wetherell insightfully note that it would be incorrect to read Neil and Keith's criticism of the lads as representing a resistant masculinity. Instead, by taking up hegemonic masculine themes of strength and self-control, they are complicit in the perpetuation of a kind of masculinity that sees other masculinities as inferior and—crucially—un-masculine.

To sum up, by classifying hegemonic, complicit, and subordinate masculinities Connell theorized gender as a *hierarchical* and relational system. But Connell also underscored variability in masculinities across space and time. Connell thought of hegemonic masculinity as a historically moving target. For instance, Connell argues that in the 1950s United States men like Humphrey Bogart or John Wayne represented a culture-wide emphasis on a tough, stoic kind of masculinity. But it would be a mistake to think that this particular hegemonic masculinity spreads itself over the United States, evenly distributed into each and every nook and cranny of the Eisenhower era. Hegemonic masculinity varies from profession to profession, neighborhood to neighborhood, and household to household. While some families might value intellectual or rational pursuits as emblematic of masculinity, others might prize athleticism and physical prowess. And, crucially, masculinities vary across racial, sexual, and gendered lines. To examine how those statuses shape masculinities, we will now visit intersectional theory.

For Consideration

Think back to your experience in high school or grade school. What kind of variety in masculinities was there in your school?

- Try coming up with a list of names that were used to talk about groups of boys at your school. Examples might include things like "jocks," "bros," "nerds," or "softboys."
- Were some groups of boys more socially powerful than other groups? In what ways did that power manifest?
- What groups seemed less powerful or less popular? What made those groups seem less popular? How did those groups know or how were they told that they were less popular?

Intersectionality

Intersectionality theory emerged in the 1970s as an offshoot of feminism that challenged the perceived invisibility of women of color within the broader women's movement. The Combahee River Collective (1977/2014), a group of Black (and largely queer) female activists observed that they had been sidelined in both antiracist *and* antisexist movements. They argued that their sidelining resulted from an intellectual shortcoming in both the civil rights movement and second wave feminism. Each movement focused on only one **axis of difference**—race or gender, respectively. This emphasis on only one kind of identity *necessarily* contributed to the erasure of groups that experience multiple types of oppression, like Black women who face both racism and sexism. Among African-American activists, these activists were marginalized as women. And, among feminists, they were marginalized as Black. They reasoned that the only way to highlight their marginalization was a way of looking at the world that did not boil down to single axes or single categories—a way of seeing race and gender as acting simultaneously.

In the years since the development of intersectionality, the concept has been applied to many different identity communities beyond Black women. For instance, Bowleg (2013) conducted interview research that examined how these intersectional dynamics play out for gay and bisexual Black men. One of her participants, Charles, reported that being gay and Black made him feel pervasively isolated in a way that goes beyond just racism and homophobia. He claimed, "There are few places that I can go where I can feel completely whole; in the African American communities as well as the gay White communities" (p. 761). While straight Black men and gay White men might have safe spaces to which they can retreat, Charles, by virtue of his interlocking identities, felt constantly on alert. This is the essence of intersectionality: a rejection of either/or, gender versus race logic, and a turn to both/and stance towards an interlinking system of gender and race.

While intersectionality is an increasingly visible concept in intellectual and public discourse, it is frequently misunderstood (Cole, 2009). A common oversimplification of intersectionality is the idea that understanding someone's identity as intersectional really just means acknowledging that a person has different identities, piled up on top of each other like a stack of discrete pancakes. For example, this misunderstanding of intersectionality would approach Black masculinity by viewing Black men's male privilege as being tempered by racial disadvantage. By this reading, intersectionality simply entails doing addition and subtraction.

Intersectional scholars reject this approach to studying oppression and privilege. They argue that race and gender, for example, are not *separate* aspects of Black men's lives. Instead, race fundamentally changes the way that Black men experience masculinity, and, by the same coin, anti-Blackness is also, inextricably, gendered. Identities do not only layer—they also interact and dissolve into one another. Or, as Nigel, another gay Black man participant in Bowleg's (2013) study put it: "It's hard for me to separate [my identities] … Like once you've blended the cake you can't take the parts back to the main ingredients" (p. 758). Thinking intersectionally means taking seriously the possibility that different identities are mixed in ways that cannot be easily teased apart.

With that said, we will now discuss two different masculinities in more depth: Black masculinities and Neo-Nazi masculinities. But first a caveat. It is important to recognize that there is no one Black masculinity or one Neo-Nazi masculinity. Like "masculinity" at large, these two groups are themselves internally fragmented—constantly changing in response to both internal and external pressure and contesting competing notions of masculinity.

For Consideration

When you look in the mirror, how would you describe your identity? Try to not give this much thought and just write down the things that come to you immediately.

Now consider your list in light of these questions:

- What does your list say about the privileged or oppressed status of your identities?
- Are there any identities that came to you more quickly or more easily? Why might some identities jump out at you more quickly and others less quickly?

Black Masculinities

A common trope in research on masculinities is the idea that hegemonic masculinity sets standards that are at times mutually contradictory or even impossible for men to meet. While this is true in general of hegemonic masculinity, it is particularly salient for Black American men. The data on personal income are particularly striking here. A recent analysis of the American Communities Survey looked at Americans born between 1978 and 1983, and found the median Black males born between those years earn $18,220 in personal income: $2,180 lower than the median Black female, and $12,590 less than the median White male (Chetty, Hendren, Jones, & Porter, 2018). It is particularly noteworthy that earnings appear to be equal or even slightly lower for Black men than they are for Black women. Insofar as hegemonic masculinity places a premium on men being the primary financial provider, the economic reality of Black American life puts hegemonic masculinity out of reach for many Black men. The question for many Black masculinities, then, is how to respond to or contest this out-of-reach gender ideal.

One way that Black masculinities might accommodate this predicament is through the enactment of violence. Consider, for example, the more militant elements of the civil rights movement. bell hooks (2004) suggests that men like Eldridge Cleaver, a key member of the early Black Panther Party, or George Jackson, a co-founder of the Black Guerrilla Family, turned to violent resistance to racism as a way of asserting their manhood and claiming respectability. hooks sees this violence as fundamentally rooted in the simultaneous bind placed on Black men by racism and hegemonic masculinity, and warns that it will continue so long as:

> *Black males are socialized from birth to embrace the notion that their manhood will be determined by whether or not they can dominate and control others and yet the political system they live within (imperialist white-supremacist capitalist patriarchy) prevents most of them from having access to socially acceptable positions of power and dominance, then they will claim their patriarchal manhood, through socially unacceptable channels. They will enact rituals of blood, of patriarchal manhood by using violence to dominate and control.*
>
> (pp. 53–54)

Similar dynamics can be seen playing out in particular contemporary rap music scenes where homophobia and misogyny are commonplace. Belle (2014) writes that "often in mainstream hip-hop, one has to prove his manhood by committing violent acts in order to maintain his 'street credibility.' You gain 'street credibility' by being hyperviolent, homophobic, and heteronormative, while degrading women" (p. 296).

This process of subordination illustrates just one of the ways that hegemonic masculinities are constructed in opposition to other less valued masculinities. But it would be a mistake to say that this is the *only* way of enacting masculinity as a Black male or that Black masculinities are over-determined by hegemonic norms and social structures. Men whose masculinities are marginalized are also *actively* involved in the construction of their own masculinities—and they may respond to their marginalization by re-enacting hegemonic norms as well as by resisting them.

While some Black men enact variations of hypermasculinity, other Black men have crafted progressive Black masculinities that embrace feminism and LGBT rights. White and Peretz (2010) describe the journeys of two Black men, Albert and Carlos, who experienced a transformation in the way they constructed themselves as men after entering into pro-feminist organizations. Notably, these Black men repositioned emotionality in a way that undermines the traditional association of emotional expression with weakness and femininity. Carlos explained that, "by learning to express yourself emotionally, you become more effective in looking out for your interests and the interests of others. Plus, you learn to act more successfully against injustices because you are not emotionally blocked" (p. 413). Carlos found that he was able to share his emotions and his experiences of pain as a way of building solidarity with other activists and as part and parcel of being an effective participant in a struggle against hegemonic masculinity.

Here, again, it is important to pay attention to the ways that masculinities emerge in *relation* to one another. Just as Black men construct their own masculinities in relation to dominant White masculinities and subordinate masculinities and femininities, those dominant White masculinities also engage in a process of relational self-definition. This is highlighted in the pressing question once posed by novelist James Baldwin, who asked White viewers of a television program to consider, "why was it necessary to have a Negro in the first place?" (WGBH, 1963). For Baldwin, Black masculinity was not merely subordinated to White masculinity. Black masculinity *does* symbolic work for White masculinity. Or, as he wrote, "the White man's masculinity depends on a denial of the masculinity of the Blacks" (Baldwin, 1962). Bob Dylan identified precisely this function of Blackness in his song *Only a pawn in their game*, in which he accused segregationist politicians of mollifying working-class White men by stoking White supremacy: "A South politician preaches to the poor White man/ 'You got more than the Blacks, don't complain/You're better than them, you been born with white skin,' they explain" (Dylan, 1964). Importantly "the poor White man" is not powerful in isolation—only when Black men are put in relief is he conferred a position of dominance. As we will see in the next section, the ultimate extension of this kind of racial othering is the contemporary Neo-Nazi movement.

Neo-Nazis

On a warm summer evening in 2017, over 100 individuals, nearly all White and male, gathered in the middle of the campus of the University of Virginia. These men had flocked to Charlottesville to attend a "Unite the Right" rally scheduled for the next day to protest the removal of a statue of a Confederate general (Heim, 2017) A White supremacist website, *The Daily Stormer*, had encouraged those of its readers who planned on attending the rally to bring tiki torches (Toy, 2017). And so, at around 8:45p.m. on August 11, 2017, a torch-lit parade began marching towards a statue of Thomas Jefferson, filling the nearly empty campus with the echoes of Neo-Nazi slogans: "Blood and soil!" "Jews will not replace us!" The next day, James A. Fields, a 20-year-old White man, drove his car into a crowd of counter-protesters, killing one and injuring 35 others.

In the Neo-Nazi movement and associated threads of White nationalism, racial dynamics are front and center. Gender might at first seem completely irrelevant to understanding White supremacy. Yet examining the gendering of Neo-Nazism is precisely what sociologist Michael Kimmel did in his book *Angry White Men* (2013). Kimmel's argument is simple yet surprising and provides a good case illustration of how intersectional thinking can be applied to the analysis of hegemonic masculinities and not just marginalized masculinities.

Kimmel considers the right-wing extremism on display in Charlottesville as driven by several interweaving forces. First among these are structural changes in the American economy that have gradually eroded manufacturing jobs that once offered men well-paying jobs without the need for a college degree. Second are the social changes brought on by feminism, civil rights, and LGBT rights that have gradually expanded the number of women, Black people, and gender minorities competing for well-paying jobs. Finally, and most crucially, are the traditional masculine norms that tell men that they need to be self-reliant, powerful, bread-winners. Traditional masculinity, Kimmel forwards, leaves some White men stuck between a rock and a hard place. They are trying to enact a masculinity that prizes "the self-made man" (p. 14) above all else, but doing so in the context of downward social mobility. This bind sets some men up to experience the emotion they are socialized to express: anger. Kimmel argues that this anger can get misdirected towards an easy scapegoat: those oppressed groups, like migrants or racial minorities, that now have access to places that used to be the privileged domain of White men. White supremacist violence, Neo-Nazi rallies, and the like become a way for some White men to enact masculinity when other options for enacting masculinity seem to have evaporated. Kimmel's point here is, of course, not to justify Neo-Nazism as a reasonable response to a changing world. His aim is simply to understand the roots of contemporary White supremacy in terms that are neither purely racial nor purely economic, but also gendered.

The gendering of White supremacy is evident in the case of Anders Behring Breivik, an extremist convicted of massacring 77 people in Oslo, Norway, most of them teenagers at a Labour Party summer camp. While commentators frequently explained Breivik's attack as the result of mental illness, Breivik provided his own rationale in a compendium of White supremacist writings. There are fundamental though subtle currents of patriarchal masculine norms that also run through the document underneath the denunciations of Jews and Islam. The very first paragraph of the document begins by looking back on an earlier time in the history of the European family:

> *Most Europeans look back on the 1950s as a good time. Our homes were safe ... Public schools were generally excellent ... Most men treated women like ladies, and most ladies devoted their time and effort to making good homes, rearing their children well and helping their communities through volunteer work. Children grew up in two-parent households, and the mother was there to meet the child when he came home from school.*
>
> (Breivik, 2011, p. 19)

That a Neo-Nazi manifesto should start with a nostalgic description of the nuclear family, with its patriarchal head of household, is quite striking. The manifesto could have started by painting a picture of eroding Christian values, an influx of immigration, or a cabal of liberal elites. But, instead, this first paragraph foregrounds patriarchal authority and feminine subordination. The document then goes on to describe how this nuclear family has been upended by modernity. If this manifesto calls for avenging a loss, it is clear that it is a distinctly masculine loss.

Elsewhere, Breivik's manifesto places the blame for this loss of traditional gender relations on "cultural Marxism" and, specifically, on feminism. It proclaims that,

> *the female manipulation of males has been institutionalised during the last decades and is a partial cause of the feminisation of men in Europe .... European women, in light of the feminist revolution, are now considerably more influential than men due to the sum of all forms of capital.*
>
> (Breivik, 2011, p. 118)

This language, albeit packaged in violent extremism, is not a far cry from the men's rights movement in the United States and elsewhere. The idea is that something has gone wrong in the lives of men, and that traditional masculinity is under threat by feminism and needs to be defended. Violence becomes not only a means to achieving a renewed organic society, but a masculine end in itself: a way of enacting a traditional patriarchal authority in the face of encroaching "feminisation."

Research on Other Marginalized Groups

The previous sections have provided an overview of what it means to consider multiple masculinities and to study men from an intersectional perspective. We also considered two specific examples: Black masculinities and White Neo-Nazis. Yet psychologists and other social scientists have done a considerable amount of research into the social construction and social learning of masculinities in more than just these two groups, examining ethnic minorities, sexual minorities, and other marginalized groups (see recent chapters by Hammond, Flemming, & Villa-Torres; Iwamoto & Kaya; Ojeta & Organista; Rouse; and Sánchez in the (2016) *APA Handbook on Men and Masculinities*). We review some of this rapidly emerging literature research below.

Research on gay masculinities has produced an accumulating body of evidence that suggests that conformity to traditional masculine norms plays a particularly pronounced role in the gay community. For example, gay men's personal advertisements tend to include more masculine self-descriptors than those of heterosexual men (Logan, 2010). Moreover, gay men generally tend to seek partners that they view as more masculine than themselves (Sánchez et al., 2010). Pezzote notes the tragic irony "that gay men use the same masculine standards they were excluded by to exclude each other" (Pezzote, 2008, p. 63). Sánchez and Vilain (2012) found that gay men's anti-effeminacy is in part explained by internalized homophobia. Harry (1983) suggests that adult gay men's anti-effeminacy may also reflect a defensive overcompensation in response to being bullied as gender nonconforming during childhood and adolescence. Of course, these generalizations do not apply to all gay men, and there are many gay subcultures, such as bear subculture (Sánchez, 2016), which embrace a much more flexible masculinity.

Latinx culture is incredibly diverse, spanning from the United States down to the tip of South America. Nevertheless, Ojeda and Organista (2016) find several themes that seem common to Latino-American masculinities: *familisimo, personalismo, simpatía,* and *respeto. Familisimo* refers to valuing family above oneself. *Personalisimo* is about making genuine connections with others rather than viewing relationships as instrumental. *Simpatía* refers to minimizing conflict and facilitating social cohesion. Lastly, *respeto,* Ojeda and Organista write, is about respecting individuals higher in a social hierarchy. These norms are notably less individualistic than masculine norms are among White Americans. Still, studies show that *machismo,* that is, conformity to negative aspects of those Latino norms (such as over-reacting to others' failures to display *respeto*) is associated with the same sort of negative mental health outcomes experienced by White American men who conform more strongly to traditional masculine norms (Fragoso & Kashubeck, 2000).

Scholarship on East Asian and Asian American men provides more evidence for the heterogeneity of masculinity norms. For instance, Chua and Fujino (1999) found that, unlike White Americans, neither U.S.-born Asian Americans nor first generation Chinese and Japanese immigrants viewed masculinity as being opposed to femininity. Not only do the components of masculinity, such as anti-femininity, differ in the Asian American community, but the salience of masculinity as a social identity also appears to differ, and is on average relatively unimportant for Asian American men compared with White American men (Chua & Fujino, 1999). Studies find that Asian Americans nevertheless face systemic and harmful gender stereotyping by broader society at large as desexualized, weak, or submissive. Lu and Wong (2013) note that these emasculating stereotypes are strikingly distinct from stereotypes of other racial minorities who are frequently positioned as hypermasculine. To the extent that Asian American men feel stereotyped along these lines, they tend to experience heightened symptoms of depression (Wong, Owen, Tran, Collins, & Higgins, 2012).

This scholarship shows that masculinities vary across groups not only in form—how masculinity is defined and what norms make it up—but also in its importance. It bears noting that the bulk of the research cited above on gay masculinities, Latino masculinities, and Asian American masculinities does not adopt an intersectional framework. However, we can only imagine that even more heterogeneous masculinities might emerge by looking at how these different identities overlap.

Multiple Masculinities in Society

Intersectionality has become an increasingly widely used term in contemporary discourse. For example, the online magazine EverydayFeminism. com, which promotes itself as "helping people apply intersectional feminism and compassionate activism to their real everyday lives," received approximately 30 million visitors in 2017. Intersectionality is invoked by both social justice communities and by political commentary on the apparent excesses of those communities. But on both sides, intersectionality is often oversimplified. For many on the left, intersectionality serves as an "everything but the kitchen sink" approach to inclusivity. For many on the right, intersectionality is positioned as a dogmatic orthodoxy that preaches hate for straight White men. For example, an article in the conservative *National Review* called intersectionality a "religion of deep-blue America" (French, 2018).

When it comes to public conversations about men and masculinity, however, intersectionality has been notably absent. While intersectionality has been taken up to discuss men that experience multiple forms of oppression, it is rarely used to discuss the ways men's *privileged* status as men intersects with other oppressed (or other privileged) statuses.

Why might intersectional and multiple masculinities perspectives have failed to make their way into public discussions of masculinity? There are a couple of barriers to entry here that are worth considering. One challenge is that discussing masculinity through an intersectional lens is a fairly complicated way of looking at the world, one that may challenge cognitive biases. For instance, researchers have suggested that humans have a bias towards *essentialist* thinking about identity (Haslam & Whelan, 2008). As we discussed in Chapter 3, thinking essentialistically about men means viewing them as possessing some common, internal, unchanging quality that causes them to be fundamentally masculine. Intersectional thinking directly dismisses this intuitive essentialistic thinking as imposing a kind of homogeneity on men that is not warranted. Intersectionality also discourages the sort of *categorical* thinking that researchers claim is a common feature of social cognition (Macrae & Bodenhausen, 2001). Intersectional thinking requires a tremendous tolerance for ambiguity: it rejects a black-and-white conceptualization that sees the world made up of an oppressor class and an oppressed class. People can be privileged in one domain and oppressed in another. Likewise, people can be oppressed and, simultaneously, complicit in their own subordination.

Another challenge to thinking about men intersectionally is the challenge of making privileged identities visible. As we discussed in the previous chapter, one of the features of male privilege is that it allows men to avoid seeing that they themselves are gendered beings. They do not experience the same type of discrimination that women face that reminds them, day to day, that they are women. This same logic applies to White privilege, heterosexist privilege, and any other sort of privilege.

Despite these cognitive roadblocks, the relative absence of intersectionality in public discourse about men and masculinity is still surprising given the amount of attention that White working-class men—a group explicitly defined by race, class, and gender (as well as, occasionally, religion)—have received in the wake of the 2016 United States presidential election. There has been a large public debate (paralleled by scholarly debate in political psychology) about whether this group of voters' apparent enthusiasm for Donald Trump was motivated by economic insecurity or by racial animus (Mutz, 2018). The first group insists that White working-class men were motivated to vote for Trump because of financial hardships—unemployment, stagnant wages, rising health insurance costs—trends that Trump promised to reverse (MacGillis & ProPublica, 2017). The second side of this debate argues that these men who pivoted toward Trump did so for fear of losing their traditionally dominant status, under threat of immigrants, women, and people of color (Lopez, 2017).

Using an intersectional lens, we might reapproach this debate about working-class White men's voting behavior. First, we should notice that the question of "economics versus culture" constitutes a fairly black and white either/or way of making sense of the world. Thinking intersection-ally would instead encourage us to apply a both/and logic to the debate. For example, let's revisit what James Baldwin (1962) said about White masculinity needing Black masculinity as its foil: we might reason that working-class White men's need for symbolic dominance over Blacks becomes all the more acute when their traditional economic privilege dis-appears alongside the shrinking manufacturing sector. Just as racial animus can legitimize the economic disadvantage of Black men, economic transformations in the lives of White men can fuel further racial animus. Thus, the discussion goes from being a question of the importance of class versus race to an examination of how Whiteness *and* working-class status might simultaneously produce a change in political behavior.

Beyond providing a potentially more nuanced description of contem-porary masculinity, there are other potential, untapped ways that intersec-tionality and the multiple masculinities perspectives could be leveraged in challenging conversations about social justice. For instance, acknowledging that people can simultaneously occupy privileged *and* oppressed statuses might be helpful for disarming men who might feel defensive at the idea that they are in a position of total power. Arguments that hegemonic mas-culinity is *not* a characteristic of the majority, or an insistence on the multiplicity of masculinities, might also calm the outrage that some men feel at words such as "toxic masculinity." By suggesting that "toxic mascu-linity" is not necessarily synonymous with their masculinity, a multiple masculinities perspective might be used to address perceptions that docu-ments like the American Psychological Association's guidelines for psycho-logical practice with boys and men constitute a "war on men."

Summary and Conclusion: One Masculinity or Many?

Hegemonic masculinities, complicit masculinities, marginalized masculin-ities, subordinate masculinities, Black masculinities, gay masculinities, pro-gressive masculinities, Neo-Nazi masculinities. Where does the list end? After examining the breadth of masculinities on display in this chapter, the reader may wonder: if it is true that there are so many masculinities, what is the use of grouping them under the category of "masculinities" at all? Why aren't they all simply "different human identities"? What makes multiple masculinities hang together as "masculinities"?

The answer is perhaps somewhat unsatisfying: from both a multiple mas-culinities perspective and from an intersectional perspective, there is noth-ing universal we can say about masculinities per se, beyond an obvious statement such as "masculinities are the ways society has constructed what it means to be a male as opposed to a female." Multiple masculinities hang together as "masculinities" quite simply because they all are constructed as different ways of being men. Or, as Connell (2005) puts it, *'masculinity', to the extent that the term can be defined at all, is simultaneously a **place** in gender relations, the **practices** through which men and women engage that place in gender, and the **effects** of these practices in bodily experience, personality and culture.*

(p. 71, emphasis added)

Any given manifestation of "masculinity" emerges as a position in a web of gender relations, as well as in networks of racial, class, and sexual relations. Masculinity is constructed differently across groups according to all of these lines of difference. But which lines matter, when they matter, and how they matter is continually in flux.

Not only do our understandings of masculinity change across time and place. So too does one person's masculinity change situation to situation. For example, when Ethan delivers talks as a researcher on the psychology of men, he can occupy a hegemonic masculine status by positioning himself as rational and occupationally successful. However—as a mental health professional generally open with his emotions—when he goes to high school reunions and spends time with "the bros" of his teenage years, he is more likely to get joked about as nerdy or as sensitive. Laughing along with their jokes, he can no longer claim hegemonic position for himself and instead acts, complicitly, in support of the hegemonic masculinity dominant in that particular local context. As the multiple masculinities and intersectional perspectives contend, masculinity is never constant.

Although heterogeneous, historically contingent, and situationally variable, if we narrow our lens beyond *all* masculinities and hone our focus on hegemonic and complicit masculinities, there is one key element that unites masculinities as a unique kind of identity. That element is power. Hegemonic and complicit masculinities function to establish and maintain hierarchies over subordinate masculinities and femininities. As a consequence, hegemonic and complicit masculinities are invariably bound up with anti-femininity and the subordination of other men.

There are also a few universal lessons that the multiple masculinities and intersectional perspectives say about gender more broadly. They suggest that in order to understand gender and power we cannot look simply at the relationship between men and women: we should also examine the ways that oppressed races, classes, and sexual orientations also get cast as ideological foils against the background of hegemonic masculinity. In other words, to understand men, we need to look beyond the category of "men."

References

Baldwin, J. (1962, November 17). Letter from a region of my mind. *New Yorker*. Retrieved May 16, 2018, from: www.newyorker.com/magazine/1962/11/17/letter-from-a-region-in-my-mind.

Belle, C. (2014). From Jay-Z to Dead Prez: examining representations of Black masculinity in mainstream versus underground hip-hop music. *Journal of Black Studies, 45*(4), 287–300.

Bowleg, L. (2013). "Once you've blended the cake, you can't take the parts back to the main ingredients": Black, gay and bisexual men's descriptions and experiences of intersectionality. *Sex Roles, 68*(11–12), 754–767.

Breivik, A. (2011). *2083: a European declaration of independence* [Compendium]. Retrieved from: www.washingtonpost.com/r/2010-2019/WashingtonPost/2011/07/24/National-Politics/Graphics/2083+-+A+European+Declaration+of+Independence.pdf?noredirect=on.

Chetty, R., Hendren, N., Jones, M. R., & Porter, S. R. (2018, March). *Race and economic opportunity in the United States: an intergenerational perspective.* Washington, DC: Center for Economic Studies, U.S. Census Bureau.

Chua, P. & Fujino, D. C. (1999). Negotiating new Asian-American masculinities: attitudes and gender expectations. *The Journal of Men's Studies, 7*(3), 391–413.

Cole, E. R. (2009). Intersectionality and research in psychology. *American Psychologist, 64*(3), 170–180.

Combahee River Collective (1977/2014). A Black feminist statement. *Women's Studies Quarterly, 42*(3/4), 271–280.

Connell, R. W. (2005). *Masculinities* (2nd ed.). Los Angeles, CA: University of California Press.

Connell, R. W. & Messerschmidt, J. W. (2005). Hegemonic masculinity: rethinking the concept. *Gender & Society, 19*(6), 829–859.

Crenshaw, K. (1989). Demarginalizing the intersection of race and sex: a Black feminist critique of antidiscrimination doctrine, feminist theory, and antiracist politics. *University of Chicago Legal Forum, 1989*(1), 139–167.

Dylan, B. (1964). *Only a pawn in their game. On* 'The times they are a-changin'. New York, NY: Columbia.

Edley, N. & Wetherell, M. (1997). Jockeying for position: the construction of masculine identities. *Discourse & Society, 8*(2), 203–217.

Fragoso, J. M. & Kashubeck, S. (2000). Machismo, gender role conflict, and mental health in Mexican American men. *Psychology of Men & Masculinity, 1*(2), 87–97.

French, D. (2018, March 6). Intersectionality, the dangerous faith. *National Review.* Retrieved from: www.nationalreview.com/2018/03/intersectionality-the-dangerous-faith.

Hammond, W. P., Fleming, P. J., & Villa-Torres, L. (2016). Everyday racism as a threat to the masculine social self: framing investigations of African American male health disparities. In Y. J. Wong & S. R. Wester (Eds), *APA handbook of men and masculinities* (pp. 259–283). Washington, DC: American Psychological Association.

Harry, J. (1983). Gay male and lesbian relationships. In E. D. Macklin & R. H. Rubin (Eds), *Contemporary families and alternative life styles* (pp. 216–234). Beverly Hills, CA: Sage.

Haslam, N. & Whelan, J. (2008). Human natures: psychological essentialism in thinking about differences between people. *Social and Personality Psychology Compass, 2*(3), 1297–1312.

Heim, J. (2017, August 14). Recounting a day of rage, hate, violence and death. *Washington Post*. Retrieved from: http://pshs.psd202.org/documents/hedwards/1504102116.pdf.

hooks, b. (2004). *We real cool: Black men and masculinity*. New York, NY: Routledge.

Iwamoto, D. K. & Kaya, A. (2016). Asian American men. In Y. J. Wong & S. R. Wester (Eds), *APA handbook of men and masculinities* (pp. 285–297). Washington, DC: American Psychological Association.

Kimmel, M. (2013). *Angry white men: American masculinity at the end of an era*. London, England: Hachette.

Logan, T. D. (2010). Personal characteristics, sexual behaviors, and male sex work: a quantitative approach. *American Sociological Review, 75*(5), 679–704.

Lopez, G. (2017, December 15). The past year of research has made it very clear: Trump won because of racial resentment. *Vox*. Retrieved from: www.vox.com/identities/2017/12/15/16781222/trump-racism-economic-anxiety-study.

Lu, A. & Wong, Y. J. (2013). Stressful experiences of masculinity among US-born and immigrant Asian American men. *Gender & Society, 27*(3), 345–371.

MacGillis, A. & ProPublica (2017, September). The original underclass: poor White Americans' current crisis shouldn't have caught the rest of the country as off guard as it has. *The Atlantic*. Retrieved from: www.theatlantic.com/magazine/archive/2016/09/the-original-underclass/492731.

Macrae, C. N. & Bodenhausen, G. V. (2001). Social cognition: categorical person perception. *British Journal of Psychology, 92*(1), 239–255.

Mutz, D. C. (2018). Status threat, not economic hardship, explains the 2016 presidential vote. *Proceedings of the National Academy of Sciences, 115*(19), E4330–E4339.

Ojeda, L. & Organista, K. C. (2016). Latino American men. In Y. J. Wong & S. R. Wester (Eds), *APA handbook of men and masculinities* (pp. 299–318). Washington, DC: American Psychological Association.

Pezzote, A. (2008). *Straight acting: gay men, masculinity and finding true love*. New York, NY: Kensington Publishing Corporation.

Rouse, L. M. (2016). American Indians, Alaska Natives, and the psychology of men and masculinity. In Y. J. Wong & S. R. Wester (Eds), *APA handbook of men and masculinities* (pp. 319–337). Washington, DC: American Psychological Association.

Sánchez, F. J. (2016). Masculinity issues among gay, bisexual, and transgender men. In Y. J. Wong & S. R. Wester (Eds), *APA handbook of men and masculinities* (pp. 339–356). Washington, DC: American Psychological Association.

Sánchez, F. J. & Vilain, E. (2012). "Straight-acting gays": the relationship between masculine consciousness, anti-effeminacy, and negative gay identity. *Archives of Sexual Behavior, 41*(1), 111–119.

Sánchez, F. J., Westefeld, J. S., Liu, W. M., & Vilain, E. (2010). Masculine gender role conflict and negative feelings about being gay. *Professional Psychology: Research and Practice, 41*(2), 104–111.

Toy, S. (2017, August 11) Charlottesville braces itself for yet another white nationalist rally on Saturday. *USA Today*. Retrieved from: www.usatoday.com/story/news/2017/08/11/charlottesville-braces-itself-yet-another-white-nationalist-rally-saturday/560829001.

WGBH (1963). A conversation with James Baldwin. *The Negro and the American promise* [television program]. Boston, MA: WGBH Media Library & Archives. Retrieved May 16, 2018, from: http://openvault.wgbh.org/catalog/ V_C03ED1927DCF46B5A8C82275DF4239F9.

White, A. M. & Peretz, T. (2010). Emotions and redefining black masculinity: movement narratives of two profeminist organizers. *Men and Masculinities, 12*(4), 403–424.

Wong, Y. J., Owen, J., Tran, K. K., Collins, D. L., & Higgins, C. E. (2012). Asian American male college students' perceptions of people's stereotypes about Asian American men. *Psychology of Men & Masculinity, 13*(1), 75–88.

PART THREE
Things to Look At

8

RELATIONSHIPS

The psychology of men and masculinity exists not only in the minds of individuals, but also in the space between them. Men's relationships—with each other, with friends, with family members, and with intimate partners—are all contexts where psychologists have turned their attention for theory and research. And for good reason. If we think of gender as a largely social phenomenon, the impetus for studying how men's gender plays out in relationships becomes obvious: without relationships there would be no one from whom men could learn masculinity and no one with or against whom men could construct masculinity. For instance, different-sex romantic relationships are a particularly important focus of study if we want to understand how *gender difference* between men and women gets constructed in real day-to-day life, whereas same-sex relationships are an opportunity to see how men take up and/or push back against dominant conceptions of what it means to be a man. Male–male friendships are a productive site for understanding masculinity: they are frequently the crucible in which boys learn how to be like men. The same can be said of sons' relationships with their parents and fathers' relationships with their children: these connections form the building blocks of not only gender socialization, but of all future relationships.

In this chapter, we examine each of these kinds of relationships in turn. We follow the life course of the child, starting by looking at how boys' relationships to their parents develop in the early years of life. We then examine friendships, focusing in particular on same-sex (or homosocial) friendships. We also review research on men's romantic relationships and sexuality, and end our discussion by examining fatherhood.

Boys' Relationships to Parents

Masculine gender socialization begins in infancy and is mediated through boys' first relationships: with parents. Although parents typically treat male and female children in roughly equivalent ways in the first years of life (Bell & Carver, 1980; Stockard, 2006), some differential behavior towards boys and girls is evident in the first months. For instance, boys generally get dressed in different colored clothes, receive more trucks and fewer dolls as toys, and are spoken to with less soft voices by their parents (Stewart, Cooper, Stewart, & Friedley, 1996; Witt, 1997). Even this kind of subtle difference in how children are spoken to sends a message that shapes men's psychology: that it is better to communicate with harder rather than softer emotions.

As boys mature, the father–son dyad becomes a key relationship that shapes boys' masculinity (Odenweller, Rittenour, Myers, & Brann, 2013). By *modeling* (a term you'll recall from Chapter 4 on social learning), boys learn much of what it means to "be a man" from their fathers (Witt, 1997). This modeling ripples across men's future relationships, molding behavior in romantic relationships and parenting throughout the lifespan and, of course, throughout the lifespans of their own children.

Despite the importance of the father–son relationship, there is only limited research on the topic. What research there is focuses almost exclusively on the father's perspective and what types of father characteristics and behaviors are most conducive to child development. There is scant research on *sons'* side of the relationship: how sons view their fathers (Levant, Gerdes, Jadaszewski, & Alto, 2018). One of the only studies that does examine sons' experiences of their fathers considered how young Black men navigated the transition to fatherhood (Perry & Lewis, 2016). The researchers found that fathers frequently featured centrally in these stories, starring as either the hero or the villains. Interview participants who had a close relationship with their fathers explained that they sought to emulate them. But men whose fathers were more absent from their childhood reported a pendulum swing in the opposite direction: these participants constructed their idea of good fatherhood *in opposition* to their own fathers. While limited, this research shows that fathers, not just mothers, can leave a profound impact on boys.

Friendships

As boys enter school, their social bonds expand beyond immediate family members or caregivers and begin to include friendships with other children. Research shows that, starting at around age three, boys begin to associate predominantly with other boys when given the option. This phenomenon, ***sex segregation***, is surprisingly universal, occurring not only across cultures but among many primate species as well (Maccoby &

Jacklin, 1987; Ruble, Martin, & Berenbaum, 2006). The preference continues largely unabated until adolescence, when boys increasingly form relationships with people of other genders; although young adults that endorse more masculine gender norms continue to have a preference for same-sex friends (Reeder, 2003).

Research does not indicate large sex differences between the structure of boys' and girls' same-sex friendships. While there is strong evidence that school-age (5–12) boys have larger play groups than girls (Rose & Rudolph, 2006), this difference appears to disappear quickly, with only mixed evidence for any sex difference in numbers of friends among middle- and high-school-age children (Benenson, 1990; Smith, 2011). Research shows that school-age boys and girls both value closeness in relationships. However, as children mature into adults, women have larger social networks than men (McLaughlin, Vagenas, Pachana, Begum, & Dobson, 2010). Men are more likely than women to see narrowing circles of friends, particularly later in life as they establish long-term romantic relationships—which leaves men potentially vulnerable to isolation and at greater risk of health problems after the death of a spouse (Stroebe, Stroebe, & Schut, 2001). Recent surveys suggest that adult heterosexual men report, on average, only two friends with whom they can discuss personal matters. Moreover, the modal number of friends that adult men have (the number that occurs most frequently in the data) is zero.

Sex differences appear not only in the quantity of friendships, but also in their quality. Research shows quite consistently that, when compared with same-age peers, adult men report less satisfying and less intimate friendships than women (Demir & Orthel, 2011; Fehr & Harasymchuk, 2017). Greif (2008) notes that men's friendships tend to be more "shoulder-to-shoulder" than "face-to-face," based on shared activities rather than ongoing dialogue and sharing intimate secrets. Journalist Ezra Klein (as quoted in Fessler, 2018) discussed the challenges that "shoulder-to-shoulder" friendships presented to him while growing up:

> *If your friendship is based on activities—on hanging out, playing video games, doing sports, or whatever manly things we're supposed to be doing— then as your life changes, as you move away, have children, or you get married, and you have a job, then how do you keep those friendships up? Because the material that they were based on is no longer there. And so the friendships fall away.*

Men's lower friendship quality and quantity appears to be driven substantially by their conformity to masculine norms. Bank and Hansford (2000) examined several aspects of masculinity that might be at play. They used *multiple regression*, a statistical technique that allows researchers to examine which variables are most strongly related to an outcome of interest, controlling for all other variables. In this case, Bank and Hansford were interested in intimacy in friendship as an outcome. They found that two variables—emotional restrictiveness and homophobia—jumped out as the biggest predictors of lower levels of intimacy for men. And for good reason: comfort expressing vulnerability, sharing worries, or seeking support for challenging experiences is a keystone of close friendship. Emotional restrictiveness makes this aspect of a relationship much harder to navigate. But why exactly might this other variable, homophobia—that is, an aversion to same-sex *sexual* relationships—be related to less close *platonic* relationships? The easiest explanation here is that more homophobic men are also more driven to avoid even the slightest appearance that they might be gay, a pattern of avoidance that Anderson (2009) calls **homohysteria**. The specter of being viewed as gay thus keeps such men who endorse higher levels of homophobia from getting close to other men, lest they be accused by a third party of being romantically involved. As Lewis (1978) writes, such men cannot "love and care for a friend without the shadow of some guilt and fear of peer ridicule" (p. 108).

Overall, the trend in friendship quality as boys and girls age is clear: while each starts out with similar degrees of friendship quality, boys' friendships become increasingly less satisfying in adolescence. So what happens? Why do boys go from having seemingly close friendships to distanced friendships? Developmental psychologist Niobe Way (2011) has conducted dozens of studies over the last two decades that attempt to answer this question. Her research shows, against dominant views of men as emotionally inexpressive and averse to intimacy, that teenage boys desire intimacy just as much as girls do. Despite this desire, boys begin to drift away from each other in high school. In her book *Deep Secrets* (2011), she described a particularly revealing interview with a high school senior:

> *Jason had a close male friend in his freshman year with whom he shared all his secrets and believed friendships were important because 'then you are not lonely ... you need someone to turn to when things are bad.' Three years later, when asked if he has any close friends, he says no and immediately adds that while he has nothing against gay people, he himself is not gay ... Jason, however, adds at the end of the interview that he 'wouldn't mind' having a close male friendship like the one he had when he was younger.*

(p. 19)

The fact that Jason's denial of being gay comes quickly and seemingly out of nowhere shows just how threatening close male–male friendships can be to boys. At the same time, there is a clear conflict between this fear of being labeled as gay and a desire for more closeness.

For some readers, this research may speak directly to personal experience. It certainly did for Ethan. As he reviewed it he found himself getting defensive at the idea that men's friendships tend to lack depth. "That's not true!" he mused to himself, "I've had many heart-to-hearts with my friends, in elementary, middle, and high school, as well as college and beyond." He remembered, in particular, one conversation with a group of three other male friends at a middle school sleepover. Late into the night, they took turns sharing anxieties, feelings about unrequited crushes, and, quite novel to Ethan at the time, direct statements about how much they appreciated each other's company. To this day, Ethan typically ends phone calls with close male friends by saying "I love you." And he is quick (sometimes, he worries, too quick) to share his anxieties with the friends whose support he has come to count on.

But, then again, there were many moments that seemed to fit what the literature says about men's friendships. Even now when Ethan reconnects with high school friends, he is struck by how they fall into routines of "playfully" disparaging one another, subtle digs at one another's heterosexuality; out of a world of depth and onto a plane of superficiality. What shapes each of these interactions—some profoundly close, some flat and distant—is the context. Larger groups, same-sex groups, public places where drinking is aplenty might evoke a very different social repertoire than private one-on-one conversations.

But what does the research say about male–male friendships that *are* intimate? What, indeed, about bromance? Recent years have seen increasing expressions of the bromance theme in Hollywood: Jason Siegal and Paul Rudd in *I Love You, Man* (Hamburg, 2009) or Frodo Baggins and Samwise Gamgee in *Lord of the Rings* (Jackson, 2003). Robinson, Anderson, and White (2018) write that as homophobia declines in contemporary society, young men increasingly feel more comfortable with such close, intimate relationships. As one participant in Robinson and colleagues' study explained, "It's that guy or two that you need, who is always there for you. You can talk to him about anything. It doesn't matter what you tell him, he is always there to listen" (np, online only). The research on this more *inclusive masculinity* also suggests an increasing comfort for physical intimacy between men of a sort much more common among female friends. Thus, while historically adult men's friendships may have tended to be limited by masculine norms of homophobia, as those norms change, the nature of men's friendships may be undergoing dramatic transformations and opening up new possibilities in men's same-sex friendships.

Reflecting on your own life, how do you see the issues discussed here playing out with any male friends you might have? Have you had any male best friends with whom you discussed vulnerable emotions? Why or why not? How did those conversations first start occurring?

How have your friendships with women or people of other genders differed from those you've had with men? What made them different?

Sex, Dating, and Romantic Relationships

When we talk about men and masculinity with people outside the field of psychology topics surrounding men's intimate relationships are usually among the first to arise. The same curiosity is evident in the success of self-help books like John Gray's bestselling (1992) *Men Are from Mars, Women Are from Venus*. This book, billed as a "guide to understanding the opposite sex" promises to help (decidedly *heterosexual*) couples develop a closer relationship by understanding the purportedly profound differences between men and women. Gray's book was an astonishing success, selling more than any other non-fiction book in the 1990s (CNN, 1999), and generating a series of follow-up books, interactive CD-ROMs, and expensive seminars. But what does psychological research say about men's romantic relationships? Are men really so different from women?

Researchers coming from an evolutionary psychological perspective have attempted to understand men's sexuality and romantic relationships according to selection pressures in the history of the species. For instance, along the lines of the evolutionary reasoning we described in Chapter 3, Buss and Schmitt (1993) proposed the **sexual strategies theory** as a framework for understanding how men's and women's sexual and romantic preferences have evolved in different ways in order to maximize reproductive success. For example, Buss and Schmitt found that, across cultures, men tend to be more likely to prefer short-term mating than women do; they explain that this difference arises because men can invest as little as a single sexual act in reproduction, while women must carry a child to term and ensure that it is well fed and protected. Nevertheless, they argue that men may instead prefer long-term mating strategies when doing so makes more reproductively valuable partners available, when the costs of short-term mating are high, or when women's mate preferences preclude them from pursuing short-term partners. In the context of long-term relationships, they argue that emotions like jealousy are profoundly shaped by sex: women are predicted to be more jealous of emotional infidelity, which threatens a loss of protection or material resources; men are expected to be more concerned with sexual infidelity, which raises the possibility that they might unwittingly devote resources towards raising a child that is not their own.

Qualifying these sex differences even further, social learning research has tentatively suggested that masculine gender socialization may account for some of the differences in sexual preferences and behaviors. For instance, men who more strongly adhere to masculine social norms such as toughness are more likely to prefer casual sex or to report many partners (Danube, Vescio, & Davis, 2014; Sánchez, Bocklandt, & Vilain, 2009). Gender socialization also appears, as with friendships, to influence the quality of long-term intimate relationships. Research finds consistent evidence that masculine norms predict less relationship satisfaction for both men and their partners (Burn & Ward, 2005; Wade & Coughlin, 2012). This appears true across same-sex and non-same-sex partnerships.

Exactly how conformity to masculine social norms impacts intimate relationships in the long term is not entirely clear and it likely does so through several channels. One possibility is that it affects the way emotions and vulnerability are communicated between partners. For example, Ethan worked with a couple, "Adam" and "Sherrie" (whose account below we have altered to protect their confidentiality), who came into therapy because they felt that their communication had broken down. Sherrie felt that Adam's moods were unpredictable and that he often was mad at her —that he never gave her any hints that he was having a hard day and would simply lash out or withdraw when she attempted to garner more information about why he looked down. She also felt that he was taking pains to avoid spending more time with her by working long hours building a deck for their house by himself—a project which, as she watched him struggling to drag heavy planks of lumber up the lawn, seemed like it would have been easier as a two-person job.

Adam, in contrast, felt constantly pressured by Sherrie. Carrying a long-time diagnosis of generalized anxiety disorder, he felt embarrassed by being made to "spill the beans" on his emotions and worried that she would be unattracted to his insecurities if he *really* opened up to her. He also resented Sherrie's suggestions that he *ask her to help him* work on building the deck, taking her offer as evidence that she thought he wasn't up to the job. The truth was, he wanted to build it for her as a gift.

As you can see, both emotional restrictiveness and self-reliance norms helped contribute to a challenging relationship for Adam and Sherrie. Adam's emotional inexpressiveness not only created a blank onto which Sherrie projected her own insecurities (e.g., his supposed disdain for her), but also prevented them from having an open discussion about his intention to build the deck as an act of service to her.

If Adam and Sherrie's relationship provides an example of how masculinity can influence heterosexual relationships, what then about gay relationships? In general, research on same-sex relationships shows that they are more similar than different from heterosexual ones. The same things that make for long-lasting, intimate, and satisfying relationships for same-sex pairs also do so for people in non-same-sex pairs (Balsam, Rothblum, & Wickham, 2017). And, just like for men in heterosexual relationships, higher conformity to masculine norms predicts lower relationship satisfaction among gay couples (Wade & Donis, 2007).

Research shows that men's internalization of homophobic masculine norms has consistent negative effects for gay men who are single and in relationships (Frost & Meyer, 2009). As one Black man who has sex with men put it, "manhood is just about, you know, getting all the girls, having kids, you know, doing what you want" (Fields et al., 2015, p. 126). But if masculinity is all about getting girls *and* all about doing what you want, what happens when what you want is somebody of the same sex? The strong symbolic link between masculinity and heterosexuality presents obstacles for many men in coming out of the closet and navigating relationships with other men.

Television portrayals of gay couples often gender the couple along heterosexual lines—with one partner assuming a more masculinized or dominant role and one partner assuming a more feminine or submissive role (Holz Ivory, Gibson, & Ivory, 2009). In reality, however, being gay can sometimes be liberating from these kinds of heterosexualized differences between partners. With no clear-cut cultural script on how to divide responsibilities and roles between two men in a relationship, some men in relationships with other men reject taking on stereotypically "male" and "female" roles, and instead negotiate more egalitarian relationships in which household labor, emotional caretaking, and important decisions are shared more evenly (Rostosky & Riggle, 2017). One recent study suggests that the more closely same-sex partners score on measures of masculinity–femininity, the more satisfying those relationships tend to be (Bártová et al., 2017). At the same time, research suggests that some gay men may find it hard to maintain intimate monogamous relationships because of the perception that men value physical attractiveness and casual sex (Sánchez et al., 2009).

Fatherhood

Remarkably, fathers' relationships with children were once not thought of as particularly important in child development. Historically, fatherhood was considered to revolve mostly around men's instrumental role in the family as the person providing money and/or protection. However, things have begun to change in the last several decades. This change is paralleled by many broader historical changes that have accompanied shifts from single-earner to dual-earner households, the feminist movement, and greater recognition of the unequal burden placed on mothers. Increasingly, activists and social science researchers recognize that fathers' emotional connection to their children can be just as important as the mother's relationship with the children (Levant & Wimer, 2010).

Researchers in the mid-20th century studied fatherhood using more or less one variable: the degree to which the father was involved in home life. Of particular concern was the phenomenon of the absentee father. Psychodynamic theorists speculated that the absence of a strong father figure at home might predispose boys to becoming homosexual later in life (West, 1959). Others investigated the possibility that boys without a father at home might be more likely to exhibit aggressive behavior, drop out of school, or develop mental health problems (Furstenberg & Harris, 1993; Stevenson & Black, 1988). Such hypotheses were challenging to verify because it is difficult to tease apart the effect of an absent father from the effect of a single parent. In other words, if there is a negative effect is it because the father is absent, or because there is only one parent present? However, decades of research on lesbian parents does not suggest that the absence of a father per se has any negative effect on child development (Manning, Fettro, & Lamidi, 2014). Meta-analyses comparing children raised in father-absent and father-present households also find no significant effect of father absence (Stevenson & Black, 1988).

Research since the 1990s has turned from the question of absent fathers to examining what role fathers *do* play in children's development. Indeed, fathers serve multiple roles in the family, including the traditional role of breadwinner, moral standard-bearer, emotional supporter of their partners, and nurturer of their children (Lamb, 2000). While it was once thought that fathers needed to act as a masculine role model for healthy child development, fathers' *masculinity* now appears much less important than basic processes of emotional support and involvement in the child's life (Pleck, 2010). Put another way, it's more important that men be good parents than that they be "good men."

The transition to fatherhood entails several profound shifts in men's lives. Regardless of whether children are adopted or conceived biologically, men's self-identity and relationships to their partners must change when a child arrives on the scene (Genesoni & Tallandini, 2009). Men whose partners may have been their closest attachment prior to having a child must now balance that relationship with a new one. Masculine norms too are challenged in this transition. Enacting norms of taking charge during pregnancy, and particularly during labor, is not always possible (or desirable?) for men. For example, one interview participant stated that he questioned:

Why was I there? I mean, what was the purpose? To do what? I did not know what I was supposed to do. Give encouragement to [my wife]? She was in too much pain to listen to me. I was scared. It ended up like theatre, and I was the audience. It is not as if it was my first time. I asked one of the nurses later, "Why are men there?" Her response sums it up, "To teach men a lesson!"

(Johnson, 2002, p. 174)

The experience of being a passive observer to birth, a spectator in the "theatre," clearly runs against the grain of proactive problem-solving masculinity. The birth of a child also puts a strain on what men may have previously viewed as their priorities, forcing them into a tricky rebalancing of work, play, and family. This challenging transition can take a toll on men's mental health. Evidence has increasingly accumulated showing that new fathers, like new mothers, are at risk of experiencing post-partum depression. (Strikingly, the sex difference between men's and women's rates of depression—two women experience post-partum depression for every one male—appears to be the same as the baseline difference in depression between men and women (Sundström Poromaa, Comasco, Georgakis, & Skalkidou, 2017).)

How does adherence to gender norms affect men's parenting behaviors? And how do men navigate traditional notions of stern fatherhood against new, warmer, and connected constructions of what it means to be a father? Research on the first question has found several broad patterns: conformity to traditional masculine norms is related (1) to less involvement in childcare (Sanderson & Thompson, 2002), (2) to less warmth and emotional support of children, and (3) to the use of more aggressive disciplinary techniques like spanking (Petts, Shafer, & Essig, 2018).

An example of research on the second question comes from a study by Jennifer Randles (2018) on how men in government-sponsored parenting classes redefined fatherhood beyond the narrower role of caregiver. As one participant explained, becoming a father meant learning, "A real man knows when to cry and when not to cry. What makes a man is he's aware of his emotions, he is in control, he is self-aware. What makes a good dad is a good man" (p. 533). Randles' analysis exemplifies feminist approaches to research: it underscores that while on the one hand accounts like the one above promote a more balanced division of household labor and a more flexible account of masculinity, on the other hand they suggest that "fathers' parental value derives from gender" (p. 531) rather than more universal human qualities.

Work by Randles (2018) and others suggests that a large shift is occurring in how men view fatherhood, driven in part by changing gender norms. These shifts not only will affect men's relationships with their children, but also, as we saw at the beginning of the chapter, will likely shape the gendered development of future boys. Thus, the life cycle of men's relationships begins anew.

Summary and Conclusion

You may have noticed in this chapter that as we discussed different aspects of men's relationships we drew on some theoretical perspectives more than others. This is no accident. Particular approaches to the psychology of men and masculinity lend themselves better to particular questions. For example, biological and evolutionary approaches tend to get used to study sex differences in men's and women's motivations and preferences in intimate relationships (Buss & Schmitt, 1993). Questions about how parents influence boys' gendered development, how boys and men learn about sex and relationships, and how men take cues on how to act in friendships, are all questions that might be framed through a *social learning* lens since they focus on how relationships shape men. Research on the meaning of relationships to men fall within a more *social constructionist* lens as they underscore how men shape and experience those relations. And *feminist* and *intersectional* lenses help bring focus onto the contexts of race and sexual orientation, and onto the ways that men resist or reshape traditional notions of boyhood, fatherhood, friendship, and partnership.

Throughout, several themes appear consistent. First, there are some reliable small sex differences in how individuals behave in relationships, particularly in romantic or sexual relationships. Second, social location—in terms of race, sexuality, generation, to name but a few—all shape how men *do* relationships. Finally, even in the context of romance and sexuality, we can see that there is enormous variability among men in terms of their preferences, with at least some of the variability explained by masculine gender socialization. The same holds true in the domains of friendship and parenting relationships. While masculinities shape men's relationships, those relationships are precisely the same place where masculinities can be molded, transformed, and enacted to allow men to relate to others in new and often surprising ways.

References

Anderson, E. (2009). *Inclusive masculinity: the changing nature of masculinities.* New York, NY: Routledge.
Balsam, K. F., Rothblum, E. D., & Wickham, R. E. (2017). Longitudinal predictors of relationship dissolution among same-sex and heterosexual couples. *Couple and Family Psychology: Research and Practice, 6*(4), 247–257.
Bank, B. J. & Hansford, S. L. (2000). Gender and friendship: why are men's best same-sex friendships less intimate and supportive? *Personal Relationships, 7*(1), 63–78.
Bártová, K., Štěrbová, Z., Nováková, L. M., Binter, J., Varella, M. A. C., & Valentova, J. V. (2017). Homogamy in masculinity–femininity is positively linked to relationship quality in gay male couples from the Czech Republic. *Archives of Sexual Behavior, 46*(5), 1349–1359.
Bell, N. J. & Carver, W. (1980). A reevaluation of gender label effects: expectant mothers' responses to infants. *Child Development, 51*(3), 925–927.
Benenson, J. F. (1990). Gender differences in social networks. *The Journal of Early Adolescence, 10*(4), 472–495.
Burn, S. M. & Ward, A. Z. (2005). Men's conformity to traditional masculinity and relationship satisfaction. *Psychology of Men & Masculinity, 6*(4), 254–263.

Buss, D. M. & Schmitt, D. P. (1993). Sexual strategies theory: an evolutionary perspective on human mating. *Psychological Review, 100*(2), 204–232.

CNN (1999, December 31). Grisham ranks as top-selling author of decade. Retrieved November 17, 2018, from: http://archives.cnn.com/1999/books/news/12/31/1990.sellers/index.html.

Danube, C. L., Vescio, T. K., & Davis, K. C. (2014). Male role norm endorsement and sexism predict heterosexual college men's attitudes toward casual sex, intoxicated sexual contact, and casual sex. *Sex Roles, 71*(5–8), 219–232.

Demir, M. & Orthel, H. (2011). Friendship, real–ideal discrepancies, and well-being: gender differences in college students. *The Journal of Psychology, 145*(3), 173–193.

Fehr, B. & Harasymchuk, C. (2017). A prototype matching model of satisfaction in same-sex friendships. *Personal Relationships, 24*(3), 683–693.

Fessler, L. (2018, May 1). Ezra Klein explains why men are so bad at friendship. *Quartzy.* Retrieved January 3, 2019, from: https://qz.com/quartzy/1265765/ezra-klein-explains-why-men-are-so-bad-at-friendship.

Fields, E. L., Bogart, L. M., Smith, K. C., Malebranche, D. J., Ellen, J., & Schuster, M. A. (2015). "I always felt I had to prove my manhood": homosexuality, masculinity, gender role strain, and HIV risk among young Black men who have sex with men. *American Journal of Public Health, 105*(1), 122–131.

Frost, D. M. & Meyer, I. H. (2009). Internalized homophobia and relationship quality among lesbians, gay men, and bisexuals. *Journal of Counseling Psychology, 56*(1), 97–109.

Furstenberg, F. F., Jr. & Harris, K. M. (1993). When fathers matter/why fathers matter: the impact of paternal involvement on the offspring of adolescent mothers. In A. Lawson & D. L. Rhode (Eds), *The politics of pregnancy: adolescent sexuality and public policy* (pp. 189–215). New Haven, CT: Yale University Press.

Genesoni, L. & Tallandini, M. A. (2009). Men's psychological transition to father-hood: an analysis of the literature, 1989–2008. *Birth, 36*(4), 305–318.

Gray, J. (1992). *Men are from Mars, women are from Venus: a practical guide for improving communication and getting what you want in your relationships.* New York, NY: HarperCollins.

Greif, G. (2008). *Buddy system: understanding male friendships.* London, UK: Oxford University Press.

Hamburg, J. (Director) (2009). *I love you, man* [Motion picture on DVD]. United States: Paramount Home Entertainment.

Holz Ivory, A., Gibson, R., & Ivory, J. D. (2009). Gendered relationships on television: portrayals of same-sex and heterosexual couples. *Mass Communication and Society, 12*(2), 170–192.

Jackson, P. (Director) (2003). *The return of the king* [theatrical release]. New Zealand: New Line Cinema.

Johnson, M. P. (2002). An exploration of men's experience and role at childbirth. *The Journal of Men's Studies, 10*(2), 165–182.

Lamb, M. E. (2000). The history of research on father involvement: an overview. *Marriage & Family Review, 29*(2–3), 23–42.

Levant, R. F., Gerdes, Z. T., Jadaszewski, S., & Alto, K. M. (2018). "Not my father's son": qualitative investigation of US men's perceptions of their fathers' expectations and influence. *The Journal of Men's Studies, 26*(2), 127–142.

Levant, R. F. & Wimer, D. J. (2010). The new fathering movement. In C. Z. Oren & D. C. Oren (Eds), *Counseling fathers* (pp. 3–21). New York, NY: Routledge.

Lewis, R. A. (1978). Emotional intimacy among men. *Journal of Social Issues, 34*(1), 108–121.

Maccoby, E. E. & Jacklin, C. N. (1987). Gender segregation in childhood. In H. W. Reese (Ed.), *Advances in child development and behavior* (pp. 239–287). San Diego, CA: Academic Press.

Manning, W. D., Fettro, M. N., & Lamidi, E. (2014). Child well-being in same-sex parent families: review of research prepared for American Sociological Association Amicus Brief. *Population Research and Policy Review, 33*(4), 485–502.

McLaughlin, D., Vagenas, D., Pachana, N. A., Begum, N., & Dobson, A. (2010). Gender differences in social network size and satisfaction in adults in their 70s. *Journal of Health Psychology, 15*(5), 671–679.

Odenweller, K. G., Rittenour, C. E., Myers, S. A., & Brann, M. (2013). Father–son family communication patterns and gender ideologies: a modeling and compensation analysis. *Journal of Family Communication, 13*(4), 340–357.

Perry, A. & Lewis, S. (2016). Leaving legacies: African American men discuss the impact of their fathers on the development of their own paternal attitudes and behavior. *Journal of Family Social Work, 19*(1), 3–21.

Petts, R. J., Shafer, K. M., & Essig, L. (2018). Does adherence to masculine norms shape fathering behavior? *Journal of Marriage and Family, 80*(3), 704–720.

Pleck, J. H. (2010). Paternal involvement: revised conceptualization and theoretical linkages with child outcomes. In M. E. Lamb (Ed.), *The role of the father in child development* (pp. 58–93). Hoboken, NJ: John Wiley & Sons Inc.

Randles, J. (2018). "Manning up" to be a good father: hybrid fatherhood, masculinity, and U.S. responsible fatherhood policy. *Gender & Society, 32*, 516–539.

Reeder, H. M. (2003). The effect of gender role orientation on same- and cross-sex friendship formation. *Sex Roles, 49*(3–4), 143–152.

Robinson, S., Anderson, E., & White, A. (2018). The bromance: undergraduate male friendships and the expansion of contemporary homosocial boundaries. *Sex Roles, 78*(1–2), 94–106.

Rose, A. J. & Rudolph, K. D. (2006). A review of sex differences in peer relationship processes: potential trade-offs for the emotional and behavioral development of girls and boys. *Psychological Bulletin, 132*(1), 98–131.

Rostosky, S. S. & Riggle, E. D. (2017). Same-sex couple relationship strengths: a review and synthesis of the empirical literature (2000–2016). *Psychology of Sexual Orientation and Gender Diversity, 4*(1), 1–13.

Ruble, D. N., Martin, C. L., & Berenbaum, S. A. (2006). Gender development. In N. Eisenberg, W. Damon, & R. M. Lerner (Eds), *Handbook of child psychology: social, emotional, and personality development* (pp. 858–932). Hoboken, NJ: John Wiley & Sons Inc.

Sánchez, F. J., Bocklandt, S., & Vilain, E. (2009). Gender role conflict, interest in casual sex, and relationship satisfaction among gay men. *Psychology of Men & Masculinity*, *10*(3), 237–243.

Sanderson, S. & Thompson, V. L. S. (2002). Factors associated with perceived paternal involvement in childrearing. *Sex Roles*, *46*(3–4), 99–111.

Smith, R. L. (2011). Sex differences in peer relationships. In K. H. Rubin, W. M. Bukowski, & B. Laursen (Eds), *Handbook of peer interactions, relationships, and groups* (pp. 379–393). New York, NY: Guilford Press.

Stevenson, M. R. & Black, K. N. (1988). Paternal absence and sex-role development: a meta-analysis. *Child Development*, *59*(3), 793–814.

Stewart, L., Cooper, P., Stewart, A. D., & Friedley, S. A. (1996) *Communication and gender* (3rd ed.). Scottsdale, AZ: Gorsuch Scarisbrick.

Stockard, J. (2006). Gender socialization. In J. Saltzman Chafetz (Ed.), *Handbook of the sociology of gender* (pp. 215–227). Boston, MA: Springer.

Stroebe, M., Stroebe, W., & Schut, H. (2001). Gender differences in adjustment to bereavement: an empirical and theoretical review. *Review of General Psychology*, *5*(1), 62–83.

Sundström Poromaa, I., Comasco, E., Georgakis, M. K., & Skalkidou, A. (2017). Sex differences in depression during pregnancy and the postpartum period. *Journal of Neuroscience Research*, *95*(1–2), 719–730.

Wade, J. C. & Coughlin, P. (2012). Male reference group identity dependence, masculinity ideology, and relationship satisfaction in men's heterosexual romantic relationships. *Psychology of Men & Masculinity*, *13*(4), 325–339.

Wade, J. C. & Donis, E. (2007). Masculinity ideology, male identity, and romantic relationship quality among heterosexual and gay men. *Sex Roles*, *57*(9–10), 775–786.

Way, N. (2011). *Deep secrets*. Cambridge, MA: Harvard University Press.

West, D. J. (1959). Parental figures in the genesis of male homosexuality. *International Journal of Social Psychiatry*, *5*(2), 85–97.

Witt, S. D. (1997). Parental influence on children's socialization to gender roles. *Adolescence*, *32*(126), 253–259.

9

VIOLENCE AND AGGRESSION

Violence is ancient. Older even than sex: it has been a persistent feature of life since primordial time. Even seemingly inanimate animal species such as coral heads violently attack one another when they grow too close (Richardson, Dustan, & Lang, 1979). Many of the great swings of human history—the European colonization of the Americas, the Mongol conquests, or the French Revolution—have been marked by profound acts of violence. And, throughout history, these large-scale acts of violence have been the nearly exclusive domain of men.

Recent commentary in the United States has suggested a link between men's gender and the growing epidemic of mass shootings, from Sandy Hook, to Isla Vista, to Marjory Stoneman Douglas High School. The magazine *Mother Jones* (Follman, Aronson, & Pan, 2018) tallied 110 mass shootings since 1982 (a number sure to be outdated by the time you read this sentence). "What do these shootings have in common?" asked Michael Ian Black in a *New York Times* op-ed. "Guns, yes. But also, boys. Girls aren't pulling the triggers. It's boys. It's almost always boys" (Black, 2018). Indeed, only two of the 102 shootings in *Mother Jones*' database involved a female shooter.

The overwhelming gender disparity in destructive violence is evident in crime statistics as well as attention-grabbing headlines. The United States Department of Justice's (2016) data show that men represent approximately:

- 97% of all rape arrests
- 89% of all murder and manslaughter arrests
- 86% of all robbery arrests, and
- 77% of all aggravated assault arrests.

Although research shows that men and women are both capable of violence (after all, these statistics can be flipped: women comprise 23% of all assault arrests), it is also clear that men contribute to an outsize proportion of the world's violence.

At the same time, this is not to suggest that *all* men are violent. Although there are no available estimates of the percentage of men that will get involved in a violent encounter, in terms of more severe violence, the estimates are that around 6% of men commit rape (Lisak & Miller, 2002) and around 7% of men are convicted of violent crimes (Falk et al., 2014). In other words: although most violence is committed by men, the vast majority of men do not appear to be seriously violent. This fact presents many challenges for research on masculinity and violence: if masculinity has a relationship with violence, why might this relationship seem to emerge in only a small proportion of men?

There are numerous perspectives to unraveling the paradox of men's disproportionate share in violent behavior. Consider just a few reader comments in response to Black's (2018) op-ed on men and mass shootings quoted above:

- I See It Every Day: "The first step in helping broken boys is to turn off the Xbox. The majority of boys play video games and most of those games are violent … The games are available 24/7 and the boys can play endlessly … They do this every day, for years, starting in elementary school. This is what is changing the way our boys think—and act."
- Oh Please: "Stop blaming boys. Buy car insurance for a teenage boy and see what the actuaries say about it. Boys develop differently. That is not an excuse to permit violence, but we ignore the realities of biology at our own peril. The gun laws are broken, our boys are not."
- Juanita: "It seems that some affluent parents overindulge their sons to the point of giving them a huge sense of entitlement and failing to build character and humanity. Maybe that is why so many of these mass shooters seem to come from the upper middle class, and not from the poor. These young men literally feel so entitled that they feel entitled to kill other people."

These comments convey three remarkably distinct ways of thinking about masculinity and its relationship to violence. Take I See It Every Day's comment. This reader uses what we can easily recognize as a *social learning* perspective by focusing on how video games teach boys and men. This perspective sees men's violence as possibly reversible, by turning off "the Xbox." In contrast, Oh Please draws on a *biological* point of view that sees men's violence as intrinsic to men and the "realities of biology." Finally, Juanita's comment takes a more *intersectional* lens by putting mass shootings in a class context. Her comment also echoes Michael Kimmel's explanation of mass shootings as the result of "aggrieved entitlement" (2013): men's violence as a kind of retribution for a perceived loss of status caused by post-industrialization and expanding economic participation by women and racial minorities.

In this chapter, we will use these different perspectives to unpack the relationship between violence and masculinity and explore the question of just why men seem to be so much more violent than women. First, we will define what exactly counts as violence. Clearly warfare is violent, but do sports like wrestling qualify as violent? We will then examine how masculinity relates to aggression more broadly, as well as to specific forms of violence such as sexual violence, intimate partner violence, and school bullying.

What Is Violence?

From a cursory glance, studying masculinity and violence should be simple: measure how masculine a sample of men are and how many violent acts they've committed, and then run the correlation. If more masculinity is associated with more violence, then bingo, you've got your relationship. Yet, as we've already seen, measuring things like masculinity is not nearly so simple, with varying scales and differing conceptions of masculinity leading us to a potentially very different conclusion. The same goes for violence. Although we might have an intuitive sense of what violence is, systematically defining violence for the purpose of research requires making a set of judgment calls.

Some acts are clearly violent. Murder, assault, warfare: these are all clear-cut examples of violence. All three are cases of actions that intentionally inflict physical injury to another person. But what about other behaviors that at first glance look like violence in a *formal* sense but arise in a very different *functional* context. For example, if you were an extraterrestrial suddenly dropped on the middle of a football gridiron, you'd probably assume that the heavily armored men wearing blue on the scrimmage line were trying their darndest to pulverize the guys wearing white—the *game* aspect would likely escape you. In its formal appearance, the athletes' behavior closely resembles prototypical violence. However, its function *is* distinct from that of violence, because it arises in the context of a consensual game, where the ultimate goal is not to inflict harm. Trash talking in sports is similar in this regard. While the immediate goal of trash talking may be to hurt another player's feelings, this serves the larger goal of distracting the opponent and winning the game. As the basketball player Kevin Durant opined after one of his teammates was penalized by a referee, "Come on man, *it's part of the game!*" (Poole, 2017).

The line between what is violent and what is not gets even blurrier when you think about first-person shooter video games: here, the consensual game is to "kill" other players, albeit in a virtual, simulated context. Context, it turns out, is key. For instance, we would likely view one person shooting another in a bank as the violent act *par example*. But what if we knew that the person who was shot was themselves waving around a machine gun threatening to murder everyone else inside? We might then conclude that the shooting was actually a justifiable act of defense. While the form might be the same, in its functional context self-defense has an entirely different aim than violence.

And what about acts that formally look *nothing* like violence but play a very similar function? For example, much of school-yard bullying is non-physical. However, teasing, name-calling, and other insults share many of the same functions as prototypical examples of violence do: the function and intention of name-calling is to cause (psychological) harm to another person. The same could be said of yelling racial epithets out of a car window or a manager firing an employee out of spite.

Because of the formal ambiguity of violence, we think it is helpful to distinguish **aggression**, behavior that intentionally harms another, from **violence**, behavior that intentionally causes *physical* harm to another. You'll note that both our definitions here involve the idea of intentionality. This element of intentionality is itself controversial. Drunk driving accidents, comments that unintentionally demean others (e.g., complimenting a Black man for being eloquent), creating laws that say spouses cannot legally commit rape—each of these does real harm, but without intention. This goes to show just how complicated the task of defining violence really is!

Men's Aggression and Violence in Context: Biology and Social Context

Recall the reader comment at the start of this chapter that men's violence results from the "realities of biology." Thinking back to the chapter on biology, we can see that this position involves two separate claims: (1) there is something *different* about the way men are wired hormonally, neurologically, or anatomically, and (2) that these differences *cause* the disparities in rates of violence. Showing that there are baseline differences between men and women in testosterone, for example, is not enough to show that men are "naturally" inclined to be more violent. To demonstrate this, one would also need to identify *how* differences in baseline testosterone produce different rates of aggression and violence. And, as we reviewed in Chapter 2, "baseline" testosterone is not a particularly meaningful concept for predicting behavior, as testosterone levels fluctuate enormously even within a single day and can also produce dramatically different kinds of behavior depending on the context that a testosterone spike occurs in.

Nevertheless, it stands to reason that a temporary spike in testosterone might cause an increase in aggressive behavior. One influential explanation for the role of testosterone is the *challenge hypothesis* (Archer, 2006). According to the challenge hypothesis, men have evolved such that they experience spikes in testosterone in actual or potential mating situations and that these spikes facilitate competition with other males. The idea is that increased aggression would offer an evolutionary edge in mating situations. If a male can prevent other males from mating, their own genes might have a higher chance of getting passed down to further generations. Research on humans does offer solid evidence that testosterone increases in sexual situations. However, the connection between testosterone and aggression is not a simple line from A to B, and is likely mediated by many other hormones and neurotransmitters (Kilmartin & McDermott, 2016).

The "reality of biology," then, is complex—triggered only in certain situations and through a multi-layered cascade of hormones. For example, research suggests that boys experience a spike in testosterone immediately after playing violent video games, but only when they are competing against people they view as opponents and not when training with teammates (Oxford, Ponzi, & Geary, 2010). So, while the "realities of biology" may provide a hormonal machinery for violence, the social context is also key if we want to understand why that machinery is firing.

What then is the social context of men's violence? Scholars from gender studies have noted the central role that aggression plays in demonstrating or performing masculinity. In the language of social learning, masculinity serves as a *discriminant stimulus* for the enactment of violence. When masculinity is "in the room," men are more likely to act violently. Or, in the language of social construction, doing violence is a way of doing masculinity—a part of the performance of signifying manhood. As a participant in an interview study of working-class men put it:

> *A lot of men feel the need to prove their masculinity by different means, you know, by the car they drive, by the house they live in, by the women that they date, marry, sleep with, by, you know, the amount of people that they can beat up. I think that's a huge part of it, the ego, the male ego is a powerful thing.*

(Dagirmanjian et al., 2017, p. 2782)

Cars, houses, women, fights—all these can constitute a kind of test of one's masculinity. However, failure on just one of these tests is enough to flunk the course. As Vandello and Bosson (2013) suggest, masculinity is "hard won and easily lost" (p. 101).

In the past decade, Vandello and Bosson's research on **precarious manhood** has provided compelling evidence that men's aggressive behavior operates as a way of asserting masculinity in situations of threat. Bosson et al. (2009) demonstrated this function of aggression in a clever experiment in which male participants were randomly assigned to either a masculinity-threatening situation or a non-threatening situation. To operationalize masculinity threats, the researchers had participants braid hair while control participants were asked to tie two pieces of rope together. Crucially, both conditions involved the *exact* same physical movements—the only difference was that the hair-braiding activity was supposed to threaten masculinity while the rope-tying activity was not. Afterwards, participants were given the choice between either completing a puzzle or punching a punching bag. This choice allowed researchers a rough measurement of aggression. And here's what they found: participants whose masculinity was threatened were much more likely to punch the punching bag. Moreover, in a follow-up study in which *all* participants punched the punching bag, the researchers found that masculinity-threatened men punched the punching bag with greater force than the non-threatened men. These effects held consistent across all their participants: masculinity threats seem to lead men to act more aggressively regardless of how much they *explicitly* endorse masculine norms on a questionnaire measure.

In the chapter on intersectionality, we also explored the idea that violence might serve as a way of compensating for a perceived deficiency in masculinity. You may recall that sociologists of Black masculinities have argued that marginalized groups sometimes enact a violent masculinity when systemic inequality precludes other dominant avenues for performing masculinity, like breadwinning. This dynamic can also play out on the individual level: just as communities that have fewer opportunities for men to enact traditional masculinity tend to see more aggressive behavior, so individuals who seek recognition as masculine may default to the ever-available avenues of violence or aggression when that recognition is not forthcoming. For example, research shows that boys who are more frequently bullied in school—whose manhood is repeatedly called into question—tend, over time, to exhibit more aggression (Kupersmidt, Griesler, DeRosier, Patterson, & Davis, 1995).

At the same time that violence and aggression can compensate for perceived deficits in masculinity, it can also be a context for challenging masculine norms. Journalist Thomas Page McBee (2018) writes about becoming the first transgender man to fight in Madison Square Garden. He embarks on this journey with ambivalence—he wants to explore the idea of masculinity through boxing, but hopes to keep a critical distance from what he views as its toxic features. Yet he finds that, for all its brutality, boxing can make space for a more open way of being a man:

Boxing breaks many of the binaries that men are conditioned to believe about our bodies, our genders, ourselves. With its cover of "realness" and violence, it provides room for what so many men lack: tenderness, and touch, and vulnerability ... In gyms all over the world, men are sharing their worst fears, men are asking for help, men are sparring one another with great care.

(p. 236)

His account demonstrates that while fighting may be an eminently masculine form, it does not always function in the same way. McBee finds that at the same time as the boxing gym is a place where homophobic slurs get tossed around, it is also a place where he bonds with men who come to accept him not just as a man but as a transgender man as well.

Sexual and Intimate Partner Violence

Violence within families is sadly an all too common occurrence. Approximately 17% of Americans will be physically assaulted or raped by an intimate partner at least once over their life (Tjaden & Thoennes, 2000). This violence not only impacts the immediate victims, but also the entire family. Approximately 32% of American children witness an act of domestic violence while growing up (Finkelhor, Turner, Shattuck, & Hamby, 2015), an experience that can result in lasting behavioral disturbances, trouble at school, and unstable social relationships (Holt, Buckley, & Whelan, 2008).

Traditionally, intimate partner violence (IPV) was thought to be rare—something that only disturbed men did (Gelles, 1980). However, research in the 1970s and 1980s demonstrated that it was much more widespread than social scientists had previously realized: one study even put the estimate as high as 60% of all couples (Kornblit, 1994). Intimate partner violence was also thought to be something that was almost exclusively the province of male perpetrators, with women as the perennial victims. This assumption flows directly out of gender stereotypes of men as aggressive and physically dominant and women as passive and submissive. But here too research returned another particularly surprising result. When researchers surveyed men and women and asked whether they had ever slapped, beat up, thrown something at their partner, and so on, it appeared that both men and women were *equally* violent to one another (Kimmel, 2002). These findings have sparked a contentious debate about whether there is **gender symmetry** or **gender asymmetry** in IPV. At stake in this controversy is a question of how central a role gender plays in IPV: advocates of gender symmetry view gender as just one among many variables while the advocates of gender asymmetry argue that gender plays a primary role in IPV and worry that constructing IPV as symmetrical obscures the patriarchal context in which it occurs (Hines, Douglas, & Straus, 2016).

174 Things to Look At

Here is our perspective on this hotly contested debate. While it is true that hundreds of surveys show that rates of perpetration are roughly equal between men and women, and that IPV is more frequently bidirectional than unidirectional (Dutton, 2012), these findings obscure the gender asymmetry in the severity and effects of IPV. For instance, men are approximately 20 times more likely to murder their intimate partner (Caman, Kristiansson, Granath, & Sturup, 2017). Research also shows that women are 2–3 times more likely to be injured, miss work, need to call emergency services or be left with PTSD symptoms (Smith et al., 2018). It is clear that sexual violence and IPV is something that both men and women do, and something that produces disproportionately negative effects for women's mental and physical health. Moreover, we do not view these data as threatening the cause of gender equality: as long as violence remains a central component of the construction of masculinity, it will be one way that men assert superiority over women.

The question of how gender relates to IPV need not be and should not be confined to looking at sex differences. While the question of "who has it worse" draws a lot of attention, it does not help us actually understand *how* gender creates a context for violence—how masculinity might lead *some* men to be violent *some* of the time. Even if it is true that rates of violence are equal across sexes, gender may play a unique role in violence committed by men and violence committed by women. In other words, symmetry does not rule out the possibility that gender is a key part of understanding violence.

From a social learning perspective, we might consider whether men who adhere more strongly to masculine norms are more likely to commit IPV. Research here is largely inconclusive, with few studies showing a relationship between overall masculine gender socialization and IPV perpetration (Murnen, Wright, & Kaluzny, 2002). However, Locke and Mahalik (2005) found that men who engage in problematic drinking *and* more strongly endorse masculine norms such as power over women, dominance, being a playboy, homophobia, violence, and taking risks are more likely to commit sexual violence. Other studies have shown that the kinds of sex-related stimuli that men are exposed to shape their feelings about the acceptability of sexual aggression. One study, for instance, found that college fraternity men that watch pornography—particularly pornography depicting sadomasochism and masochism or rape scenarios—report a higher likelihood of raping or sexually assaulting women than men that do not watch pornography (Foubert, Brosi, & Bannon, 2011). These effects appear to be consistent in other studies of sexual aggression and porn use (Wright, Tokunaga, & Kraus, 2015). Similarly, the likelihood of committing IPV appears to be shaped by the home environment: children with parents who are violent to one another are more likely themselves to be violent towards a partner later in life (Ehrensaft et al., 2003).

Although not directly related to sexual assault, masculine gender social-ization appears to be related to sexual assault perpetration via endorsement of what researchers call *rape myths*. Rape myths are not "mythical" in the sense that we might commonly mean when referring to stories like Zeus' rape of Europa. Rather, rape myths are a set of generalized beliefs that both excuse rapists and delegitimize rape survivors. For example, beliefs that "although most women wouldn't admit it, they generally find being physically forced into sex a real 'turn-on'," or that "many so-called rape victims are actually women who had sex and 'changed their minds' after-wards," promote the idea that women's rape claims are not valid, and that the men that do rape are really just giving women what they supposedly want (Payne, Lonsway, & Fitzgerald, 1999, p. 49).

The two rape myth beliefs quoted above actually come directly from a scale used to measure rape myths: the Illinois Rape Myth Acceptance Scale (IRMA; Payne et al., 1999). Studies show that the more men tend to endorse rape myths, as measured by the IRMA, the more likely they are to admit to having committed a sexual assault in the past (Murnen et al., 2002). Moreover, rape myth acceptance appears to be correlated with measures of male gender role socialization (Lutz-Zois, Moler, & Brown, 2015). This research finds specifically that negative attitudes towards women *statistically mediate* the relationship between male gender role socialization and rape myth acceptance. For readers unfamiliar with statis-tical mediation, in a nutshell, it is a way of showing whether the relation-ship between two variables can be accounted for by variation in a third variable. For example, while a hypothetical study might find that owning a Ferrari is statistically correlated to longer lifespan, this effect would likely be mediated by a third variable—like socio-economic status—which is related to both Ferrari ownership and health outcomes. Thus, with male rape myths and masculinity, we can say that while higher endorsement of masculine norms tends to be associated with rape myth acceptance, it is not masculinity per se but rather specific components of masculinity, like anti-femininity, that are more associated with rape myth acceptance.

From a feminist perspective, the question is less about how men's socialization leads to IPV, but instead about how IPV reflects and contrib-utes to broader societal patterns of inequality. In her controversial book *Against Our Will*, Susan Brownmiller (2013/1975) argues that we should not think of rape as a singular act committed by an individual man against an individual woman. Rather, she argues that rape should be understood as "nothing more or less than a conscious process of intimidation by which *all men* keep *all women* in a state of fear" (p. 15). In particular, Brownmiller stresses that it is not simply the frequency of rapes themselves that result in widespread fear—but also, crucially, the existence of culture that is generally tolerant of rape. One might consider here the relative rarity of punishment for rapists. First, consider that only 5–20% of rapes are reported to the police. Of those reported, roughly 7–27% result in an arrest and prosecution. Of those prosecuted, approximately 60% result in a conviction. Adding these numbers up, researchers find that only 0.2%–3% of rapes result in criminal punishment.

Not only is rape a crime often committed with legal impunity, it is also one that—at least in some contexts—is legitimized through a *rape culture*. When he was in college, Ethan reported on rape-legitimizing graffiti on the interior walls of the Beta Theta Pi fraternity (Hoffman, 2014)—a fraternity described in a 2012 federal lawsuit as a "rape factory." Ethan found that phrases like, "she said stop, I said hammertime" (a reference to MC Hammer's 1990 hit) were commonplace throughout the building. The walls were, in short, evidence of a rape culture and of the tacit acceptance of rape mythology. This story was almost prevented from being published: in the process of reporting the story, the fraternity student president threatened to use the fraternity's legal resources to prosecute Ethan for libel. Although the libel threat eventually proved empty, it is highly illustrative: it exemplified the ways that the fraternity's entrenched power could be leveraged in a way to resist critique and allow rape culture to go underscrutinized.

Bullying

The experience of bullying or being bullied is something that affects the lives of practically all children. National surveys suggest that among American adolescents, over half will be involved in bullying: either as a victim, a bully, or both (indeed, one of the strongest predictors of bullying is having been bullied). Among boys, as many as 32% are called mean names or hurtfully teased and 17% are pushed, hit, shoved, or kicked in just a two-month period (Wang, Iannotti, & Nansel, 2009). Victimization is particularly widespread among younger adolescents and tends to decrease by the mid-teens (Craig et al., 2009). Although bullying does not always leave the same kind of physical injuries that we associate with violence, its effects are still acutely felt and can persist well past school age. Adults bullied as children are more likely to experience depression and anxiety. They are also nearly 19 times more likely to experience suicidality (Copeland, Wolke, Angold, & Costello, 2013). Even merely witnessing bullying is related to a host of other negative mental health outcomes (Rivers, Poteat, Noret, & Ashurst, 2009).

Researchers typically divide bullying into four separate types: *physical,* *verbal* (name-calling, teasing), *relational* (exclusion, spreading rumors), and *cyber* (verbal, relational, or threats of physical bullying that occur online). These kinds of bullying tend to be experienced at different rates by boys and girls. For instance, it is commonly accepted that boys' bullying is more *actively* aggressive than girls' more *passive* aggression: boys use sticks and stones, girls use texts and phones. However, this perception is a bit off the mark. While research does suggest that girls are significantly more likely to use social exclusion or spreading rumors to bully other girls, it appears that boys are equally likely to engage in name calling or other forms of verbal bullying (Wang et al., 2009). Research suggests that boys' teasing is often explicitly gendered in its content: boys' teasing frequently contains homophobic or anti-feminine themes (Farkas & Leaper, 2016).

Through a social constructionist lens, we can think about bullying— particularly bullying with gendered content—as a way that masculinity gets constructed. Social constructionism is a particularly useful perspective for examining bullying because it is a clear case in which masculinity is not imposed from the top-down (from teachers, parents, or the media) but instead is created through horizontal interactions, peer on peer. Writing about schoolyard homophobia, Pascoe (2013) states:

> *It is not just gay kids who are bullied because they are gay; rather, this sort of homophobic bullying is a part of boys' gender socialization into normatively masculine behaviors, practices, attitudes, and dispositions. In other words, it is through this kind of homophobic behavior that boys learn what it is to "be a boy."*
>
> (p. 88)

The threat of being labeled "gay" can change the courses of boys' lives as they seek to avoid homophobic stigma. A former male dancer explained:

> *When I was in elementary school, I did a lot of ballet. … And that sort of [homophobic] stigma … followed me into high school. And that was followed with comments continually—"fag," you know, "fag." I think that was actually … one of the reasons why I eventually gave up ballet was just because of the constant harassment.*
>
> (Smith, 1998; as cited in Risner, 2014, p. 182)

Of course, male–male teasing and insulting expands past homophobia. In addition to disdain for homosexuals, many other male norms form the basis for bullying. Reigeluth and Addis (2016), in a series of interviews with students at an all-boys' high school, found that in addition to homophobic or misogynistic insults boys also (albeit less frequently) insult each other's intelligence, physical appearance, and disabilities. Just as homophobic insults enforce heterosexuality, calling another boy a "retard" implicitly constructs intelligence and rationality as masculine. Reigeluth and Addis found that bullying often trades on a mélange of masculine themes. For instance, "you throw like a girl" not only demeans a boy's physical *strength* but also positions that boy as *feminine*. In doing so, anti-femininity and physicality are linked together as male norms.

This process of social construction is not just researchers reading too deeply between the lines. The bullies themselves are well-aware of this fact: that what they are doing functions to shape their victims' behaviors. As one of Reigeluth and Addis' participants explained:

> PARTICIPANT: I guess there is an image of what a guy should be like. And, uh, through the teasing, they probably, like, get each other closer to that image. I guess it could be good, could be bad.
>
> INTERVIEWER: And what is that image?
>
> PARTICIPANT: Uh, like athletic, outgoing, smart I guess … good around girls, you know. (p. 78)

A social learning perspective also helps us elaborate a flip side of the social constructionist perspective. While a social constructionist perspective highlights how bullying shapes masculinity, a social learning perspective allows us to see more clearly how boys' learning history relates to bullying. If we think that homophobic insults construct a particular kind of masculinity, it should follow that homophobic insults result in changes in boys' behavior. And this is precisely what researchers find. For instance, a study found that boys whose peers use more homophobic insults were more likely to mimic the behavior. Moreover, boys who were teased with homophobic name-calling were themselves, at a later date, more likely to bully others with homophobic name-calling (Birkett & Espelage, 2015). Indeed, it appears that bullying itself is part of what boys learn. Research shows that boys who more strongly endorse masculine characteristics are more likely to bully other children (Gini & Pozzoli, 2006).

Violence in Media

Let's jump back to where we opened this chapter, with reader comments from *The New York Times*. Specifically, let's examine I See It Everyday's argument that **violent videogames** contribute to men's violence by "changing the way our boys think—and act." This is an argument that you are likely familiar with.

After seemingly every major school shooting, commentators and journalists raise the possibility that violent videogames are to blame. This is not an altogether unreasonable hypothesis. After all, videogames like *Grand Theft Auto* offer people a simulated (but increasingly realistic) way to practice raining bullets into crowds of innocent civilians. The availability and growth in sales of these games coincides almost exactly with the increase in mass-casualty gun violence in the United States. Professional organizations such as the American Psychological Association (2015) and the American Academy of Pediatrics (2009) have taken note and issued statements decrying the damaging effects of violent videogames on young people. Their concerns are backed up by some amount of research. A recent meta-analysis that analyzed 76 experimental studies found that violent video games have a small but significant effect on aggressive thoughts, feelings, and behaviors (Ferguson, 2007).

However, other data are not so clear. In fact, the question of how virtual violence is related to real-life violence is hotly contested among researchers. Key predictions that would support the idea that violent videogames cause violent criminality are not borne out by the data. For example, while it is true that the 2000s and 2010s have seen a simultaneous explosion in mass shootings and in the availability of violent videogames, youth violence more generally is in a precipitous decline. The rate of arrests of minors for violent crimes declined a whopping 63% from 1996 to 2016. The same trend holds for adult violent criminality. Even if violent videogames do lead to greater violence, there are clearly other forces at play that outweigh the negative impact of the games.

An overriding problem in trying to study whether any *particular* kind of media—be they violent videogames, war movies, or *South Park*—actually lead to greater aggression among boys is that the construction of masculinity-as-aggression is widespread across media *in general*. True, crime shows like *The Sopranos* are pretty obvious examples of the ways that masculinity gets constructed as violent. But this construction is actually much more widespread and takes place even in seemingly "peaceful" genres like advertisements, political rhetoric, or everyday metaphors. Violence is an ever-present theme in media and public discourse.

Consider the beer advertisement. Beer advertisements commonly feature highly sexualized women (the message being "drink this beer and women will swoon into your arms! You will be a man!"), but they also sometimes feature violent imagery. For example, the beer company Dos Equis ran an ad campaign from 2006 to 2018 about "The Most Interesting Man in the World," which featured an image of a grey-bearded, suave, older man dubbed over with a voice that humorously details a list of impossible accomplishments, such as teaching his horse to read his emails. Alongside the humor, the commercials deliver a subtle dose of aggression and violence as the narrator notes that the most interesting man in the world has also "punched a magician" and "slammed a revolving door" (jec20721, 2009). In another commercial for Carlton Draught (funkuncle999, 2013), we see two giant crowds of men dressed in battle regalia charging at each other *à la Lord of the Rings*, only for an overhead shot to reveal that the crowds are not forming a battle line but rather the shape of a man and an approaching beer bottle. Here, just like in a classic sexualized beer commercial, masculinity is directly on display, and, we are promised, readily available to us with the simple purchase of a bottle of beer.

Themes of masculine violence also crop up in movies that are not obviously violent, filled with guns, or dominated by action sequences. For example, the movie *Back to the Future* (Zemeckis, 1985)—a film about a boy, Marty McFly, a mad scientist, "Doc" Brown, and a time-machine—contains some covert messages about violence and masculinity. Through a series of mishaps, Marty and "Doc" Brown end up stuck in the 1950s, in Marty's parents' hometown. The film is largely comedic and lighthearted, but its central coming-of-age story also underscores the theme of becoming a man through violence. In the film, the character that undergoes the most change is Marty's (high-school-aged) father, George, depicted at the beginning as a skinny, glasses-wearing, effete victim of the bully, Biff. Through Marty's scheming intervention, George undergoes a masculine transformation into the man who will become Marty's father. George's development gets crystalized in the film's final scene, when he knocks Biff out with a punch and, in so doing, wins the respect and attraction of Marty's mother. Through violence, the boy both becomes the man and gets the girl. And all this in what is essentially a family-oriented, comedic, feel-good film with no guns, violent videogames, or other more conspicuous symbols of violent masculinity.

Political journalism is another venue that frequently plays host to masculine aggression even under the guise of (aspirationally) level-headed debate. There is evidence of this aggression even in the titles of political shows, which have names like *Hardball* or *Crossfire* (or, as comedian Jon Stewart [Zillich, 2004] once added in jest, "*I'm going to kick your ass*"). The aggression of political journalism is not a recent innovation. William Buckley Jr., a normally genteel conservative public intellectual who hosted another aggressively named show, *Firing Line*, had a debate in 1969 with the linguist Noam Chomsky about the then-raging Vietnam War (Dietrick, 1969). In the following exchange, Buckley praises Chomsky for keeping his emotions under control during their discussion:

BUCKLEY:	I recognize what an act of self-control this must involve.
CHOMSKY:	It does it really does, it really does, I mean I think ….
BUCKLEY:	You're doing very well, you're doing very well.
CHOMSKY:	Sometimes I lose my temper, maybe not tonight.
BUCKLEY:	Maybe not tonight (*Chomsky laughs*). Because if you would I'd smash you in the goddamn face (*Chomsky and audience laugh*).
CHOMSKY:	That's a good reason for not losing my temper.

Masculinity enters this conversation not only in the half-humorous threat of physical force, but also in the subtle undercutting of Chomsky's rationality by suggesting that he has an irrationality (emotions) that he is struggling to control. Such violent speech also frequents the lips of contemporary American politicians. Witness the Presidential Election of 2016. Future-president Trump told an audience of supporters that he wanted to punch a protestor in the face, and outgoing Vice President Joe Biden said the following about Trump: "I wish we were in high school and I could take him behind the gym" (Neidig, 2016). (If you ever doubt whether this kind of rhetoric is gendered, just imagine how the largely bemused public would have reacted if a *female* politician had uttered such words.)

Violent imagery also peppers the media in the form of metaphor. The culture *wars*. The *battle* for LGBT rights. Doctors stationed on the *frontlines* of the *fight* against cancer. Even in the work of the ancient Roman poet Ovid, men's seduction of women was frequently depicted through the language of battle and conquest (Cahoon, 1988). In the Spanish language, the association of war and love goes beyond metaphor: the verbs for "marry" and for "hunt," "casar" and "cazar," are nearly indistinguishable in most forms of Spanish spoken in the Americas (although they share distinct etymologies). It is clear that when the discussion about media violence and men's aggression focuses narrowly on violent videogames, a great deal gets missed about the ways that masculinity is constructed for men and boys in media writ-large, and also in language itself.

Violence is often used to humorous effect in movies and television shows. For example, one of the recurring jokes in the cartoon comedy series *South Park* is that the quiet character Kenny ends up being killed in practically every other episode—his head cut off, run over by an ambulance, or electrocuted by an undercover Saddam Hussein. Violent themes are also present in cartoons marketed for younger audiences. The cartoon *Tom & Jerry*—a show about a cat, Tom, and his futile endless attempts to capture and kill the mouse, Jerry—depicts the two fighting each other with everything from explosions and poisons to lawnmowers and waffle irons.

- What distinguishes these forms of comedic violence from "more serious" representations of violence?
- In what ways do you see comedic violence being gendered?
- What kinds of lessons do you think boys might learn from watching these kinds of violent cartoons?

Summary and Conclusion

Violence is gendered, not only in the sense that men are statistically more likely to be violent. The relationship between violence and gender goes beyond sex differences. Masculinity is a key context for understanding violence: violence gets used as a way of asserting masculinity and deviations from masculine norms frequently elicit aggressive responses from other men. Violence also shapes the performance of masculinity, indeed it symbolizes masculinity. From Achilles to Terminator, Hannibal Lecter to Darth Vader, men are celebrated as well as reviled for their willingness to engage in violence.

While violent people are much more likely to be men, this of course does not imply that all men are violent. Nevertheless, in day-to-day life, perceived or actual male violence can affect the way children comport themselves on the playground, how individuals relate to their male romantic partners, how men relate to each other, and the way men assert their own manhood. The mere threat of aggression, physical or verbal, can be a powerful force in enforcing traditional masculinity—just as the threat of intimate partner violence can be a force for control in romantic relationships. Understanding men's relationship to violence is thus a crucial part of understanding how masculinity is constructed, how men learn about masculinity, and how larger social inequities are perpetuated. And in each of these questions of social construction, of social learning, and of power structures, we see how the topic of violence captivates researchers from across different theoretical perspectives.

References

American Academy of Pediatrics (2009). Media violence. *Pediatrics*, *124*(5), 1495–1503.

American Psychological Association (2015). *Resolution on violent video games*. Retrieved from: www.apa.org/about/policy/violent-video-games.aspx.

Archer, J. (2006). Testosterone and human aggression: an evaluation of the challenge hypothesis. *Neuroscience & Biobehavioral Reviews*, *30*(3), 319–345.

Birkett, M. & Espelage, D. L. (2015). Homophobic name-calling, peer-groups, and masculinity: the socialization of homophobic behavior in adolescents. *Social Development*, *24*(1), 184–205.

Black, M. I. (2018, February 21). The boys are not alright. *New York Times*. Retrieved from: www.nytimes.com/2018/02/21/opinion/boys-violence-shootings-guns.html.

Bosson, J. K., Vandello, J. A., Burnaford, R. M., Weaver, J. R., & Wasti, S. A. (2009). Precarious manhood and displays of physical aggression. *Personality and Social Psychology Bulletin*, *35*(5), 623–634.

Brownmiller, S. (2013/1975). *Against our will: men, women and rape* [epub]. New York, NY: Open Road Media.

Cahoon, L. (1988). The bed as battlefield: erotic conquest and military metaphor in Ovid's Amores. *Transactions of the American Philological Association (1974–)*, *118*, 293–307.

Caman, S., Kristiansson, M., Granath, S., & Sturup, J. (2017). Trends in rates and characteristics of intimate partner homicides between 1990 and 2013. *Journal of Criminal Justice, 49,* 14–21.

Copeland, W. E., Wolke, D., Angold, A., & Costello, E. J. (2013). Adult psychiatric outcomes of bullying and being bullied by peers in childhood and adolescence. *JAMA Psychiatry, 70*(4), 419–426.

Craig, W., Harel-Fisch, Y., Fogel-Grinvald, H., Dostaler, S., Hetland, J., Simons-Morton, B., Molcho, M., Gaspar de Mato, M., Overpeck, M., Due, P., Pickett, W., & the HBSC Violence & Injuries Prevention Focus Group and the HBSC Bullying Writing Group (2009). A cross-national profile of bullying and victimization among adolescents in 40 countries. *International Journal of Public Health, 54*(2), 216–224.

Dagirmanjian, F. B., Mahalik, J. R., Boland, J., Colbow, A., Dunn, J., Pomarico, A., & Rappaport, D. (2017). How do men construct and explain men's violence? *Journal of Interpersonal Violence, 32*(15), 2275–2297.

Dietrick, G. (1969, April 3). Vietnam and the intellectuals [Television broadcast]. *Firing line.* New York, NY: WOR-TV.

Dutton, D. G. (2012). The case against the role of gender in intimate partner violence. *Aggression and Violent Behavior, 17*(1), 99–104.

Ehrensaft, M. K., Cohen, P., Brown, J., Smailes, E., Chen, H., & Johnson, J. G. (2003). Intergenerational transmission of partner violence: a 20-year prospective study. *Journal of Consulting and Clinical Psychology, 71*(4), 741–753.

Falk, Ö., Wallinius, M., Lundström, S., Frisell, T., Anckarsäter, H., & Kerekes, N. (2014). The 1% of the population accountable for 63% of all violent crime convictions. *Social Psychiatry and Psychiatric Epidemiology, 49*(4), 559–571.

Farkas, T. & Leaper, C. (2016). The psychology of boys. In Y. J. Wong & S. R. Wester (Eds), *APA handbook of men and masculinities* (pp. 357–387). Washington, DC: American Psychological Association.

Ferguson, C. J. (2007). The good, the bad and the ugly: a meta-analytic review of positive and negative effects of violent video games. *Psychiatric Quarterly, 78*(4), 309–316.

Finkelhor, D., Turner, H. A., Shattuck, A., & Hamby, S. L. (2015). Prevalence of childhood exposure to violence, crime, and abuse: results from the national survey of children's exposure to violence. *JAMA Pediatrics, 169*(8), 746–754.

Follman, M., Aronson, G., & Pan, D. (2018, January 24). US mass shootings, 1982–2019: data from Mother Jones' investigation. *Mother Jones.* Retrieved from: www.motherjones.com/politics/2012/12/mass-shootings-mother-jones-full-data.

Foubert, J. D., Brosi, M. W., & Bannon, R. S. (2011). Pornography viewing among fraternity men: effects on bystander intervention, rape myth acceptance and behavioral intent to commit sexual assault. *Sexual Addiction & Compulsivity, 18* (4), 212–231.

funkuncle999 (2013, July 13). Carlton Draught "Big Ad" (HI-DEF) best version online [Advertisement]. *YouTube.com.* Retrieved from: www.youtube.com/watch?v=_wM2c3WtDjQ.

Gelles, R. J. (1980). Violence in the family: a review of research in the seventies. *Journal of Marriage and the Family, 42*(4), 873–885.

Gini, G. & Pozzoli, T. (2006). The role of masculinity in children's bullying. *Sex Roles, 54*(7–8), 585–588.

Hines, D. A., Douglas, E. M., & Straus, M. A. (2016). Controversies in partner violence. In C. A. Cuevas & C. M. Rennison (Eds), *The Wiley handbook on the psychology of violence* (pp. 411–438). Chichester, UK: John Wiley & Sons.

Hoffman, E. (2014). How I got banned from Beta Theta Pi. *Wesleying.org*. Retrieved from: http://wesleying.org/2014/04/29/the-writing-on-the-wall-or-what-i-learned-at-beta-theta-pi.

Holt, S., Buckley, H., & Whelan, S. (2008). The impact of exposure to domestic violence on children and young people: a review of the literature. *Child Abuse & Neglect, 32*(8), 797–810.

jec20721 (2009, September 16). *Dos equis – the most interesting man in the world.* [video file]. Retrieved from: www.youtube.com/watch?v=U18VkI0uDxE.

Kilmartin, C. & McDermott, R. C. (2016). Violence and masculinities. In Y. J. Wong & S. R. Wester (Eds), *APA handbook of men and masculinities* (pp. 615–636). Washington, DC: American Psychological Association, doi:10.1037/14594-028.

Kimmel, M. (2013). *Angry white men: American masculinity at the end of an era.* New York, NY: Nation Books.

Kimmel, M. S. (2002). Gender symmetry" in domestic violence: a substantive and methodological research review. *Violence Against Women, 8*(11), 1332–1363.

Kornblit, A. L. (1994). Domestic violence: an emerging health issue. *Social Science & Medicine, 39*(9), 1181–1188.

Kupersmidt, J. B., Griesler, P. C., DeRosier, M. E., Patterson, C. J., & Davis, P. W. (1995). Childhood aggression and peer relations in the context of family and neighborhood factors. *Child Development, 66*(2), 360–375.

Lisak, D. & Miller, P. M. (2002). Repeat rape and multiple offending among undetected rapists. *Violence and Victims, 17*(1), 73–84.

Locke, B. D. & Mahalik, J. R. (2005). Examining masculinity norms, problem drinking, and athletic involvement as predictors of sexual aggression in college men. *Journal of Counseling Psychology, 52*(3), 279.

Lutz-Zois, C. J., Moler, K. A., & Brown, M. J. (2015). Mechanisms for the relationship between traditional masculine ideologies and rape myth acceptance among college men. *Journal of Aggression, Maltreatment & Trauma, 24*(1), 84–101.

McBee, T. P. (2018). *Amateur: a true story about what makes a man* [epub]. New York, NY: Scribner.

Murnen, S. K., Wright, C., & Kaluzny, G. (2002). If "boys will be boys," then girls will be victims? A meta-analytic review of the research that relates masculine ideology to sexual aggression. *Sex Roles, 46*(11–12), 359–375.

Neidig, H. (2016, October 21). Biden blasts Trump: I wish 'I could take him behind the gym'. *The Hill*. Retrieved from: http://thehill.com/blogs/ballot-box/presidential-races/302257-biden-blasts-trump-i-wish-i-could-take-him-behind-the-gym.

Oxford, J., Ponzi, D., & Geary, D. C. (2010). Hormonal responses differ when playing violent video games against an ingroup and outgroup. *Evolution and Human Behavior, 31*(3), 201–209.

Pascoe, C. J. (2013). Notes on a sociology of bullying: young men's homophobia as gender socialization. *QED: A Journal in GLBTQ Worldmaking, 0,* 87–103.

Payne, D. L., Lonsway, K. A., & Fitzgerald, L. F. (1999). Rape myth acceptance: exploration of its structure and its measurement using the Illinois Rape Myth Acceptance Scale. *Journal of Research in Personality, 33*(1), 27–68.

Poole, M. (2017, April 28). Durant makes plea to NBA officials: 'S-- talking is part of the game'. *NBC Sports.* Retrieved from: www.nbcsports.com/bayarea/warriors/durant-makes-plea-nba-officials-s-talking-part-game.

Reigeluth, C. S. & Addis, M. E. (2016). Adolescent boys' experiences with policing of masculinity: forms, functions, and consequences. *Psychology of Men & Masculinity, 17*(1), 74–83.

Richardson, C. A., Dustan, P., & Lang, J. C. (1979). Maintenance of living space by sweeper tentacles of Montastrea cavernosa, a Caribbean reef coral. *Marine Biology, 55*(3), 181–186.

Risner, D. (2014). Bullying victimisation and social support of adolescent male dance students: an analysis of findings. *Research in Dance Education, 15*(2), 179–201.

Rivers, I., Poteat, V. P., Noret, N., & Ashurst, N. (2009). Observing bullying at school: the mental health implications of witness status. *School Psychology Quarterly, 24*(4), 211–223.

Smith, S. G., Zhang, X., Basile, K. C., Merrick, M. T., Wang, J., Kresnow, M., & Chen, J. (2018). *National intimate partner violence and sexual violence survey: 2015 data brief—updated release.* Atlanta, GA: National Center for Injury Prevention and Control, Centers for Disease Control.

Tjaden, P. G. & Thoennes, N. (2000). *Extent, nature, and consequences of intimate partner violence: findings from the National Violence Against Women Survey.* Rockville, MD: National Institute of Justice.

U.S. Department of Justice, Federal Bureau of Investigation (2016, Fall). *Uniform crime report: crime in the United States, 2015.* Washington, DC: U.S. Department of Justice. Retrieved from: https://ucr.fbi.gov/crime-in-the-u.s/2015/crime-in-the-u.s.-2015/tables/table-42.

Vandello, J. A. & Bosson, J. K. (2013). Hard won and easily lost: a review and synthesis of theory and research on precarious manhood. *Psychology of Men & Masculinity, 14*(2), 101–113.

Wang, J., Iannotti, R. J., & Nansel, T. R. (2009). School bullying among adolescents in the United States: physical, verbal, relational, and cyber. *Journal of Adolescent Health, 45*(4), 368–375.

Wright, P. J., Tokunaga, R. S., & Kraus, A. (2015). A meta-analysis of pornography consumption and actual acts of sexual aggression in general population studies. *Journal of Communication, 66*(1), 183–205.

Zemeckis, R. (1985). *Back to the future* [Motion picture]. Universal City, CA: Universal Pictures.

Zillich, J. (2004, October 15). *Crossfire* [Television broadcast]. Washington, DC: CNN.

10

MENTAL AND PHYSICAL HEALTH

On May 2, 2012, award-winning former NFL linebacker Junior Seau died from a self-inflicted gunshot wound to his chest (Steeg, 2012). Friends and family were stunned. On the field, Seau was known for his leadership and never-quit attitude. Off the field, he had a reputation as a friendly, easy-going, and generous person. It was nearly impossible to understand why such a successful, well-liked, and apparently happy man would take his own life.

An autopsy found no evidence of drugs or alcohol involved in his death. But over the next year, observers wondered whether Seau, like an increasing number of former professional football players, had likely suffered from chronic traumatic encephalopathy (CTE), a brain condition caused by repeated concussions or subconcussive blows to the head. Researchers are sharply divided on whether CTE represents a real disease and on how prevalent it is among football players, who, skeptics note, live longer lives and commit suicide at lower rates than the general public (Randolph, 2018). Nevertheless, a number of players go on to experience a cluster of neurocognitive symptoms like memory impairment, disorientation, physical pain, trouble planning activities and making decisions, depression, anger, and suicidal impulses. Although Seau did not leave a suicide note, his girlfriend found a piece of paper near his body containing lyrics to his favorite song, "Who I Ain't," that describe a person who is unhappy with the man he has become (Steeg, 2012).

Junior Seau's suicide generated a tremendous amount of media attention in the U.S., presumably because of his status as a widely known and well-respected professional athlete. But other than the fact that he was famous, the circumstances surrounding his death are not unfamiliar to those who study the psychology of men's well-being. Several aspects of traditional masculine gender norms have been linked to physical and psychological damage (O'Neil, 2012; Wong, Ho Ringo, Wang, & Miller,

2017). In this case, the repeated beating that Seau's body took was revered by the culture as evidence of masculinity. Generally speaking, masculine gender norms surrounding toughness, emotional stoicism, and endurance of pain can encourage men to engage in a wide range of health-risk behaviors, many of which we address throughout this chapter.

Of course, not all men are professional football players, and most do not experience repeated concussions or other types of violent injuries. In that sense, Junior Seau's story is somewhat extreme. But in another sense, it is more mundane, if not common. Seau's severe emotional and physical pain was largely silent and invisible to those around him. For a variety of reasons that we explore throughout this chapter, men often experience psychological and social pressure to keep their vulnerability hidden from others (Addis, 2011). Such pressure can make it difficult for individuals to seek professional help, to share concerns with others, and at times even to recognize themselves that things are not right.

Facts About Men's Mental and Physical Health

As we saw in Chapter 5, the social construction of masculinity often entails highlighting men's power and strength and hiding their vulnerabilities (real or imagined). As a result, the obstacles to recognizing mental and physical health problems affect not only individual men but also our collective awareness of men's well-being. There are several consequences of this neglect including, (a) relatively few health promotion efforts targeted specifically at men and masculinity, (b) widespread acceptance (if not endorsement) of the gender stereotype, "Men don't go to the doctor," and (c) difficulty noticing boys' and men's anger, social withdrawal, and substance abuse as outward signs of hidden distress.

Perhaps as a result of this societal invisibility, many people are unaware of some basic facts about men's mental and physical health. For example, as of 2015, global epidemiological data showed that men live an average of roughly five years less than women. The rates are remarkably consistent over time (since data started being collected) and across cultures. Many scientists take these data as evidence that biology plays a role in sex differences in lifespan, and particularly testosterone (Austad & Fischer, 2016). For example, eunuchs are incapable of producing testosterone and there is evidence that they live longer than males who still possess their testes (Min, Lee, & Park, 2012).

Health behaviors also play a significant role in sex differences related to mortality. First, there are differences in *health-protective behaviors*. On average, women use healthcare in the U.S. more than men (Bertakis, Azari, Helms, Callahan, & Robbins, 2000). In the year 2011, women reported 4.44 healthcare visits (family practice, hospital, and emergency room) per person. The rate for men was 3.54 (Centers for Disease Control and Prevention, 2017). Second, as we will see later in the chapter, both sex differences and individual differences in conformity to masculine gender norms are associated with a wide range of *health-risk behaviors* such as smoking, substance abuse, not wearing a seat belt, poor diet, and so on.

Although women are more likely to attempt to take their own lives, men are four times more likely to complete suicide (Bilsker & White, 2011; Nock et al., 2008). One reason is that men tend to choose methods with greater lethality (e.g., guns), but shame and self-stigma regarding depression and mental illness more broadly may also play a role (Mackenzie, Visperas, Ogrodniczuk, Oliffe, & Nurmi, 2018). Social learning and social construction of masculinity may in part drive shame associated with emotional vulnerability. In a recent meta-analysis of 78 studies with 19,453 research subjects, Wong et al. (2017) found that conformity to specific masculine norms is consistently negatively associated with positive mental health-related outcomes. In other words, the more likely individual men are to buy into gender norms such as emotional stoicism, self-reliance, and toughness, the less likely they are to report indicators of positive mental health. Notably, the results were stronger for social aspects of mental health (e.g., relationships/social support) than for psychological functioning per se, although both relationships were statistically significant. The results were consistent across age, race, and sexual orientation.

Masculine Hearts and Minds: The Costs of Emotional Restriction

The role of masculinity in the ways men experience, express, and respond to emotional distress has been extensively studied in the psychology of men. Most people have an intuitive sense of what emotions are (e.g., feelings), but psychological research takes it further, considering the questions of exactly how emotions operate and also how they are involved in human health and well-being. One common view is that emotions are evolved mechanisms that provide ongoing feedback about an organism's relation to its environment; a sort of social-emotional "barometer" or signal, if you will (Barrett, Mesquita, Ochsner, & Gross, 2007, p. 378; Russell & Barrett, 1999). When things are going well, we feel content or happy and it makes sense to continue doing what we're doing. When we feel negatively, this is an indicator that our relationship to our environment may be problematic and it could make sense to change what we're doing. Thus, emotions provide vital ongoing feedback in daily life. One consequence of this is that although we're often motivated to reduce the impact of negative or painful emotions in our lives, a longer-term strategy of ignoring or suppressing emotions can have detrimental effects on our well-being (e.g., Gross & Levenson, 1997). Put another way, there are numerous situations in life where pushing feelings down or keeping a stiff upper lip may make sense, temporarily.

However, when people become rigidly wedded to emotional restriction regardless of the situation, they often forego other coping options such as expressing their feelings or sharing problems with others.

As we saw in Chapter 4, boys are often taught from a very young age that expression of vulnerable emotions such as sadness, fear, and grief is shameful and feminine (e.g., "big boys don't cry"). Although there are racial and cultural differences in the degree to which males are held accountable to this gender norm, its effects appear to be pervasive; many adult men have difficulty experiencing strong emotions and/or communicating about them with others. In 1973, psychoanalyst Peter Sifneos coined the term *alexithymia*, a word whose Greek etymology essentially means "without words for feelings," to describe a pattern of difficulty in identifying and communicating emotional states (Sifneos, 1973). Although alexithymia is not considered a mental disorder per se, research over the last few decades has shown that it is associated with a wide range of emotional and interpersonal difficulties, as well as symptoms of depression, anxiety, and other psychiatric problems (Kim et al., 2008; Yelsma & Marrow, 2003).

These links are not surprising considering the adaptive feedback that emotions provide. Fortunately, research suggests that the prevalence of alexithymia is generally less than 10% of the population. However, as might be expected, men tend to score higher on measures of alexithymia than women, although the size of that difference is fairly small (Levant, Hall, Williams, & Hasan, 2009). In recent years Ron Levant and his colleagues have suggested that there may be a particular subtype of alexithymia that is much more common in males. Levant describes *normative male alexithymia* as a socialized pattern of restrictive emotionality influenced by traditional masculine ideology which results in difficulty identifying, describing, and communicating emotions (Levant, Allen, & Lien, 2014).

The central idea here is that the existence of a widespread ideology supporting the notion that *feeling emotions and communicating about them with others is antithetical to masculinity* places many men at risk for a wide range of health-related problems. This does not mean that every man everywhere detests emotions and has no idea what he is feeling or how to talk about it. Nor does it mean that *all* women are deeply emotionally intuitive. Scientific data and our everyday experiences refute these gender stereotypes. Nonetheless, small average differences can produce meaningful effects when they apply to large numbers of people. So while not all men are alexithymic, there does appear to be a widespread trend in that direction. Put another way, anyone who considers masculinity to be an important part of their identity may be, to varying degrees, at risk of the kinds of problems that arise from lack of awareness of their emotions.

In addition to individual differences in awareness of emotions, researchers in social and clinical psychology have also studied the effects of emotional suppression. Suppression is a strategy for regulating the experience of emotions and involves active attempts to prevent oneself from experiencing and/or expressing what one is feeling. Perhaps not surprisingly, there are consistent sex differences in the degree to which people use suppression as a coping strategy, with men reporting higher rates than women (Buck, 2003). Suppressing feelings can be useful in some circumstances. Yawning, or blurting out, "Wow, is this lecture boring!" in the middle of a class will probably cause more harm than good. On the other hand, the long-term inflexible use of suppression as a coping strategy can have potentially serious negative consequences. In one study, emotional suppression was measured in a wide variety of ways in students making the transition to college. Over time suppression was consistently associated with lower social support, more loneliness, and less satisfaction with relationships (Srivastava, Tamir, McGonigal, John, & Gross, 2009). The negative effects of suppression are not limited to relationships. Studies have shown that suppression is associated with increased mortality, including death due to cancer (Chapman, Fiscella, Kawachi, Duberstein, & Muennig, 2013).

The links between masculinity and emotional restriction can be viewed from the variety of theoretical perspectives explored in the first half of this book. From a social learning perspective (Chapter 4), it seems clear that what young boys learn about the value (or lack of value) of emotions, as well as how to express (or not express) them, can affect their well-being in a variety of ways that extend into adulthood. There is a clear need to shift cultural practices that reinforce male emotional restriction and stoicism and instead support men in experiencing, identifying, and communicating their emotions to others.

A feminist perspective (Chapter 6) would likely consider how power is negotiated individually and societally when it comes to the various roles of emotion in men's mental and physical health. For example, keeping one's inner life hidden from view is one way to maintain power via perceived invulnerability. If I keep my problems to myself and insist that I am not bothered by any kind of real emotional or physical pain, I place myself in a more dominant position in relation to those around me; I have constructed a self (see Chapter 5) that is immune to pain and does not need help from others. I also place the burden of emotional labor—of tending to others' emotions and the consequences of my own—onto female partners and friends who are not so unemotional. Similar processes can occur through the social construction of masculinity at a symbolic level. The gender stereotype of men as stoic and rational, and women as sensitive and emotional, serves to reinforce an ideology in which men and masculinity are cast in a more positive light when it comes to allocation of resources, decision-making, and so on (consider the widespread notion that we should never let emotions cloud our judgment when it comes to important decisions). This relative advantage for men comes at a cost, what sociologist Michael Kaufman (1994) has referred to as "men's contradictory experience of power." As Kaufman says:

> *There are many things men do to have the type of power we associate with masculinity: We have to perform and stay in control. We're supposed to conquer, be on top of things, and call the shots. We have to tough it out, provide, and achieve. Meanwhile we learn to beat back our feelings, hide our emotions, and suppress our needs.*
>
> (p. 148, italics added for emphasis)

An intersectional perspective (Chapter 7) might begin with the observation that not all men have equal access to power in society, nor to the specific types of power associated with enacting emotionally restricted versions of masculinity. Gay men, for example, are frequently negatively stereotyped as overly emotionally expressive. As a result, regardless of their tendencies toward emotional expressiveness or inexpressiveness, individual men must contend with an identity that is created for them by society; the "feminine, emotionally expressive gay man." At the same time, gay men are subjected to the same hegemonic masculine norms as all men and thus, broadly speaking, are expected to keep their emotions under control in ways that are congruent with traditional masculinity. In one large study ($N = 547$) gay men spontaneously reported more negative than positive effects of masculine norms on their well-being, including difficulty being emotional and affectionate and pressure to appear masculine (Sánchez, Greenberg, Liu, & Vilain, 2009).

Performative Machines: Masculinity and Men's Bodies

Men's Health magazine is the second most widely read men's-oriented publication in the world, with 25 editions in 35 countries (Hearst, 2019). Based on these numbers, one might infer that men are deeply interested in their own health, and that the magazine provides a diverse and substantial amount of information about men's well-being. Browsing through an issue you might expect to see numerous articles on preventing testicular cancer, cardiovascular disease, diet, and other health-related concerns known to affect men's physical and emotional well-being.

In fact, the magazine covers very little in the way of health in any traditional sense. The cover photo almost invariably features a bare-chested White male with six well-defined abdominal muscles providing the focal center. Visually speaking, the message is clear: health = large, well-defined muscles and tanned, white hairless skin. Verbally speaking, judging by the articles highlighted on the cover, being a healthy man is a matter of sexual performance, working out, and being competitive in career and in sport (Labre, 2005).

What exactly is going on here? From our perspective, the content in *Men's Health* and related publications reflects the dominant social construction of men's bodies in Western society: the body as a *performative machine* (Addis, 2011). Men's bodies are expected to perform feats of strength and endurance, to withstand extreme pain, to physically dominate other men (and sometimes women), to always be capable of sexual "performance" (narrowly defined), to party hard at night and work strenuously the next day, and to do all of this with little to no preventative healthcare or attention to the body's inherent vulnerabilities.

Consider the context of professional sports. Male athletes are repeatedly praised and at times worshiped for subjecting their bodies to extreme risks in the pursuit of victory. The health consequences can be severe. For example, former NFL football players are at increased risk for Alzheimer's disease (Kerr, Marshall, Harding, & Guskiewicz, 2012). It appears that the risk of dying from a neurodegenerative disease is particularly acute for football players who play in positions that involve more high-speed collisions with the opposing team (Lehman, Hein, Baron, & Gersic, 2012). As with the case of Junior Seau, illustrated at the beginning of this chapter, such neurodegeneration is associated with a wide range of severe mental and physical health problems.

What about the vast majority of men who are not professional athletes? Is their physical and psychological well-being unaffected by the social learning and social construction of masculinity? Anecdotal and research evidence suggests otherwise. For example, from 2000 to 2002, the popular American television show *Jackass* displayed nothing more than repeated episodes of young adult men engaging in a variety of physical stunts that frequently produced, or appeared to produce, potentially severe bodily injuries. For example, one episode featured a cast member being catapulted through the air inside an outhouse filled with feces. Another showed a cast member being given a tattoo while riding in an off-road vehicle. Throughout each episode, grunts and groans suggesting severe pain are clearly audible. The show was enormously popular and produced several spinoff films. One could argue over how realistic or extreme it was, but the fact remains that the entire premise would be nonsensical *if not for the widespread understanding that men can be expected to engage in a wide range of risky, if not self-abusive activities as a way of establishing their masculinity.*

For Consideration

Where and when do you see men's bodies affected by hegemonic masculine norms?

What are the consequences?

How aware are you and others you know of these issues?

Is humor involved? If so, how?

Other links between masculinity and men's mental and physical health are less sensationalistic and more mundane, but carry equally important implications. One recent study found that men in the U.K. often choose from a variety of health-related behaviors based on how each behavior fits their conception of "masculine capital" (De Visser & McDonnell, 2013). In other words, men appear to be sensitive to the potential gender-based meanings of different health behaviors. This sensitivity can at times lead to actions that are health promoting and research has shown that some masculine norms, under the right circumstances, are associated with positive health and well-being (Hammer & Good, 2010; Levant & Wimer, 2014). Whether such effects are best understood as "positive masculinity" is a complex issue that we take up in some detail below. For now, it's worth noting that things can also go in the opposite direction. For example, Mahalik and Burns (2011) found that men who scored higher on conformity to masculine norms perceived more barriers to, and engaged in less, heart-healthy behaviors.

Sex

As we saw in Chapter 8, men's romantic relationships are influenced by masculinity. But what about sex and sexuality? Men's insecurities are evident in the existence of whole industries of seduction artists, stamina enhancement drugs, or penis enlargement devices and surgeries. Research shows that a majority of men in heterosexual relationships are unsatisfied with the size of their penis—and this despite the fact that 85% of women report being satisfied with their partner's size (Lever, Frederick, & Peplau, 2006). Men's insecurity about penis size may be fodder for jokes about middle-age men's motivations for buying luxury cars, but it can also have very dramatic consequences for self-esteem. Consider the following testimony on reddit.com:

> *I hate having a small dick, and I'm suicidal over it … Honestly, I just can't bring myself to believe that size doesn't matter to women. I just absolutely cannot … sex with me will NEVER be as pleasurable to any woman as it would've been with anyone better endowed she's been with. Which means that I will always be settled for sexually. I will always be emasculated. I will always be second best.*

u/smallpenisvent (2016, March 20),
www.reddit.com/r/smalldickproblems/comments/4b7l2v/
i_just_want_to_vent_i_hope_yall_dont_mind/

One thing that is particularly striking in this man's account is the automatic link between having a small penis and being "emasculated." This is in a sense not surprising in a culture that uses "manhood" as a euphemism for the male genitalia. Another arresting feature of this account is the insistence that women could never (in all caps) be pleasured by him. Where do men learn such messages about what matters in sex?

American boys on average first receive formal sex education in middle school (Martinez, Abma, & Copen, 2010). However, by this time, boys have already been exposed to information about sex from a variety of sources: from peers, media, and often porn. Thus, trusted adults like teachers or parents are typically not boys' first or main source of information. Boys report receiving less information about sex from teachers, doctors, or same-sex parents than girls do (Sprecher, Harris, & Meyers, 2008). According to recent surveys, only approximately 27% of British boys cited their parents as a source of *any* information about sex. Far more boys stated that they received information about sex from the media (47%) or friends (66%) (Tanton et al., 2015). And, as internet pornography becomes ever more accessible, it too is a source for information about sex. An Australian survey showed that 70% of boys have been exposed to pornography by age 14 (Lim, Agius, Carrotte, Vella, & Hellard, 2017).

Pornography may be a problematic information source about sex for a variety of reasons. As a pseudo-educational material, pornography frequently portrays sex in ways that are unrealistic. Foreplay is typically minimal, and male actors are depicted as having greater stamina than is reasonable for most men. Such unrealistic depictions may lead men to assume that, if they cannot last as long as porn stars, or their partner is not interested in the same variety of sex acts, then something is wrong. Among other effects, pornography also potentially reinforces traditional gender stereotypes of men as dominant and women as submissive and is related to stronger perceptions of women as sexual objects (Barron & Kimmel, 2000; Brown & L'Engle, 2009). One study of 50 of the most popular videos available from the Adult Video Network found that 88% of sex scenes involved physical violence against women (spanking, gagging, etc.) and 49% depicted men insulting women. By contrast, only 10% of scenes included any kind of behaviors the researchers coded as "positive," like kissing, statements of affection, or cuddling (Bridges, Wosnitzer, Scharrer, Sun, & Liberman, 2010). Perhaps most significantly, a recent meta-analysis shows that men's (but not women's) pornography use is linked to less satisfying relationships (Wright, Tokunaga, Kraus, & Klann, 2017).

At the same time that research suggests negative effects, the long-term effects of porn consumption are less clear (e.g., Landripet & Štulhofer, 2015; Park et al., 2016; Stark, Klucken, Potenza, Brand, & Strahler, 2018). Some studies find pornography consumption to be associated with sexual dysfunction whereas other studies fail to find such an association. In addition, many individual men appear to report positive effects of porn use. For example, in one study of men who have sex with men participants reported positive effects of viewing porn on their sex lives (Hald, Smolenski, & Rosser, 2013).

Information from peers about sex can also be problematic. Ethan recalls, for instance, that before he had his first sexual experience as a teenager, a male friend took him aside and explained the "mechanics and techniques" of sex. The friend seemed quite confident in his advice, and Ethan took it sincerely. It was only several months later that Ethan learned that his friend was as inexperienced as he was. Anecdotes aside, research also suggests that we frequently misunderstand what is typical within our peer group and fall victim to a phenomenon researchers call *pluralistic ignorance*. In one study of pluralistic ignorance about desires for casual sex, for example, Lambert, Kahn, and Apple (2003) asked college men and women to estimate how comfortable the average male and female student would be with hooking up—typically defined as a sexual interaction outside a monogamous relationship. Students of all genders consistently expressed being less comfortable hooking up than they imagined would the typical student of their own gender. In other words, college men (and women) tend to overestimate how comfortable others are hooking up. This misperception may lead men to seek out more hookups than they really want, or to overestimate how far their partners want to go.

The media too is rife with depictions of male sexuality and men's romantic lives that may mislead more than enlighten. Consider classic male film heroes like James Bond. In addition to playing into norms of men as violent and, simultaneously, cool-headed—Bond represents a true Casanova character. The typical Bond film involves anywhere from two to nine encounters between James Bond and a "Bond girl" (Neuendorf, Gore, Dalessandro, Janstova, & Snyder-Suhy, 2010). Bond is portrayed both as seductive and charming, and, simultaneously, as distant and indifferent to the women he pursues. In *The Spy Who Loved Me* (Gilbert, 1977), he interrupts lovemaking when he receives a message from MI6 command. In the laugh line that follows, Bond's lover pines, "But James, I need you!" to which he responds, unperturbed, "so does England."

What were some of the early messages you learned about sex and about how men are supposed to approach sex?

How have those early messages affected what you do or what you expect in sex? How and why might your views on sex have changed?

How do you think these messages might affect men in same-sex relationships?

Is Help a Four-Letter Word?

In the 2011 book *Invisible Men* (Addis, 2011) Michael tells the story of Patrick, a financially successful, handsome, middle-aged White man, whom he first met in an inpatient psychiatric hospital. Michael was serving as a psychology intern there and typically spent his mornings reviewing charts of people admitted the previous evening so he could conduct an initial assessment interview to help determine what the problems were and what might be a helpful approach to treatment. Many of the patients admitted had attempted suicide. Of those, not surprisingly, the majority were women. Many had extensive histories of previous suicide attempts and, with most, their families and friends were well-aware of their struggles.

Patrick's story was different. In many ways his recent life experiences were not unlike those of the character Willy Loman in Arthur Miller's (1996) classic play, *Death of a Salesman*. Patrick had built a very successful business over many years, from which he and his family enjoyed the benefits. But he had begun to run into financial trouble over the previous couple of years. The situation slowly escalated to the point where creditors and unpaid clients were pursuing Patrick. While such a situation would be extremely stressful for anyone, in Patrick's case one thing made it much worse: he had told no one in his family about his struggles. Instead, he dressed for work each day as if nothing had changed (even though he had long since stopped actually going to work), and returned each evening with a forced smile on his face. Eventually, things got so bad that he decided to take his own life. If his teenage son had not come home early one evening and discovered his father with a shotgun pointed at himself, Patrick never would have made it to the hospital. When Michael interviewed him the next morning he was silent and withdrawn, saying only that *dying was better than having to admit failure and ask for help*, "like a sniveling little boy."

In 1989, Good, Dell, and Mintz published a study that quickly became a classic in the psychology of men and masculinity and set in motion three decades of research. The researchers gave surveys measuring attitudes toward stereotypic male roles, gender role conflict (see Chapter 4), and attitudes toward professional help-seeking to 401 undergraduate men enrolled in an introductory psychology course at a large mid-western university in the U.S. Statistical analyses revealed that men who reported more positive associations with traditional masculinity and higher levels of gender role conflict also reported more negative attitudes toward seeking psychological help from a professional. Since this first study, dozens of others have documented links between masculinity and negative attitudes toward help-seeking (Addis & Hoffman, 2017; Addis & Mahalik, 2003).

As the studies cited above show, men's relative reluctance to seek help from healthcare professionals extends beyond their attitudes and into actual behavior. Men utilize virtually all forms of healthcare at a lower rate than women. Researchers and therapists who specialize in working with men have suggested that masculine norms such as self-reliance and emotional stoicism make the process of seeking help shameful, particularly for those men who are more heavily invested in masculinity as a part of their identity (Addis & Mahalik, 2003; Brooks, 1998; Englar-Carlson & Stevens, 2006). On the other hand, everyone probably knows individual men who have sought help from a physician or a mental health professional. And at the risk of pointing out the obvious, many men may seek help for other kinds of problems such as home repairs, car maintenance, preparing taxes, moving, or lifting heavy objects. How can we reconcile this with the pervasive stereotype, "men don't ask for help"?

One answer is that *context* clearly matters. Research suggests that people, in general, are less likely to seek help when they believe that the issue they need help with is unusual or non-normative (Nadler, 1990; Tessler & Schwartz, 1972). Because there's nothing particularly unusual about a car breaking down, or being unable to lift a refrigerator by yourself, it may be much easier for men to ask for help in these circumstances. However, if a man believes that he should be able to keep his emotions under control, that his body should perform like a well-oiled machine, and that other men do not have the kinds of problems he's experiencing, he may be significantly less likely to ask for help when he's struggling (Addis & Mahalik, 2003).

For this reason, public health agencies, researchers, therapists, and community activists have begun developing programs and interventions that attempt to destigmatize the process of men seeking psychological or physical healthcare. These efforts typically include language, symbols, and statistical information countering the notion that asking for help is a sign of weakness and instead emphasizing to varying degrees how asking for help can make men even more masculine. Examples include the "Real Men, Real Depression" campaign by the National Institute of Mental Health and Mantherapy.org in the U.S., as well as the "Soften the Fuck Up" public health campaign in Australia, and others. Although there is some evidence that framing mental health messaging with sensitivity to men's struggles with masculinity can improve attitudes toward help-seeking (e.g., Hammer & Vogel, 2010), to date relatively little progress has been made in increasing actual help-seeking behavior (Syzdek, Addis, Green, Whorley, & Berger, 2014; Syzdek, Green, Lindgren, & Addis, 2016).

For Consideration

What have you noticed about the help-seeking attitudes and behavior of those around you? What about yourself?

How are they shaped by masculinity?

Do you know any people who identify as female and have negative attitudes toward help-seeking? If so, what might this say about how the psychology of men understands help-seeking?

What does it say about how masculinity is or is not involved?

Can women's help-seeking be affected by masculinity?

The last question above is one that regularly comes up when teaching the psychology of men. Students begin to recognize that many of the behaviors stereotypically associated with masculinity (e.g., emotional stoicism, resistance to seeking help) can also be found in women. For example, Michael had a close female friend growing up, who we'll call Sarah. Sarah was the oldest of six children. Both of her parents came from a fairly traditional White Christian background. Her father, in particular, believed strongly in pulling yourself up by your bootstraps and in the importance of financial self-sufficiency. In many ways, he raised Sarah to be the stereotypic "oldest son." As a result, although she enacted femininity in many ways, Sarah had also been exposed to a fairly heavy dose of the social learning of masculinity. One consequence was that she tended to keep problems to herself and found the prospect of seeking help shameful. She believed strongly that she should be able to handle her own problems, and that the expression of strong vulnerable emotions meant she was failing to do so.

This kind of pattern is only surprising if you assume the effects of masculinity are limited to men, and that's hardly the case. With the exception of the biological perspective, each of the theories covered in the first half of this book largely view gender as collections of ideologies, social roles, and/or performative repertoires that are, in principle, separate from biological sex. Thus, women may perform masculinity and men may perform femininity depending on the circumstances. In patriarchal societies (see Chapter 6), masculinity is typically granted more social value than femininity. As a result, masculine norms and ideologies come to signify not only what is expected of men, but also what is considered good and desirable for people in general. One consequence of this is that women are more likely to be encouraged to enact masculinity than men are to enact femininity.

Summary and Conclusion

The social construction and social learning of masculinity are associated with the way men experience, express, and respond to problems in their lives. Three decades of research have shown that men who endorse hegemonic masculine norms such as emotional stoicism and self-reliance are at increased risk for depression, substance abuse, relationship problems, and a host of other mental and physical health problems. These same masculine norms and ideologies are all associated with a greater reluctance to seek help from friends, family, and health care professionals, thus placing many men in a sort of double-bind when it comes to their well-being versus their commitment to particular notions of what it means to be a man.

Men's bodies in particular are strongly affected by societal definitions of masculinity. Generally speaking, the male body is portrayed as a performative machine and men are encouraged to abuse rather than care for their bodies. In recent years public health agencies, therapists, and health care providers have begun to understand many of the obstacles men face when it comes to taking care of themselves physically, mentally, and relationally. One approach has been to attempt to cast health care, broadly speaking, in a more masculine light. Another has been to develop and promote more health-positive definitions of what it means to be a man. Whether such approaches are effective in reducing health risks for men is ultimately an empirical question.

References

Addis, M. E. (2011). *Invisible men: men's inner lives and the consequences of silence*. New York, NY: Henry Holt.

Addis, M. E. & Hoffman, E. (2017). Men's depression and help-seeking through the lenses of gender. In R. F. Levant & Y. J. Wong (Eds), *The psychology of men and masculinities* (pp. 171–196). Washington, DC: American Psychological Association.

Addis, M. E. & Mahalik, J. R. (2003). Men, masculinity, and the contexts of help seeking. *American Psychologist, 58*(1), 5–14.

Austad, S. N. & Fischer, K. E. (2016). Sex differences in lifespan. *Cell Metabolism, 23*(6), 1022–1033.

Barrett, L. F., Mesquita, B., Ochsner, K. N., & Gross, J. J. (2007). The experience of emotion. *Annual Review of Psychology, 58*, 373–403.

Barron, M. & Kimmel, M. (2000). Sexual violence in three pornographic media: toward a sociological explanation. *Journal of Sex Research, 37*(2), 161–168.

Bertakis, K. D., Azari, R., Helms, J. L., Callahan, E. J., & Robbins, J. A. (2000). Gender differences in the utilization of health care services. *The Journal of Family Practice, 49*(2), 147–152.

Bilsker, D. & White, J. (2011). The silent epidemic of male suicide. *British Columbia Medical Journal, 53*(10), 529–534.

Bridges, A. J., Wosnitzer, R., Scharrer, E., Sun, C., & Liberman, R. (2010). Aggression and sexual behavior in best-selling pornography videos: a content analysis update. *Violence Against Women, 16*(10), 1065–1085.

Brooks, G. R. (1998). *A new psychotherapy for traditional men*. San Francisco, CA: Jossey-Bass.

Brown, J. D. & L'Engle, K. L. (2009). X-rated: sexual attitudes and behaviors associated with US early adolescents' exposure to sexually explicit media. *Communication Research, 36*(1), 129–151.

Buck, R. (2003). Emotional expression, suppression, and control: nonverbal communication in cultural context. *Journal of Intercultural Communication Research, 32*(1), 175–187.

Centers for Disease Control and Prevention (2017). *Health, United States, 2016: with chartbook on long-term trends in health*. Hyattsville, MD: National Center for Health Statistics. Retrieved from: www.cdc.gov/nchs/hus/contents2016.htm#076.

Chapman, B. P., Fiscella, K., Kawachi, I., Duberstein, P., & Muennig, P. (2013). Emotion suppression and mortality risk over a 12-year follow-up. *Journal of Psychosomatic Research, 75*(4), 381–385.

De Visser, R. O. & McDonnell, E. J. (2013). "Man points": masculine capital and young men's health. *Health Psychology, 32*(1), 5–14.

Englar-Carlson, M. E. & Stevens, M. A. (2006). *In the room with men: a casebook of therapeutic change*. Washington, DC: American Psychological Association.

Gilbert, L. (Director) (1977). *The spy who loved me* [Motion picture on DVD]. United Kingdom: Sony Pictures Home Entertainment.

Good, G. E., Dell, D. M., & Mintz, L. B. (1989). Male role and gender role conflict: relations to help seeking in men. *Journal of Counseling Psychology, 36*(3), 295–300.

Gross, J. J. & Levenson, R. W. (1997). Hiding feelings: the acute effects of inhibiting negative and positive emotion. *Journal of Abnormal Psychology, 106*(1), 95–103.

Hald, G. M., Smolenski, D., & Rosser, B. S. (2013). Perceived effects of sexually explicit media among men who have sex with men and psychometric properties of the Pornography Consumption Effects Scale (PCES). *The Journal of Sexual Medicine, 10*(3), 757–767.

Hammer, J. H. & Good, G. E. (2010). Positive psychology: an empirical examination of beneficial aspects of endorsement of masculine norms. *Psychology of Men & Masculinity, 11*(4), 303–318.

Hammer, J. H. & Vogel, D. L. (2010). Men's help seeking for depression: the efficacy of a male-sensitive brochure about counseling. *The Counseling Psychologist, 38*(2), 296–313.

Hearst (2019). Men's health. *Hearst.com*. Retrieved from: www.hearst.com/magazines/men-s-health.

Kaufman, M. (1994). *Cracking the armour: power, pain and the lives of men*. New York, NY: Penguin.

Kerr, Z. Y., Marshall, S. W., Harding, J. H., & Guskiewicz, K. M. (2012). Nine-year risk of depression diagnosis increases with increasing self-reported concussions in retired professional football players. *The American Journal of Sports Medicine*, 40(10), 2206–2212.

Kim, J. H., Lee, S. J., Rim, H. D., Kim, H. W., Bae, G. Y., & Chang, S. M. (2008). The relationship between alexithymia and general symptoms of patients with depressive disorders. *Psychiatry Investigation*, 5(3), 179–185.

Labre, M. P. (2005). Burn fat, build muscle: a content analysis of men's health and men's fitness. *International Journal of Men's Health*, 4(2), 187–200.

Lambert, T. A., Kahn, A. S., & Apple, K. J. (2003). Pluralistic ignorance and hooking up. *Journal of Sex Research*, 40(2), 129–133.

Landripet, I. & Štulhofer, A. (2015). Is pornography use associated with sexual difficulties and dysfunctions among younger heterosexual men? *The Journal of Sexual Medicine*, 5(12), 1136–1139.

Lehman, E. J., Hein, M. J., Baron, S. L., & Gersic, C. M. (2012). Neurodegenerative causes of death among retired National Football League players. *Neurology*, 79(19), 1970–1974.

Levant, R. F., Allen, P. A., & Lien, M. C. (2014). Alexithymia in men: how and when do emotional processing deficiencies occur? *Psychology of Men & Masculinity*, 15(3), 324–334.

Levant, R. F., Hall, R. J., Williams, C. M., & Hasan, N. T. (2009). Gender differences in alexithymia. *Psychology of Men & Masculinity*, 10(3), 190–203.

Levant, R. F. & Wimer, D. J. (2014). Masculinity constructs as protective buffers and risk factors for men's health. *American Journal of Men's Health*, 8(2), 110–120.

Lever, J., Frederick, D. A., & Peplau, L. A. (2006). Does size matter? Men's and women's views on penis size across the lifespan. *Psychology of Men & Masculinity*, 7(3), 129–143.

Lim, M. S., Agius, P. A., Carrotte, E. R., Vella, A. M., & Hellard, M. E. (2017). Young Australians' use of pornography and associations with sexual risk behaviours. *Australian and New Zealand Journal of Public Health*, 41(4), 438–443.

Mackenzie, C. S., Visperas, A., Ogrodniczuk, J. S., Oliffe, J. L., & Nurmi, M. A. (2018). Age and sex differences in self-stigma and public stigma concerning depression and suicide in men. *Stigma and Health*. Advance online publication: doi: http://dx.doi.org/10.1037/sah0000138.

Mahalik, J. R. & Burns, S. M. (2011). Predicting health behaviors in young men that put them at risk for heart disease. *Psychology of Men & Masculinity*, 12(1), 1–12.

Martinez, G., Abma, J., & Copen, C. (2010). Educating teenagers about sex in the United States. *NCHS data brief no. 44*. Hyattsville, MD: National Center for Health Statistics.

Miller, A. (1996). *Death of a salesman* (rev. ed.). New York, NY: Penguin (original work published in 1949).

Min, K. J., Lee, C. K., & Park, H. N. (2012). The lifespan of Korean eunuchs. *Current Biology*, 22(18), R792–R793.

Nadler, A. (1990). Help-seeking behavior as a coping resource. In M. Rosenbaum (Ed.), *Learned resourcefulness: on coping skills, self control, and adaptive behavior* (pp. 127–162). New York, NY: Springer.

Neuendorf, K. A., Gore, T. D., Dalessandro, A., Janstova, P., & Snyder-Suhy, S. (2010). Shaken and stirred: a content analysis of women's portrayals in James Bond films. *Sex Roles, 62*(11–12), 747–761.

Nock, M. K., Borges, G., Bromet, E. J., Cha, C. B., Kessler, R. C., & Lee, S. (2008). Suicide and suicidal behavior. *Epidemiologic Reviews, 30*(1), 133–154.

O'Neil, J. M. (2012). The psychology of men: theory, research, clinical knowledge, and future directions. In E. Altmaier & J. Hansen (Eds), *Oxford handbook of counseling psychology* (pp. 375–408). New York, NY: Oxford University Press.

Park, B., Wilson, G., Berger, J., Christman, M., Reina, B., Bishop, F., Klam, W., & Doan, A. (2016). Is internet pornography causing sexual dysfunctions? A review with clinical reports. *Behavioral Sciences, 6*(3), retrieved from: www.mdpi.com/2076-328X/6/3/17.

Randolph, C. (2018). Chronic traumatic encephalopathy is not a real disease. *Archives of Clinical Neuropsychology, 33*(5), 644–648.

Russell, J. A. & Barrett, L. F. (1999). Core affect, prototypical emotional episodes, and other things called emotion: dissecting the elephant. *Journal of Personality and Social Psychology, 76*(5), 805–819.

Sánchez, F. J., Greenberg, S. T., Liu, W. M., & Vilain, E. (2009). Reported effects of masculine ideals on gay men. *Psychology of Men & Masculinity, 10*(1), 73–87.

Sifneos, P. E. (1973). The prevalence of 'alexithymic'characteristics in psychosomatic patients. *Psychotherapy and Psychosomatics, 22*(2–6), 255–262.

Sprecher, S., Harris, G., & Meyers, A. (2008). Perceptions of sources of sex education and targets of sex communication: sociodemographic and cohort effects. *Journal of Sex Research, 45*(1), 17–26.

Srivastava, S., Tamir, M., McGonigal, K. M., John, O. P., & Gross, J. J. (2009). The social costs of emotional suppression: a prospective study of the transition to college. *Journal of Personality and Social Psychology, 96*(4), 883–897.

Stark, R., Klucken, T., Potenza, M. N., Brand, M., & Strahler, J. (2018). A current understanding of the behavioral neuroscience of compulsive sexual behavior disorder and problematic pornography use. *Current Behavioral Neuroscience Reports, 5*(4), 218–231.

Steeg, J. L. (2012, October 14). Junior Seau: song of sorrow. *The San Diego Union-Tribune.* Retrieved from: www.sandiegouniontribune.com/sports/chargers/sdut-junior-seau-real-story-2012oct14-htmlstory.html.

Syzdek, M. R., Addis, M. E., Green, J. D., Whorley, M. R., & Berger, J. L. (2014). A pilot trial of gender-based motivational interviewing for help-seeking and internalizing symptoms in men. *Psychology of Men & Masculinity, 15*(1), 90–94.

Syzdek, M. R., Green, J. D., Lindgren, B. R., & Addis, M. E. (2016). Pilot trial of gender-based motivational interviewing for increasing mental health service use in college men. *Psychotherapy, 53*(1), 124–129.

Tanton, C., Jones, K. G., Macdowall, W., Clifton, S., Mitchell, K. R., Datta, J., Lewis, R., Field, N., Sonnenberg, P., Stevens, A., & Wellings, K. (2015). Patterns and trends in sources of information about sex among young people in Britain: evidence from three National Surveys of Sexual Attitudes and Lifestyles. *BMJ Open, 5*(3), doi:10.1136/bmjopen-2015-007834.

Tessler, R. C. & Schwartz, S. H. (1972). Help seeking, self-esteem, and achievement motivation: an attributional analysis. *Journal of Personality and Social Psychology*, *21*, 318–326.

u/smallpenisvent (2016, March 20). I just want to vent, I hope y'all don't mind. *Reddit.com*. Retrieved November 10, 2018, from: www.reddit.com/r/smalldick problems/comments/4b7l2v/i_just_want_to_vent_i_hope_yall_dont_mind.

Wright, P. J., Tokunaga, R. S., Kraus, A., & Klann, E. (2017). Pornography consumption and satisfaction: a meta-analysis. *Human Communication Research*, *43*(3), 315–343.

Wong, Y. J., Ho Ringo, M. H., Wang, S. Y., & Miller, I. S. (2017). Meta-analyses of the relationship between conformity to masculine norms and mental health-related outcomes. *Journal of Counseling Psychology*, *64*(1), 80–93.

Yelsma, P. & Marrow, S. (2003). An examination of couples' difficulties with emotional expressiveness and their marital satisfaction. *The Journal of Family Communication*, *3*(1), 41–62.

PART FOUR

Looking Deeper/Going Further

11

PHILOSOPHY OF SCIENCE

A book about the psychology of men might seem like an odd place for a chapter on philosophy. Traditionally, learning about psychology has involved studying the field's theories and findings and gaining practical skills in *doing* psychology—running experiments, computing statistics, and writing up studies. Philosophy, by contrast, seems like a world apart. Philosophers stereotypically work in musty seminar rooms, debating distinctions like The Real versus The Ideal. In Ethan's first week of graduate school the professor introduced several readings on epistemological and ontological assumptions and was met with audible groans from the class. She reassured students: "Not to worry. You won't need to use these big words after this first week." Many researchers in psychology can lead successful careers without diving into philosophy. So what benefit could students in the psychology of men and masculinity possibly gain from learning about philosophy of science?

While the word philosophy, Greek for "love of knowledge," suggests an intellectual pursuit undertaken for its own sake, there are several ways a psychological perspective on men and masculinity can benefit from philosophy:

- First, philosophy allows us to understand the reasoning and assumptions that guide different approaches to understanding the psychology of men. In the second part of this book, we traced five approaches: biological, social learning, social constructionist, feminist, and intersectional. These different approaches are undergirded by assumptions about the status of free will, what masculinity is, whether social science is or can be objective, and so on. If you want to say more about these different perspectives than, "yes, there are many different ways of studying men's psychology," and consider *how* those perspectives are different on a fundamental level, you need to dip your toes into philosophy.

- Second, and relatedly, understanding the philosophical assumptions of scholarship is particularly important if you want to go beyond being a consumer of psychology to becoming a producer. Approaching these perspectives without a philosophical vocabulary is like buying a package of bread without being able to decipher the list of ingredients or nutritional information. While some consumers might be comfortable going ahead and buying the bread without knowing what goes into the loaf, if they want to try baking some on their own, they are in trouble. The same goes for aspiring psychological scientists: if you want to do an experiment on how masculinity relates to personality traits like openness to experience, you should be aware of the assumptions you're making about the nature of masculinity (in this case that it is a stable trait that men "have") as well as the nature of knowledge (in this case that conducting experiments and controlling for confounds leads to a presumably more objective form of knowledge).
- Third, understanding the philosophy of science is also important for being able to explore the deeper social scientific context in which psychology of men and masculinities is embedded. Historically, the five perspectives—biology, social learning, social construction, feminism, and intersectionality—derive from much broader intellectual traditions. Knowing about these can help make sense out of camp antagonisms (for example, why evolutionary psychology has received a lot of feminist criticism) and for understanding why scholars use the vocabulary they do (such as why social constructionism—given its origins in anthropology and sociology—tends to import a lot of concepts from those fields).

In this chapter we will go a little deeper, and make the philosophical distinctions in various approaches explicit. To set the table, we will tackle a few big words like "epistemology" and "ontology." Then, with this vocabulary in hand, we will examine several important philosophical questions in more detail: does psychology make progress? What's the difference between "good" psychology and "bad" psychology? And what do we do with so many competing theories of men and masculinity? Throughout the chapter, we include excerpts of dialogue between the authors to help bring this material to life and demonstrate how the philosophical concepts discussed can be used in service of a broader and deeper look at the psychology of men.

Snippet 1: Why Philosophy?

Michael and Ethan initially address the question that starts this chapter: "why philosophy?" They focus on philosophy as a critical thinking skillset that helps reveal hidden assumptions. Michael argues that the naive assumption that science can objectively and conclusively answer crucial questions about human psychology isn't borne out in practice. He notes that social forces operating behind the curtain, like fundability and popularity, drive the kind of answers we can arrive at. Ethan pivots from a focus on how psychology arrives at answers to a focus on the role assumptions play in asking those questions in the first place.

MICHAEL: This chapter is about philosophy of science and it's not a standard thing to have a chapter like that in a book like this. So, for you, why does it matter? Why are you interested in the philosophy of science?

ETHAN: The way I think about the philosophy of science is by understanding it as a way to see the water we swim in. Without having an understanding of the philosophy of science you run the risk of not critically examining the kind of assumptions that you are making, that there are assumptions you might be making that you don't realize you're making—and there can be a lot of them in psychology. So by doing philosophy of science we can try to uncover what some of those assumptions are, like the idea that what matters is the individual. Or what particularly matters is being able to predict, control, and influence behavior. Or that, for example, gender is a thing that people *have*. These are assumptions, but without seeing them that way psychologists often taken them as givens.

MICHAEL: I'm with you all the way on this but I think there is a lot there about what you said about assumptions. I think you and I care about assumptions, but I'm not sure our students always understand why they should care about them. Because it seems like an abstract logical thing. It's like, "oh, okay, we've got an assignment, now we're gonna figure out what the assumptions are, blah blah blah."

For me, here's why assumptions matter. I don't know about you, but I was sort of raised with the idea that science was gonna be the one who's gonna decide who's right. Like if there was a question at hand, "is masculinity harmful?" "Does cigarette smoking cause cancer?" "Is national security enhanced by investing in the military, or, should we, you know, buy more fruit?" It's gonna come down to "What are the data?" Right?

What I found in psychology was really interesting. It's like, when I really started to take on that identity, that practice of being a hard-nosed empiricist, the data didn't tend to answer in big ways: there's not a lot we can predict with great precision and we can't influence that much. And then you start to realize that the questions that are getting asked are often driven by what's fundable and what's popular at the time. So it's not as if science is this god-like, objective thing.

ETHAN: So, that's really interesting, I like what you're getting at, which is "where do the questions come from?" and I do think science does a really good job of answering questions like, "How are we going to determine whether or not cigarette smoking causes cancer?" Once we've got those really clear, formulated questions, science can provide somewhat clear answers. But science can't tell us what questions to ask, and I think that's more where philosophy comes in.

MICHAEL: Can you say more about that?

ETHAN: Well, for example, in the history of our own field there is this perennial question about what's different between men and women. And, you know, on its surface, it's kind of an interesting question. But it's turned out to be more or less fruitless for figuring out how gender affects people's lives. If we really want to understand gender, the question we should be asking isn't "what's the difference between men and women?" You've said this yourself before. The question is more basic: "how does gender work"?

MICHAEL: I would phrase the question differently. I would say rather than the question being "How are men and women different?" the question should be, "How does the *idea* that men and women are fundamentally different affect human functioning?" That's the question for me.

ETHAN: And there's a question that, I don't know, do you think you could get from the first question, "how are men and women different?" to this second question of "what does the idea of difference do to people?" without some understanding of philosophy?

MICHAEL: I think you could get there through theoretical debate about … questions …. So, I guess the answer would be "no" because you end up having to question what knowledge is, which eventually comes back to epistemology. But let me back up to the question "are men and women different," uhm, is that a *useful* question or not? Right, like, is that a good way to go? One answer would be, "well what do the data say?" But the data doesn't really get at it because the question is not "are men and women different?" the question is, "is this a useful question or not?"

So the traditional view of science is that science will resolve any question. And your point is—and I take this point and I think it's right—is that while science is a method for resolving questions it doesn't tell us *which* questions to ask.

ETHAN: Yeah, that's my point.

MICHAEL: And that's a really powerful point, because where *do* the questions come from then?

Epistemology

One term you're bound to run into if you take even a few steps into philosophy of science is "epistemology." Epistemology is the branch of philosophy that deals with the nature of knowledge. Key questions in epistemology include: what counts as *valid* knowledge ("what does it mean to say something is true?"), whether there are different *kinds* of knowledge ("is there a difference between scientific knowledge and non-scientific knowledge?"), what makes science "scientific" ("how do you demarcate science from pseudoscience"), and whether science is progressive ("are scientists getting closer to the truth or do they repeatedly reinvent the wheel?"). We deal with the first of these questions below, and return to the other questions later in the chapter once we've outfitted ourselves with a few more philosophical tools.

What Is True?

This is a question for which philosophers have historically had three answers. According to the **correspondence theory** of truth, we should view a statement as true *if it accurately describes the real world*. From this perspective the proposition that "conforming to masculine norms makes men less likely to ask for help" is true *if and only if* we can go out into the world and find that conforming to something called "masculine norms" actually reduces men's proclivity for help-seeking.

The second theory of truth, the **coherence theory**, states that the truth of a proposition depends on whether or not it is logically consistent with propositions that we already know to be true. Therefore, we might say that the statement (1) "men's violence is natural" is true if it is also true that (2) "the outcomes of evolutionary processes are 'natural,'" (3) "evolutionary processes lead to traits that increase an individual's odds of survival and reproduction," and that (4) "a tendency toward violent behavior increases men's likelihood of producing offspring." Note that statement (1) would not be true if any of statements (2), (3), and (4) are not themselves consistent with the larger web of propositions about men, violence, and evolution.

The third answer to the question "what is true?" is the **pragmatic theory of truth**, which essentially discards the idea of truth in favor of the concept **workability**. A proposition is workable if adopting the proposition as true leads to successfully moving toward a particular goal or value. For example, if your goal is to become accepted as a member of a hypermasculine community, the proposition "real men don't cry" is true in the sense that believing it is true will likely lead to successful working—gaining credibility—in that hypermasculine community. However, if your goal is to develop effective psychotherapeutic interventions for men, believing in this proposition might cause difficulty in compassionately responding to men who are crying and might increase men's shame. In this context, it would not be workable to take "real men don't cry" as true. More broadly, a pragmatic approach to the psychology of men and masculinity might be concerned with developing knowledge that helps move society towards increased human well-being and greater gender equality (Addis, Mansfield, & Syzdek, 2010).

Ontology

While epistemology deals with *how* we know, ontological questions are questions about *what* we know: the nature of the world and what makes it up. Key questions here concern whether and how the world might be meaningfully carved up into different phenomena and whether psychological and social phenomena are fundamentally different from physical phenomena. With regards to the second question, one of the most well-known ontological concepts is the idea of the mind–body *dualism*—that there exist two separate substances in the world: one made up of the matter of our cells, bodies, and the physical universe, and the other made up of consciousness and experience. The classical distinction between sex and gender largely parallels the demarcation of mind and body.

In addition to dualist ontologies, there are also *monist* ontologies. These tend to fall into one of two categories. Physicalist monists deny that there is anything unique about conscious experience that separates it from the material world. The idea here is that the biological, chemical, and physical underpinnings of psychological phenomena are themselves the *entirety* of conscious phenomena. Masculinity, by this reading, should ultimately be reducible to biological, chemical, and physical phenomena. In contrast, idealist monists posit that the world is fundamentally mental in nature— not just that we can *know* only our subjective experience and must remain skeptical about the physical world (an anti-realist *epistemological* position) but that *ideas are all there is in the world*. This latter position tends to be adopted, in a weaker form (i.e., we should remain completely agnostic about the physical), by scholars who take a discourse analytic approach to studying men and masculinity.

We are painting broad strokes here—there exist numerous ontological monisms, dualisms, pluralisms—but some implications for understanding different approaches to the psychology of men and masculinity should be apparent. As one example, it makes an awful lot of sense to use a biological paradigm if you have physicalist monist ontological commitments. Likewise, a dualist or idealist monist perspective leaves some room for studying the meaning of masculinities and the way men experience and navigate those meanings.

There is another ontological distinction you are already familiar with from an earlier chapter in this book. Recall our discussion in Chapter 5 of contrasting perspectives on *masculinity-as-a-noun* and *masculinity-as-a-verb*. This distinction is an ontological one—contrasting a view of masculinity as a *thing* that exists in human minds or bodies and a view of masculinity as a *process* or *type of activity*. Treating masculinity as a verb means that it lacks "thingness" the way a table or a cellular membrane have thingness. Even within the realm of *things*, however, we might still ask the question: *what kinds of things are men and/or masculinities?*

One of the central activities of psychological science is categorizing. Men and women, gender and sex, masculinity and femininity—these are all categories. Philosophers describe scientific categories that map onto world as *natural kinds*, concepts that, as Plato said, "carve nature at its joints." Saying that liquids and gasses are natural kinds is to say that there *really is* a meaningful difference between them—that they are *not* just names and that there would still be a real difference between liquids and gasses even if humans did not have the concepts "liquid" or "gas."

In psychology, it is much more difficult to discern what, if anything, counts as a natural kind. Does the world really come pre-packaged into things like thoughts, on the one hand, and feelings, on the other? Or masculinity and femininity? Although the categories "men" and "women" are potentially good examples of natural kinds, it is not exactly clear where we carve nature to get those two kinds: at the level of genotype (XX vs XY)? Or at the level of phenotype (male genitalia versus female genitalia)? And what do we make of individuals with male genotypes and female phenotypes? Or of people with three X chromosomes or people with both male and female genitalia? Deciding whether to group these individuals into a third category of sex, to call some female, or others male, involves human decision-making that leaves it hard to say whether male and female truly are natural kinds.

In contrast to the idea of natural kinds, the philosopher Ian Hacking (2006) proposed the idea of **human kinds**. Male inverts (Chapter 1), spouse batterers (Chapter 9), or alexithymics (Chapter 8) might all be considered examples of human kinds. What distinguishes human kinds from natural kinds, according to Hacking, is that human kinds are *not indifferent* to being classified and studied. Hacking argues that human kinds respond to being studied via a complex feedback loop. For example, when psychologists "discover" a category like "spousal batterers," the knowledge psychologists generate about them filters back into society, informing how the mental health and criminal justice systems (among others) treat batterers. Over time, the way we think about spousal abuse more generally changes. Where we might once have thought that intimate partner violence results from a *loss* of self-restraint and have viewed "spousal batterers" as out of control "barbarians" (Witters, 1998), psychologists now conceptualize intimate partner violence as a way that batterers *exercise* control over their partners. Thus classifications, as well as psychologists' knowledge about those classifications, also change the way humans get classified. They might seek to redefine themselves: "spousal batterers" might, instead, re-label themselves as "old fashioned," "alcoholic," or "just asking for respect." Hacking writes that although:

> We think of these kinds of people as given, as definite classes defined by definite properties ... it is not quite like that. They are moving targets because our investigations interact with the targets themselves, and change them. And since they are changed, they are not quite the same kind of people as before ... Sometimes our sciences create kinds of people that in a certain sense did not exist before.
>
> (p. 293)

Human kinds, then, are fundamentally different from natural kinds not only because they are human but because they are locked in a kind of never-ending dance with psychological science, each stepping in response to the others' lead. We can see exactly this kind of dance at play when society takes up different ways of thinking about masculinity, like when men organize in reaction to feminism or when workshops draw on social learning theory to try to reform men, bringing new "kinds" of men and masculinities, like new fatherhood, into being.

Snippet 2: How Do We Best Know Masculinity? And What Is Masculinity?

In the following sidebar, Michael again presses the question of why we should care about the philosophy of science, and, in particular, why we should be concerned with epistemology. He begins by raising the issue that data can be explained by many theories. He also notes that, in practice, the psychology of men and masculinity has frequently failed to meaningfully represent the real world. The subsequent quick conversational pivot from epistemology to ontology—in the context of a messy world—exemplifies the ways that what we think it means to "know" depend largely on what we think exists. Ethan and Michael conclude this snippet by discussing different ways researchers might approach studying a messy world.

MICHAEL: We've got five different chapters about why men do what they do. And at a certain point if you want to know how to proceed with that information, how to make use of it, how do you choose? Which one is right? Is it gonna be resolved by the data? Well it turns out the data don't bare out the question of whether *cognition* really matters in a particular moment, or whether it's more about *reinforcement* history, or whatever it may be. On top of that, the other thing is that those different theories come with different methods in support of them and different epistemologies.

So I guess, so let me back up with a practical question for you. We spend a lot of time in the chapter on epistemology. Why does that matter in the psychology of men? Like, why is that such a big deal and why should people be thinking about it?

ETHAN: Well I think it matters because, well, you just said it: each of these different theories has different standards and different methods to evaluate what's true or not.

As scientists I think we are pretty well versed

in the kinds of epistemologies that are used in biological theories and in, to some extent, social learning theories. The idea is that we make hypotheses and we go and collect data, and if the data support our hypotheses we look for any sort of remaining mysteries, generate new hypotheses, and proceed ad infinitum. "There's a real world out there and we need to test our knowledge against it. We need to make contact with that real world." If you apply *that* understanding of truth to something like social constructionism or feminism or intersectionality the methods seem like they aren't the best way of getting at the truth, if that's what the truth is.

MICHAEL: Well and here's the thing too is that, even within theoretical perspectives that are more open to that sort of positivist methodology, it doesn't work real well. So, for example, if you're studying the consequences of the social learning of masculinity and you're finding that there is a correlation between people's reports of their beliefs about masculinity and their behavior, those various variables still rarely account for more than maybe 9% of the variance in each other, even though we plop them all together in big diagrams with lots of arrows. So, it makes me wonder, even with those methods that think they are relying on the idea that we need to track the world in some way, are we really tracking the world that well?

ETHAN: Yeah, well I think the question is what do you do when you ... when you encounter a mess?

MICHAEL: Yes.

ETHAN: When you encounter a mess do you do the best you can to clean up, even if the best you can do is not terribly well? Or do you acknowledge, "Hey there's a mess here, and let's proceed with the knowledge that we're not gonna clean up this mess."

MICHAEL: So what's in the mess for you? In terms of trying to understand the psychology of men and masculinities, what's messy? I think that's another way to think about epistemology and ontology.

ETHAN: When you think about it from a positivist methodology it's ... yeah, lots of variance, a ton of variance that—

MICHAEL: A *ton* of variance.

ETHAN: —drives human behavior. But then there's another dimension of messiness which really interests me, which is the fact that we are human beings studying human behavior. In particular you and I are interested in popular beliefs about masculinity but we also have beliefs ourselves about masculinity.

MICHAEL: Right, right. So let's unpack that for a minute. For me, when I think about that, that's the idea that we are both trying to understand masculinity but as people trying to understand it we are also constructing it, so we are part of the thing that we are trying to understand.

ETHAN: Right, and our theories are about what *we're* doing, in a sense.

MICHAEL: Well couldn't someone operating from a correspondence theory of truth say that's just error variance?

ETHAN: It is. Well, I would, to use the statistical parlance, say it is *systematic* variance, it's systematic error.

MICHAEL: Systematic error, right. Things we haven't accounted for. So doesn't it sort of, on some level, come down to whether you want to put your faith in discovering reality even though it's complicated, or you want to put your faith in trying to be a more adept and comprehensive thinker about the problem of reality and our job in it?

Advanced Questions in Philosophy of Science

What Separates "Good" Psychology From "Bad" Psychology?

Our society is replete with magazine articles, self-help guides, and television gurus offering apparent psychological wisdom that often turns out, on inspection, to have no firm grounding in research or scholarship. Figuring out what is good psychology and what is bad psychology is important for several reasons. First, the presence of junk psychology seeping into the field's intellectual bedrock threatens progress: if foundational research is flawed this may undermine research that builds upon it. Second, our ability to make the world a better place, to guide public policy, or to compete for scarce public funding rests on psychology's perceived legitimacy—which can be severely undermined by pseudoscientific findings.

Philosophers interested in these questions have revealed that the task of separating the wheat of science from the chaff of pseudoscience is actually a quite complicated one. There is considerable debate among philosophers who study this **demarcation problem** about what criteria distinguish science and whether there even are *any* criteria that might be up to this quality control job. And demarcation gets even more thorny in psychology relative to the natural sciences.

There are a few aspects of psychology that make this question particularly hard to answer. First, because we live in a complex, probabilistic world, even "good" psychology regularly and predictably produces false findings,[1] even if psychologists do everything right. The history of psychology is also packed with examples of dominant theories, like phrenology, that were once granted the legitimacy of science but are now dismissed as bogus. How do we know that our own theories of men and masculinity might not also meet a similar fate in the future?

Clearly, whether or not scientific theories will eventually "get it right" is a problematic way to tease apart the scientific from the non-scientific since, absent a time-machine, we do not know what the future will say about current theories. Instead, many epistemologists have argued that we should focus on the *structure* rather than the *content* of theories in figuring out which are scientific and which are not. According to Karl Popper, what makes a theory scientific is that it makes **falsifiable** predictions about the world (Thonton, 2018). By this standard, a theory that "repressed childhood memories sometimes lead men to avoid closeness with other men" is not scientific because it requires demonstrating that such men have distinct patterns of repressed memories. These would be—by definition—inaccessible to observation and measurement. Moreover, even if we were able to find many cases of men avoiding closeness that were definitively *not* caused by repressed memories, we could never rule out the possibility of eventually finding a case in which one was (after all, the memory could be repressed).

The merit of Popper's falsification criterion is that it offers scientists a good guide for how to proceed in their scholarship: to draw predictions from theories and specify the conditions under which that theory would be falsified, to test those predictions, and, if their criteria for rejecting the theory are met, to consider novel theories that can explain both old findings and the new, unexpected finding. Theories of sex roles from the mid-20th century, for instance, made a falsifiable prediction: that men who had traits on the feminine side of a masculinity–femininity spectrum were less healthy psychologically than men with more masculine traits. When Sandra Bem (1974) found that, in fact, androgynous individuals—those with high masculine *and* high feminine traits—were more well-adapted psychologically, this provided a fairly convincing falsification of the earlier theory.

Instead of looking at the *structure* of theories to determine whether or not they are scientific, other philosophers, like Thomas Kuhn (1962), argue that our focus should be on *scientific practice*. He characterized science as fluctuating between two distinct modes over time: ***puzzle-solving*** and ***revolutions***:

- During puzzle-solving, scientists work within a well-established framework of constructs and experimental procedures, testing the predictions of the dominant theory. Kuhn suggested that although falsifying theories might be ideal, in actuality, when scientists discover findings that run against theories, they tend to assume that they made a mistake or bracket the finding as an anomaly—not as evidence of a theoretical shortcoming.
- However, when anomalies build up over time, Kuhn argued, sciences enter a period of crisis in which there becomes space for new theories, methods, and constructs to compete with those previously dominant.

Finally, through a process of revolution, a new worldview emerges in which the previously anomalous appears sensible. But it is not simply that the new worldview solves old problems: it also raises new questions, shines light onto previously unarticulated phenomena, forgets old problems, and lets old concepts fade into obscurity. Kuhn provocatively claimed that after a scientific revolution, the new world (or "paradigm") cannot be understood in the terms of the old, and vice versa. From a Kuhnian perspective, "good" psychological science exists when this pattern of puzzle-solving and revolution occurs.

Kuhn himself suggested that psychology is not a mature enough science for his model to work. While we largely agree with his assessment, there are some examples of revolution-*like* events in the history of psychology. For example, the emergence of research on gender, as opposed to on sex differences, has many of the markings of a scientific revolution. As you'll recall from our discussion of the history of the psychology of men and masculinity, scientific psychology prior to the 1930s was dominated by different questions, different concepts, and different methods. In terms of questions, scholars were interested in understanding what was unique about men and women and what was universal. Conceptually, psychologists concerned themselves with *sex differences*—biological male versus biological female. Methodologically, researchers tended to take samples of men and women, measure them on a trait they were interested in, and compare the statistical mean of men to women using *t* tests. But then, starting with Terman and Miles' MF scale (1936) and a concern with sex role orientation, things began to shift. New questions were asked: are some women *more* feminine than others, some men *more* masculine than others? What are the consequences of these varying levels of sex role orientation? New concepts came to the fore: concepts of gender, socialization, social construction, role strain, and patriarchy. And new methods began to bubble to the surface.

The key point of reading the history of the psychology of gender through Kuhn's idea of a revolution is to understand that the reason for change was not that the psychology of sex was falsified. While it did encounter problems documenting significant findings in some areas, in other areas significant (but generally small) effects of sex *did* emerge. Rather, the questions asked by the psychology of sex differences became less urgent, and its methods and concepts less useful for answering newer questions.

Does Psychology Make Progress?

The progress of the natural sciences—evidenced by their massive achievements in producing technologies and medicines—has typically been taken for granted. Indeed, one of the main tasks that philosophy of science traditionally occupied itself with was explaining why science is able to make progress. Psychology, then, presents something of an interesting case. Unlike physics, we have no atom bombs and no rocket ships to tout as evidence of progress. Unlike microbiologists, we have no antibiotics and no nearly-guaranteed cures for whole classes of pathologies. Clinical psychology's most effective treatment is, arguably, cognitive behavior therapy for panic disorder, but even that proves efficacious in only around three quarters of cases (Hofmann, Asnaani, Vonk, Sawyer, & Fang, 2012). Of course, psychotherapeutic technologies, measurements like the IQ test, and concepts like implicit cognition have found many uses in society at large. Still, they lack the awe-inspiring quality or reliable ability to save lives of many technologies in medicine and the natural sciences. One might question whether psychology's products are evidence of scientific progress.

As we saw in our review of the history of the psychology of men and masculinity there is a wide diversity of ways to approach the subject matter. But is it possible to judge which theories are "better" or whether new theories have "improved" upon those from earlier in history? The issue of judging theories against each other might be resolvable if some were better at advancing us towards a particular goal than others; however, new theories have posed new questions rather than finding answers to old ones. We argued in the first and second chapters that studying sex differences—a dominant approach in the early 20th century but one that continues into the present—is limited in its ability to tell us about how masculinity affects men because it ignores differences between men and across different situations. But does that mean that studies in the gender role strain paradigm or social constructionist analyses of cross-situational variation in masculinity constitute progress? It depends, largely, on what your goals are. If your goals are to understand how masculinity "works," then you might say that some progress has been made. But if your goal really is to just understand whether men and women have differences in personality, interests, or their behaviors—the goal of many researchers that look at sex differences—then looking at variation within men is not really progress at all and sex differences is probably the way to go.

In addition to asking whether newer theories constitute progress upon old theories, we might also ask whether the *totality* of current theories constitutes progress: has the psychology of men and masculinity moved towards a more complete understanding? But this question raises another: a more complete understanding of *what*? We know more now than we did 40 years ago about how conforming to traditional masculinity relates to mental health outcomes, about the conditions under which testosterone leads to aggressive behavior, about how gender bias can affect psychological research, and about the ways that men's understanding of their gender can be influenced by their race, class, or sexuality. But are those bodies of knowledge moving towards something larger, the way that physics is moving towards understanding ever-smaller building blocks of matter? And are these different approaches fundamentally reconcilable, or are they, like Kuhn's different worldviews, incompatible?

Psychological perspectives are commensurable if they share enough common epistemological, ontological, and methodological ground that researchers can agree on criteria for evaluating the veracity or quality of different research findings. For example, if you're committed to the positions

(1) that there is a real thing called masculinity out there in the world,
(2) that researchers are capable of objectively studying masculinity, and
(3) that theories should specify specific predictions about how one variable affects another then the social learning approach offers clear benefits over an intersectional approach. The trouble is that these commitments are *not* shared between the two approaches: they belong to the social learning approach. Intersectional theorists dispute all three assumptions, arguing that masculinity is *not* a thing, that scientists can only ever study masculinity from a subjective position, and that theories should strive to destabilize politically oppressive social conditions at the same time that they aim to describe the world.

These two approaches, then, can be said to be incommensurable. There is no way of judging one as better than the other. Does this then confine us to **relativism**—the position that there is no truth, only different perspectives? Not necessarily—there are several other options. We can become partisans—advocating for our particular favorite theory's assumptions as more sophisticated, rigorous, or politically just. Or we can take the pragmatist position that while no perspective may be true in the abstract, that certain perspectives are more useful depending on your goals.

Snippet 3: What Do You Do With Competing Theories?

Below, Ethan and Michael begin to make sense of what a researcher might do when confronted with disparate and sometimes contradictory approaches to studying the psychology of men and masculinity. Michael argues that there are problems to both zeroing in on one approach to the exclusion of others, and to taking an all-hands-on-deck stance towards multiple theories. He offers functional contextualism as a middle way: different approaches get used strategically, depending on the researcher's particular goals. Ethan suggests two broad classes of goals or activities that researchers in psychology pursue: predicting versus describing. They then discuss some of the deeper ontological distinctions that facilitate those different activities.

ETHAN: So this gets back to a question we were talking about earlier, which is what do we do with all these different theories of masculinity? Do we decide between them? Or do you think that we can get a better understanding by being able to hold multiple ones? Or does that make things muddier?

MICHAEL: That's a good question because one place people often stop in studying the psychology of men and masculinity is that they read the different perspectives and say to themselves, "that all makes sense, each and every one. They all have a little to offer."

ETHAN: Mhm.

MICHAEL: And I guess for me I'm not satisfied with that because which one at which time? And for which problem? But to answer your question, you know, is it more useful to pick one or to ... how did you phrase it?

ETHAN: Does it make you a better thinker about mascu-
              linity to be able to hold multiple theories, more
              than one big picture theory? Or does it become
              a hindrance?
MICHAEL: Yeah, like, do we make more progress?
ETHAN: Yeah, what's better? To specialize in one theory
              or to embrace the multiplicity?
MICHAEL: Well, there's advantages to both. So, an advan-
              tage to embracing *one* is that you can go *further*,
              you know *deeper* ... but you're only seeing it
              one way.
ETHAN: And what's the problem with that?
MICHAEL: Well that's a good question ... what's the problem
              with only seeing it one way? Well the questions
              are sort of received, and I think you ultimately
              stop critically thinking, you know? So, for
              example, let's say you have a social learning per-
              spective on masculinity, and you are approaching
              science from a positivist perspective, so you're
              gathering quantitative data and you're doing stat-
              istical significance testing. One can make progress
              that way, by studying numerous iterations of
              slightly different variables and applying the same
              methods and never quite reaching a conclusion.
              So, from a scientific progress perspective that's
              problematic because it may be incremental but it
              doesn't seem to add up to much, or to any sort of
              Kuhnian approach to science.
              Another problem with it is that it doesn't always
              attend to some things that matter to me, like the
              political consequences of thinking differently. For
              example, much of the quantitative research on
              men and masculinity is focused on men's pain ...
              which you know, I think is very real and it's
              important to deal with, but by doing that we're
              not focusing on, or dedicating resources to, or
              maybe we're not even thinking about the way
              masculinity might be a privilege to men and con-
              tribute to other social problems that are of con-
              cern to me. I think, you can't stick with one
              theory because it doesn't allow you to jump out-
              side, so to speak. That concern about how this
              scholarship may not be attending to men's
              accountability in social problems, that for me

comes out of a feminist perspective. And if I don't have that in my toolbox, so to speak, or my background, then I'm not going to see that as a concern. So, I want to see more, I want to see more of the system.

ETHAN: So those are the pros and cons of taking a particular approach and carrying it as far as you can. But I'm curious about the pros and cons of trying to juggle multiple theories?

MICHAEL: Right. Well one con of trying to juggle that, it's sort of like, "What shirt am I gonna put on *today*?"

ETHAN: And you end up not wearing a shirt?

MICHAEL: Yeah [laughter], you end up not wearing a shirt or you don't know what your style is, you know, "what am I trying to do here?" I would say if you move rapid fire through eclecticism, you end up with a merging of style and perspective that isn't necessarily intentional or hasn't been really thought through. The alternative for me is what is called a "functional contextualist perspective" or the pragmatic perspective, which is that you lead by identifying a value or a goal and then select a theory and an epistemology that helps you make progress toward that goal. That's to me one way out. Not perfect. But one way out.
As a psychologist, I want to use the insights of different perspectives on the psychology of men but not do so randomly. I don't want to make a soup and say "I'm just gonna throw cumin in. I'm gonna throw in chili powder."

ETHAN: "Toss in a little intersectionality."

MICHAEL: Yeah! "A little intersectionality. Some feminism." That doesn't make sense to me. I want to make progress by using perspectives that work for particular problems.

ETHAN: Right. So like, if I want to understand "what's the *meaning* of depression in men?" then it's pretty clear that taking a positive approach is not the way to go, because positivism just doesn't really deal a lot with meaning and how things are constructed. That's just not in its vocabulary really. I'm not asking a question about cause and effect but just "how do I describe the world?" It's a different activity. It's *describing* the world. We're painting a picture that doesn't involve any sort of *prediction*.

MICHAEL: Well, I mean, does this come down to whether you want to count things to understand the world or do you want to talk about them to understand the world? Because if you want to understand the relationships between gender and depression and how it all gets made by humans, does it come down to whether you need to count something versus interpret something? I think that is driving a lot of the difficulty in communicating between different perspectives.

ETHAN: Right. I think some people who really prefer counting would want to look at people who do interpreting and say "that's just making stuff up." And I think people who like to interpret like to look at people who count and say "well, that's just reductionist and …".

MICHAEL: —Simple minded.

ETHAN: Yeah. "That's not actually helping you understand anything. It's not interesting at all, it's washing away what's interesting."

MICHAEL: So that's epistemology, right? It's the question of how do we know we're making progress? Which is another way of saying, what is knowledge? Those things are related, and they both link with ontology because if your ontology of masculinity is that this is a studiable thing, as an individual difference variable, and that makes sense to you, there's something called masculinity in different people and the degree to which it's in them matters, then that fits quite well with a more positivist epistemology. But if masculinity for you is more like a butterfly in a hall of mirrors, you know, it's a moving target, it's moving in the sense that it's not a thing people *have* but it's something they *do*, they do it differently in different situations and the people trying to understand them doing it are also doing it. You know, that really gets to be a butterfly in a hall of mirrors. If that's your ontological view, that lends itself more towards thick interpretation of the *doing*—of how masculinity operates.

Where We Stand: Functional Contextualism and "Positive Masculinity"

As we review these differing epistemological and ontological positions, you might wonder where we stand. Our approach to research on masculinity follows what is known as *functional contextualism*. This framework is strongly influenced by pragmatism, covered briefly above. In terms of ontology, functional contextualism remains strikingly agnostic. It does not matter what masculinity "really is" to a functional contextualist—what matters instead is how claims that masculinity is like this or that operate in context. There are two contexts that are particularly important here. First is the context of *(A) professional, academic research on men and masculinity*. The idea that masculinity *really is* reducible to hormones and gonads or that masculinity *really is* part of a structure that oppresses women is not the point. The point is how each of these perspectives enables effective research. From this perspective, wrong-headed conceptualizations of masculinity are bad for research not so much because they're false but because they don't work well. If we thought that masculinity was a physiological reaction to eating lots and lots of freshwater fish we would, first, have a hard time finding any data to support this and, second, have a hard time maintaining credibility in the wider community of researchers.

The second important context to consider is *(B) society writ large*; how our claims affect human behavior. To take a provocative example, the notion that masculinity is nothing more than having male genitals is problematic in a societal context because it might (1) de-legitimize the identities of transgender people (why worry about the experiences of people for whom gender doesn't match sex if gender and sex are one and the same?), and (2) discourage efforts to teach men about different ways of being in the world (if masculinity comes entirely from biology, then why would social learning make any difference?). Moreover, the claim would also not help us go very far in the *(A)* scientific context if we wanted to see why some men seem "more" masculine than others—since the claim that masculinity is just a matter of having a penis is categorical, it's either something you have or don't and not something that can vary by degree.

Like with pragmatist epistemology, functional contextualism holds that we should evaluate truth claims on their *workability*—how well they help us to achieve particular goals—rather than whether they directly map onto reality (Hayes, 1993). Those goals cannot be arrived at through rigorous experimentation or research. They are first principles; they are the bedrock in which we ground our research. In our own research on men and masculinities and in the writing of this book, we typically have three particular goals in mind. We seek:

(1) To predict and influence human behavior.
(2) To increase human well-being.
(3) To promote gender equality.

What do we mean by each of these goals? At base, we want to *(1) predict and influence* human behavior. If we don't know how to affect behavior, we will simply be shouting into the void—all of our writing, research, and teaching will be for naught. Being able to predict and influence means that we might be able to *(2) increase human well-being* and *(3) promote gender equality*. We mean human well-being in the broadest sense—increasing psychological and physical health and reducing suffering. And in terms of gender equality, we strive for a society in which it is not the case that some genders have more power than others and some people are more limited by their gender than others. To give you a sense of how a functional contextualist perspective affects the way we do research, we'll explore a topic we've touched on throughout the book: *if research shows that masculinity can be harmful, what do we do about it?* This is one of the most important questions currently facing the field, and one with no easy answers.

If you take the perspective that violence, emotional suppression, and excessive self-reliance are intrinsic to masculinity—that masculinity is an essential part of all men—then the most we can hope for is to *ameliorate* it. At best, we might develop strategies that help men keep their "natural" violent or competitive tendencies in check. If you instead follow a social learning perspective, the more appealing answer would be to try to *reconstruct* masculinity—to create new less harmful notions of what it means to be a man. Some researchers argue that the most effective way to improve men's well-being is to reject aspects of masculinity that are harmful and instead promote a "*positive masculinity*" centered on norms of courage, resilience, duty to others, demonstrating love through action, and so on (Englar-Carlson & Kiselica, 2013; Hammer & Good, 2010). This is an approach that has gained many supporters in recent years, and even features prominently in the new APA guidelines for psychological practice with men and boys. However, our philosophical commitments lead us to question this approach.

Consistent with a functional contextualist perspective, our central concern is how the idea of "positive masculinity" *functions* in *context*. First, in a scholarly context, the concept of "positive masculinity" shares many features that we also find problematic about masculinity as a set of norms or as a social role. The idea here is that "positive masculinity" has been defined as a static and trait-like set of attributes (like "traditional masculinity") that do not vary across situations or over time. Thinking about masculinity, positive or negative, as a stable disposition doesn't by itself give us a set of conceptual tools for asking questions like, "Why do masculine norms seem to have positive effects in some situations but not others?" or "What specific situations elicit 'positive' masculine behavior?" Of course, it's possible to expansively define "positive masculinity" to mean men flexibly enacting gender in a way that has positive effects. But if positive masculinity is so amorphous, what's the value of calling it "masculinity" at all? Why not speak more generally of healthy *human* behaviors and qualities?

We also are skeptical that "positive masculinity" will have the effects we want to see in a societal context. Psychologists Hammer and Good (2010), proponents of "positive masculinity," hope that in the context of therapy:

> *A* focus on distinguishing healthy forms of masculinity from unhealthy ones and on identifying and building upon the strengths they have as men may resonate more with traditional men than an emotion-focused, symptom-alleviation approach (Mankowski, Maton, Burke, Hoover, & Anderson, 2000); it may help men restore the possible lost sense of pride associated with being a man (Levant, 1997). Aiding men in developing healthy, flexible conceptions of masculinity may have more intrinsic appeal than would being told what not to do, though that is certainly an important component.
>
> (Good, 1998, p. 313)

We see nothing wrong with the impulse to encourage flexible behavior, and it makes sense to try to make therapy effective for all people. But with regards to the value of predicting and influencing behavior, it's first important to recognize that some of the claims here—like the idea that building on masculine strengths will be more effective for some men—are claims that need to be subjected to empirical scrutiny. If using "positive masculinity" actually makes therapy work better for increasing men's well-being, then that is a point in its favor in terms of the values of promoting human well-being and gender equality. However, until the data are in, we just don't know how workable "positive masculinity" is in the context of therapy.

However, even if "positive masculinity" is useful in the context of therapy, we are not sure how workable it is to increase men's "pride associated with being a man." We are concerned that encouraging this sort of pride will inevitably, for men that *don't* meet the mark of positive masculinity, lead to feelings of shame and in that sense are less workable in the context of society writ large. Hammer and Good are right to be skeptical of an approach that teaches individuals what "*not* to do" rather than what to do. But teaching men what not to do is *precisely* the way gender concepts seem to operate. We see no reason why "positive masculinity" wouldn't function the same way as ideas of "traditional masculinity" always have: defining one group of men as *real men* and demarcating them as in some way superior to other men, to women, and to gender minorities. This will inevitably lead to some forms of inequality along gender lines within and between genders.

For example, we imagine that it would be relatively easy to justify re-establishing an all-male military based on notions of "positive" masculine traits like courage. It's not hard to imagine because this was precisely the logic used for centuries! It's also not hard to imagine men gender-policing each other for not being sufficiently dutiful to others, or even not flexible enough in the way they do gender—perhaps devaluing men who more rigidly adhere to gender roles as *not real men*. In short, we are operating from the assumption that the *function* of socially constructing and reinforcing masculinities (positive or otherwise) is always to create expectations for conformity to certain norms and ideologies based on one's gender.

Our position is that instead of reconstructing masculinity, the most workable course of action is to **deconstruct** masculinity and gender more broadly to whatever extent we can, particularly in a societal context. By deconstruct, we mean making people's gender a less salient part of what it means to be human and reducing how often gender operates as a discriminative stimulus in the environment. We want to encourage positive *humanity*. How well this can work, is, again, an open empirical question. But in the absence of research, we see an approach of deconstruction as much more in line with our values and our philosophical commitments. And in the next chapter, we elaborate in more detail what kinds of concrete steps you might take towards deconstructing masculinity in your own life, if that is a path you wish to take.

For Consideration

As you've seen in this chapter, different philosophical assumptions can lead to very different ways of answering pressing questions about men and masculinities. Instead of arguing from your intuition or personal experience, try answering the following questions from each of the five perspectives we've covered in this book: biological, social learning, social constructionist, feminist, and intersectional.

1. We've presented research that draws on a variety of evidence in this book: questionnaire responses, measurements of testosterone levels, interview data, and much more. What differentiates evidence that can tell us more about the truth from evidence that tells us less about the truth?

2. A century ago, handedness was a much more important dimension of human difference. Left-handed children were punished in school for writing with their dominant hand until they learned to write with

the right hand (Tracy, 1979). This historical bias is embedded, for example, when we use the word "righteousness" interchangeably with "goodness," while the French use "gauche (left)" as a synonym for "awkward" or "maladroit" (literally, "bad at right"). This bias was even substantiated scientifically. The Italian doctor Cesare Lombroso concluded in a (1903) study of criminality:

> *One can without difficulty find among good men real left-handedness, as among the greatest evil-doers there are some who have not that characteristic. I do not dream at all of saying that all left-handed people are wicked, but that left-handedness, united to many other traits, may contribute to form one of the worst characters among the human species.*
>
> (p. 444)

Nowadays, this cultural attention to handedness has all but disappeared. Could the same happen for gender? Why or why not?

1. If you've studied scientific methods, or even if you've watched movies about science, you know that scientists engage in a variety of activities, from thinking up research questions, to recruiting participants, to presenting their findings to fellow researchers. Is science anything more than the sum of scientists' behaviors? Why or why not?
2. How do psychologists' own psychologies affect the psychological science they produce? How objective can we be about a psychology of men? To what degree are we discovering it, and to what degree are we inventing it? Does it matter? If so, why?
3. Can the psychology of men and masculinities be unified? If not, why not? If it can be, is it a worthwhile goal?

For even more reflection, consider the way the above questions have been posed. Do you think that some questions themselves lend themselves to certain philosophical assumptions? What assumptions seem to be operating in the questions?

Michael and Ethan end their dialogue by returning to the idea that studying philosophy of science can help uncover unacknowledged assumptions. As an example, they discuss the essentialist presuppositions guiding recent efforts to foster a more "positive masculinity."

MICHAEL: When the world is messy (like humans trying to be objective about studying humans), you're saying that having an understanding of the philosophy of science helps us to be better aware of the mess, and better able to think critically about it. So we can problematize certain notions—we can ask, "what's behind this idea? Where did it come from and what are its consequences," rather than simply, "is this idea true?"

ETHAN: Yeah.

MICHAEL: I like that. And so here's where you can go with that, here's a context where philosophy of science can help us. Where's a place where masculinity needs to be problematized?

ETHAN: Well what about the idea of positive masculinity. There's a context where masculinity could be problematized. An assumption of positive masculinity, is that, well, "masculinity is a thing men are gonna have to have, so we might as well make it good."

MICHAEL: Yeah, "men need masculinity."

ETHAN: And maybe we should problematize that. So there's a context.

MICHAEL: Let's slow down for a sec. So if we were sort of thinking "Let's get men in therapy. OK! We can make therapy masculine! It's positive masculinity! They'll buy it!" That *is* testable and a potentially useful question if the sole agenda is getting men into therapy. But what it doesn't attend to for you, in what you just said, is that it doesn't—

ETHAN: —Attend to the possibility that you don't need the masculinity.

MICHAEL: Yes, yes right. That's right.

ETHAN: There's a hidden assumption.

Summary and Conclusion

Philosophy is not simply a side-dish to psychology's entrée. It is the pan, the oven, and the farm—all the things needed to get the plate to the table. And thinking about psychology without understanding the assumptions that go into it is much like going into your kitchen, seeing the ingredients for making an omelet on the counter, and assuming that omelet-making is all there is to know about cooking. In doing so, we avoid understanding that in getting the eggs, cream, and butter out of the fridge, some fundamental choices have already been made.

Studying men and masculinity from any perspective, be it feminist, biological, behaviorist, or otherwise, is made more robust by understanding what assumptions you have already made. Becoming a gender scholar, to borrow from Donald Rumsfeld (as cited in Zizek, 2004), entails not only figuring out the *known knowns* like the 4 to 1 male to female suicide ratio, the *known unknowns* like the degree to which men under-report psychological distress, and the *unknown unknowns*, those questions we have not even yet imagined to ask. It also entails examining the *unknown knowns*, the things we know but do not realize we know: how we go about doing our scholarship, what the purpose of studying it is, and what kind of a thing, process, or idea masculinity(ies) is (or are). Without reflecting on our philosophical assumptions we not only run the risk of missing the context that our research is operating in, but we also lose a powerful vocabulary for understanding, comparing, and critiquing alternative ways of thinking about the psychology of men and masculinity.

Note

1 In quantitative research, the likelihood of finding an effect when there actually is no effect is known as the Type I error, which by convention is set at 5% in psychological research. Other kinds of mistakes in quantitative research include failing to detect an actual effect, which may be even more common than 5%.

References

Addis, M. E., Mansfield, A. K., & Syzdek, M. R. (2010). Is "masculinity" a problem? Framing the effects of gendered social learning in men. *Psychology of Men & Masculinity, 11*(2), 77–90.

Bem, S. L. (1974). The measurement of psychological androgyny. *Journal of Consulting and Clinical Psychology, 42*(2), 155–162.

Englar-Carlson, M. & Kiselica, M. S. (2013). Affirming the strengths in men: a positive masculinity approach to assisting male clients. *Journal of Counseling & Development, 91*(4), 399–409.

Good, G. E. (1998). Missing and underrepresented aspects of men's lives. *Society for the Psychological Study of Men and Masculinity Bulletin, 3*, 1–2.

Hacking, I. (2006, April 11). *Kinds of people: moving targets.* The Tenth British Academy Lecture. London, UK: The British Academy.

Hammer, J. H. & Good, G. E. (2010). Positive psychology: an empirical examination of beneficial aspects of endorsement of masculine norms. *Psychology of Men & Masculinity, 11*(4), 303–318.

Hayes, S. C. (1993). Analytic goals and the varieties of scientific contextualism. In S. C. Hayes, L. J. Hayes, H. W. Reese, & T. R. Sarbin (Eds), *Varieties of scientific contextualism* (pp. 11–27). Reno, NV: Context Press.

Hofmann, S. G., Asnaani, A., Vonk, I. J., Sawyer, A. T., & Fang, A. (2012). The efficacy of cognitive behavioral therapy: a review of meta-analyses. *Cognitive Therapy and Research, 36*(5), 427–440.

Kuhn, T. S. (1962). *The structure of scientific revolutions.* Chicago, IL: University of Chicago Press.

Levant, R. (1997). The masculinity crisis. *Journal of Men's Studies, 5,* 221–231.

Lombroso, C. (1903). Left-handedness and left-sidedness. *The North American Review, 177*(562), 440–444.

Mankowski, E. M., Maton, K. I., Burke, C. K., Hoover, S. H., & Anderson, C. A. (2000). Collaborative research with a men's organization: psychological impact, group functioning, and organizational growth. In E. Barton (Ed.), *Mythopoetic perspectives on men's healing work: anthology for therapists and others* (pp. 183–203). Westport, CT: Bergin & Garvey.

Terman, L. M. & Miles, C. C. (1936). *Sex and personality: studies in masculinity and femininity.* New York, NY: McGraw-Hill.

Thonton, S. (2018). Karl Popper. In E. N. Zalta (Ed.), *The Stanford encyclopedia of philosophy.* (Fall 2018 Edition). Retrieved from: https://plato.stanford.edu/arch ives/fall2018/entries/popper.

Tracy, L. (1979, August 13). On the other hand, consider who's left. *Washington Post.* Retrieved from: www.washingtonpost.com/archive/lifestyle/1979/08/13/on-the-other-hand-consider-whos-left/6c2c854c-42eb-44fa-b4c8-f2a04a740049.

Witters, J. (1998). Men who beat women believe they are justified. *Village Life News,* spousal abusers. Retrieved from: www.villagelife.org/news/archives/DV_coverstory/DV_menjustified.html.

Zizek, S. (May 21 2004). What Rumsfeld doesn't know that he knows about Abu Ghraib. *In These Times.* Retrieved from: http://inthesetimes.com/article/747/what_rumsfeld_doesn_know_that_he_knows_about_abu_ghraib.

12

MAKING CHANGES

A Framework for Change

In our psychology of men courses there typically comes a point when we have read and discussed all of the field's major theories and have considered research linking masculine gender norms and ideologies to a wide range of human concerns. The students have also completed several writing assignments in which they connect the material from the course to specific situations in their lives. Most of them have come to see the psychology of men and masculinities operating everywhere around them—so much so that, for some, they can't stop seeing it. Whether it's sexist or homophobic language in sports, the effects of emotional restriction on a loved one's health, or simply the desire to better free themselves or others from the restrictions imposed by particular masculine gender roles, the question is the same: what can we do about all of this?

The answers to this question are very personal. What you decide to do (or not do) with new knowledge depends on your own values and goals. Put another way, when a person learns about the psychology of men and masculinities, that knowledge doesn't get plopped down into a vacuum. Instead, it gets plugged into our existing beliefs, ideologies, and assumptions about the nature of people and the social world. At times, we must also change our belief systems in the presence of new information.

Several years ago, a student in one of Michael's courses (we'll call him Ross) wrote a paper about his visit home for spring break. Ross had grown up in a relatively traditional White Anglo-Saxon/Protestant New England family and he had become aware over the course of the semester that traditional gender roles were a standard and well-accepted part of his family context. When the family got together, women were responsible for all of the cleaning and cooking (except for grilling the meat) and the men generally watched sports on television. Gender was thus divided along not only labor lines but also physically, with the majority of men in one room and the women in another. Prior to taking the class, Ross had the sense that his family was relatively traditional, but it created no conflict for him.

Ross's paper described the cognitive and emotional dissonance he felt during the week home. On the one hand, his increasing awareness of gender made him feel distanced from his family; how could they continue to enact these stereotypic roles with seemingly little or no awareness? Was the men's privilege (e.g., being cooked and cleaned for) connected to their pain and social isolation (e.g., his father's drinking and his grandfather's apparent depression)? On the other hand, Ross loved his family and often felt comforted in their presence. These two discrepant reactions created a state of emotional conflict for Ross. He also anticipated negative consequences if he were to in any way express what he was feeling and thinking to his family. He was virtually certain that the men would mock him and the women would tell him to relax and not take things so seriously. In the end, Ross chose to share some of his observations with cousins and siblings closer to his age. To his surprise, they were open to discussing it and had experienced similar thoughts and feelings themselves.

Another student, Aiesha, described experiencing a sort of epiphany when reading about the relationship between masculinity and men's mental health. She realized that her grandfather, her father, and her younger brother all exhibited signs of depression and yet each one refused to seek professional help. Aiesha knew that she couldn't force them to change but she also felt a strong sense of responsibility to do something to help them. She spoke to her mother and her sister about it and both revealed that they too were concerned. However, both essentially said, "that's the way they are—they're not going to change so why start a fight about it." Aiesha did not share how she chose to proceed from there.

Ross and Aiesha were both confronting the question of personal change—whether and how to intervene in their own local family systems. For others, studying the psychology of men and masculinities raises questions about larger-scale societal and cultural changes. Riley, a transgender male student, put it this way:

> *This stuff is so huge I don't even know where to begin. It's everywhere. Misogyny, homophobia, men killing themselves with drugs, alcohol, and violence, the way our politicians interact. I almost wish I wasn't aware of it, but I am. It feels like an enormous weight on my shoulders. What can one person do about any of this?*

Riley's question is sensible; if gender is understood as a set of processes that is tightly interwoven into daily life at all levels of the social world, how can individual change make much of a difference? The same question can be posed in relation to race and class, and there are no simple answers. Nonetheless, when the prospect of meaningful change seems hopelessly daunting it can be helpful to bear a few things in mind. First, large and pervasive social processes are in some respects the collective results of individual actions. The social construction of masculinity, for example, relies upon individuals and groups continuously configuring, reconfiguring, enacting, and re-enacting different ideas about how men should think, act, and feel. The social learning of masculinity is influenced by larger social products like film and social media, but it is also heavily influenced by those around us. When we change our ideas about what is appropriate or inappropriate for people of different genders, we also necessarily provide different types of experiences for those around us. In doing so, we affect their social learning as well as our own.

It is also helpful to remember the power of human agency. As we saw in Chapter 5, people are not only passively shaped by social norms and ideologies around them. We are also capable of making conscious, intentional decisions about whether, when, and how to support or refute the social learning and social construction of masculinity. Although it may not be easy, and it might make us or those around us uncomfortable, we are capable of saying, "I don't agree," or, "with all due respect, I'm uncomfortable with what you just said." We can also be more proactive and less reactive; rather than waiting to respond to problematic behavior, we can seek to create environments that are in line with our values. Although verging on a platitude at this point, the phrase "think globally, act locally" captures well an orientation to large-scale change that emphasizes the difference individual choices can make.

It should be clear by now that our approach to questions of change is grounded in the assumption that a psychology of men and masculinities is not only about discovering facts generated by research, but also about figuring out how to more effectively navigate the gendered world, by assessing how well the consequences of our actions are in line with our values and goals. In other words, it's about being intentional in how we use the information. Our perspective is also strongly influenced by the fact that we have both been trained as clinical psychologists in a scientist-practitioner orientation. As a result, we tend to be focused on change at the individual level; if we were sociologists or political scientists, we would without a doubt be more focused on structural change. But as scientist-practitioners, we rely heavily on the available evidence regarding the most effective ways to change thoughts, feelings, and actions. If there's one thing clinical psychologists have learned from scientific research it is that change rarely happens overnight. Instead, change tends to emerge from the accumulation of practice in shifting how we approach situations in our lives, and from new experiences that result from our efforts to shift our habitual patterns.

Values

The first step is gaining a clear sense of what we value. Values are the things we consider most important in life. Some examples might include health, family, financial success, friendship, justice, honesty, knowledge, power, creativity, and so on. Below are some exercises to help you get a sense of your own values, and how they relate to your understanding of the psychology of men and masculinities.

In the space below, write down the values that matter most to you. In other words, what's important to you? Don't worry about ordering them—just write down whatever come to mind.

The values that are important to me include:

_____

_____

_____

_____

_____

_____

_____

_____

What did you notice about your list of values? Any surprises? People sometimes find that their personal values are very clear to them. For others, the exercise may require some thought. Either way it can be very useful to clarify your values and try to state them explicitly. Another, dramatic way of getting at your values is to think about how you would want to be remembered after you are gone. What epitaph would you want to sum up your life (Hayes, Strosahl, & Wilson, 2011, p. 306)?

Now consider how your personal values line up with your sense of satisfaction with life in areas that may be related to a psychology of men and masculinities. For example, how are your friendships with men currently? What about intimate relationships? How may your own physical or psychological health be related to different gender norms and ideologies? Completing the following questions can help you get a sense of this.

In general, my friendships with men are …_____

_____

_____

_____

I would like my friendships with men to be …_____

_____

_____

_____

In general, my psychological well-being is …_____

_____

_____

_____

I would like my psychological well-being to be …_____

_____

_____

_____

These same kinds of questions can be used to get yourself thinking about other values in your life. One issue to consider is the degree to which you are living the kind of life that you value. Of course, the answer is rarely yes/no. Most people are making more or less progress on their values in different areas of life at any point in time. How are your relationships with people of your same or different genders? How well are you taking care of your body? How are your ideas about how men should think, act, and feel affecting your own and others' well-being? These are just a handful of the values-based questions that can prompt you to self-reflect and identify possible areas for change.

Masculine Norms and Ideologies as Cognitions in Daily Life

Masculine gender norms and ideologies exist not only "out there" in society but also "in here"—in our own beliefs and thought processes. Our beliefs and assumptions about how men should think, act, and feel can affect our own well-being and the well-being of those around us. Likewise, how people around us think about gender has consequences not only them, but also for us. Adam, a student in one of our courses, was on the university soccer team as well as the drama club. Over the course of the semester he described feeling increasingly uncomfortable around his teammates when they made misogynist or homophobic comments. His own changing awareness of the psychology of men and masculinities was making it more difficult to passively endorse such comments by standing by and saying nothing. In effect, Adam's personal beliefs about gender were shifting and putting him more out of sync with an important part of his life at college. Although he was committed to the team and felt a strong sense of connection to his teammates, he was also feeling increasingly distant from them. Ultimately, he decided to speak up and express his discomfort with their behavior. To his surprise, his teammates supported him and several revealed that they were also uncomfortable with that type of banter but were afraid to speak up about it.

Many clinical psychologists would interpret Adam's evolution as a *cognitive change*. Cognitive changes are shifts in our beliefs about ourselves, others, and the world around us. Cognitions can be broad and general (e.g., "My value as a person depends on my ability to be a good man"), or more narrow and specific (e.g., "My friends will think I'm screwed up and needy if I tell them I've been depressed since my parents got divorced"). Decades of research have shown that cognitive processes are intimately linked to human well-being, including our day-to-day moods, self-esteem, physical well-being, anxiety, depression, and so on. In fact, many approaches to psychotherapy and counseling focus on how to make systematic changes in the way we think about ourselves and the world around us (Beck, Rush, Shaw, & Emery, 1979; Clark, 1986; Resick & Schnicke, 1992).

An important part of the change process is identifying specific types of thinking patterns that create problems and learning to replace those patterns with more adaptive ones. For example, depression is associated with cognitive processes that are more rigid, more black and white, less flexible, and more negative and self-critical. Anxiety tends to be associated with thought patterns that emphasize danger, uncertainty, and a high probability of bad things happening in the future. Many of these ways of thinking are automatic or habitual; in other words, people do not necessarily consciously think or rationally believe them, yet the thoughts still occur and exert a strong influence on our emotions and behavior. When someone chooses to go to therapy or makes personal efforts to change their cognitions the process requires practice and the first step is becoming more aware of what exactly those cognitions are.

We suspect that masculine gender norms and ideologies can create rigid, black and white, and fear-based cognitions that affect our physical, emotional, and social well-being. For example, the thought, "Women ask for help, but men should handle their problems on their own," is both rigid and black/white. It's rigid because it makes a very general but inflexible statement ("men should …") and it's black/white because it lumps men into one category and women into another. When someone thinks this way about a problem in their lives their options for how to cope become much more limited. In contrast, the thought, "Sometimes I can handle problems on my own and sometimes it makes more sense to reach out to other people," is more flexible and contains no elements of either/or, black/white thinking.

It can be helpful to assess your own thoughts and beliefs about men and masculinity and how they impact you. Importantly, you want to develop an awareness of what you *actually tend to think*, not *what you believe is the right or rational way to think.* You may "know," for example, that it doesn't make a lot of sense to think that men should always be physically strong and dominant. But when it comes to the rapid pace of daily life, perhaps that thought crosses your mind more often than you would like to believe. To get a sense of this try completing the following sentences with the first word or phrase that comes to mind. Don't give it a lot of conscious thought or deliberation. Just write down or say whatever pops into your head.

Men should be _____

A good man always _____

Men who _____ make me uncomfortable

It's embarrassing when men _____

I expect men to_____

What do you notice? Are you surprised by any of your answers? Your immediate reactions to these and similar statements will tell you something about the general beliefs you hold regarding men and masculinity. If you identify as male this exercise may reveal something about the gendered expectations you hold for yourself. If you identify as a different gender it may begin to help you see what you expect on average from men around you.

The phrase "on average" is an important one because your thoughts about men and masculinity may be very situation-specific. You may think it's embarrassing or shameful when men cry when someone hurts their feelings, and also think it's perfectly acceptable if they shed tears at a funeral for a loved one. Likewise, you may expect men to take charge and be confident when it comes to building or fixing things, but less so when it comes to expressing emotions. Psychologists refer to this as the contextual or situation-bound nature of cognition and often represent it visually with the following diagram:

A_____B_____C

A stands for an *activating event*, B stands for *belief*, and C stands for *consequences* (Ellis, 1962). The idea is that when we are in situations we have beliefs or thoughts that affect a wide range of consequences, including how we behave, how we feel, and even how we relate to others. For example, Michael was out playing disc golf with a group of men and at one point he made a bad shot, failing to throw the disc nearly as far as the other players. One of them laughed and yelled, "You cunt-armed it!" Several thoughts quickly went through Michael's head, including, "He's right. That was lame—I'm embarrassed," then, "Hey, that's really not cool—I don't like misogynist comments," and then, finally, "Alright, this is one of those times where you need to walk the walk, and not just talk the talk."

If Michael had stuck with the thought "I'm lame," he might have felt ashamed and have withdrawn from the group. If he had only had the thought "Hey, that's not cool" he might have started an argument. With a few moments of reflection, and awareness of his own thought processes, he chose to call out the sexist comment and hopefully encourage dialogue by saying, "I don't understand. What does making a bad shot have to do with a woman's vagina? Can you explain?" Moreover, by asking a question, Michael avoided coming across as domineering or lecturing— instead, he subverted the expectation that men should always know what they are doing or always have the answer.

Researchers and practitioners in clinical psychology have identified a wide range of cognitive processes that tend to be associated with depression, anxiety, anger, and other painful emotions. While the term "cognitive errors" is often used to describe these processes we prefer to think of them as lenses or frames through which people sometimes view their experiences. Some of the more common ones include black and white thinking, all or none thinking, selective attention, and should statements (also sometimes humorously referred to as "must"urbation).

Cognitive Frames Linked to Depression and Anxiety as Applied to Gender

Black and white thinking: things are always one way or another—no grey areas.

Example: "men are competitive and women are cooperative."

Alternative frame: "not all men are the same, and neither are all women."

All or none thinking: unless everything goes the way I expect it to, it's all a failure.

Example: "unless I handle all of my problems on my own, I'm weak and dependent."

Alternative frame: "I can't handle *everything all the time* on my own. Asking for help doesn't make me any less of a man."

Selective attention: paying excessive attention to a situation or information that creates strong negative feelings.

Example: "that guy said my shirt was gay and I can't get it out of my head even though I barely know him. It's ruining my day."

Alternative frame: "his comment made me feel insecure about my masculinity, that's true, but it's really not worth my attention. I'm going to focus on what's good in my life."

Should statements: things we say to ourselves which demand that we or others act, think, or feel in particular ways.

Example: "I should know what pleases my partner sexually or I am an inadequate lover."

Alternative: "this pressure I'm putting on myself sexually is not helpful. It's fine to ask questions about what pleases my partner."

Your Behavior and the Social Construction of Masculinity

We spent a good deal of time in Chapter 5 focusing on the idea of masculinity as a verb rather than a noun. The central premise was that gender can be usefully understood as a process of active construction via human agency. In other words, much of how masculinity operates involves the real-world actions of individuals and groups actively shaping their social environments. Clinical psychology has arrived at a similar place with regard to many of the determinants of human well-being; what we do, day to day, moment to moment, has a significant effect on how we feel. Therefore, it can be tremendously helpful to develop an awareness of various ways you may "do" masculinity in your everyday life, regardless of your gender identity (recall our discussion about the pressures women sometimes experience to enact masculinity in patriarchal cultures).

What are some of the ways you do masculinity in your day-to-day life? Michael and Ethan put this question to students, friends, and family members, and here are some of their responses:

- Watching sports with my friends
- Going out for drinks when I want to talk
- Wearing the clothes I wear
- Checking out women
- Taking out the trash and fixing things around the house rather than cooking
- My beard
- Trying to keep from crying when I'm upset in a meeting
- Paying for dinner when we go out
- When am I not doing it?
- I don't know—I'm not aware of trying to be masculine in any way
- Poker night
- Making big decisions like what car we'll buy
- Joking in the locker room
- What does that mean?
- Letting the women clean up after a meal.

There are several things to notice about this list. First, it seems like doing masculinity is a very contextual process. In other words, it tends to occur in specific environments or situations (e.g., locker rooms, meetings, the house, restaurants) with particular groups of people (e.g., partners, colleagues, male friends). Put another way, we often do masculinity as a performance for or with other people. Second, the process is not always conscious or intentional. When asked for more detail about joking in the locker room, one 19-year-old African-American student said, "It's not something I think about. Like if someone makes a joke about another guy being gay, or something like that, it's not that I really think it's funny. It's just what you do—laugh at the joke." Finally, as with many relatively automatic responses, it can be helpful to increase your awareness of when and how you are doing gender. Paying attention to people and situations that tend to "pull" for doing masculinity puts you in a position to choose how you want to respond rather than being automatically drawn in.

The process of consciously choosing whether/how we do masculinity is well illustrated in a recent television advertising campaign. As we write this book there is a fair amount of buzz in the U.S. media about a new commercial from the U.S. company Gillette which makes razors, shaving cream, and other products related to shaving and self-care. For many years, Gillette's tagline has been "The best a man can get." The new ad asks the question, "Is this the best a man can get?" in the context of videos showing men cat-calling women, young boys bullying each other, and a line of grown men reciting the phrase "boys will be boys" while two young males are rolling on the ground fighting. In the last sequence an adult male, risking ridicule from the line of men standing behind him, finally steps in and pulls the fighting boys apart, saying, "This is not how to treat each other." The message seems clear: when it comes to longstanding gender norms and ideologies, men can choose to comply with them or to reject them. But either way, it's a choice.

A final word about flexibility is in order here. It would be a mistake to assume we are advocating that people never (NEVER) do gender, or that men and boys should never engage in competitive activities, never keep their emotions to themselves, never handle problems on their own, and so on. What we are suggesting is that (a) flexibility in how we react to situations is ultimately more helpful than rigid adherence to one way of being, and (b) developing the ability to consciously choose our actions, rather than acting out of habit, enhances our flexibility.

Confronting Others

In addition to focusing on your own well-being, it is possible to leverage your understanding of the psychology of men and masculinities toward social changes that are in line with your values. Some students, for example, wish to address sexism and homophobia amongst their peers or in their communities. The question of whether or not to "speak up" is a first consideration. Many students, particularly those who identify as male, anticipate significant backlash if they do.

It can help to bear a few things in mind in such situations. First, a certain degree of backlash is inevitable because the social construction and social learning of masculinity depend on their own policing in order to be sustained. In other words, change will always meet with varying degrees of resistance but this does not mean your efforts are futile. Second, the term "varying degrees of resistance" is important. The approach you choose to take and the consequences that follow will often depend on the situation. There is a big difference between, say, angrily calling out homophobic insults several hours into a rowdy late night game of beer pong, versus expressing those same concerns with questions to friends you know and trust (e.g., does it make you guys uncomfortable that we call each other "gay" and "fag" all the time?).

It is also helpful to remember that if you have concerns about misogyny, homophobia, hidden mental health concerns, or other potential masculinity-related issues amongst your friends or family, you are probably not the only one. Research shows that people tend to overestimate how much others around them conform to particular social norms (Prentice & Miller, 1993). For example, men tend to overestimate the degree to which other men hold sexist beliefs or ideologies (Dardis, Murphy, Bill, & Gidycz, 2016; Kilmartin et al., 2008). One implication of these findings is that if you speak up you may find more support for your position than you would expect. Simple questions or statements can often open up dialogue in surprising ways. For example:

- "Can I talk to you guys? I'm worried about Rico. He's been through a lot and I think he's afraid to talk to us about it. I want to reach out to him but I also want to respect his space."
- "I don't know what you all think, but it makes me uncomfortable when someone starts talking about 'scoring' or 'hitting on' a woman."
- "Help me understand. Why does it make me 'gay' if I don't want to hook up with someone tonight? Are you saying that every guy should always want to have sex with a woman every day, or else he's sexually attracted to men?"

Of course, tone counts for a lot. There are ways to say things that suggest accusation and may promote defensiveness. In particular, it can be helpful to avoid doing masculinity yourself when you confront others. There are also ways to say things that are less threatening and suggest openness and curiosity. Either way, you cannot control people's responses. Having said that, we have been consistently surprised in our own lives, and in what students tell us, by the degree to which friends, family members, co-workers, and others are willing and able to engage in dialogue.

It is possible that questioning certain masculine social norms and practices can result in a unanimously negative response. If it does, this raises additional questions: are you willing to be surrounded by friends who are deeply entrenched in misogyny and homophobia? Are they truly incapable of change, or is it possible that at least some of them "hear" you, even if they can't express it in a group setting? Do you want to develop additional relationships with other people whose values regarding gender are more in line with your own? These are not easy questions to confront but they can also provide a context for growth, not only for you but also for those around you.

Education scholar Debra Meyerson (2001) uses the term "tempered radical" to describe a stance toward social change that works "from within." Psychologist and gender scholar Chris Kilmartin (2017) applies this concept to challenging gender norms:

The radicalism of these individuals arises from their being at odds with the dominant culture of a group (such as a military unit, company, academic department, and so forth) and yet they are dedicated to the success of the group. They engage in divergent thinking because they are not fully embedded in the group culture and thus are able to view it critically. As such, tempered radicals often make others uncomfortable with their willingness to challenge the accepted assumptions of the group. Examples … include an athlete willing to interrupt stereotypical anti-feminine talk in the locker room or a fraternity president willing to bring in an expert on the prevention of gender based violence and use his position to influence the fraternity members …. They are willing to seize teachable moments and engage in deeper conversations than more embedded cultural natives (i.e., those who are less aware of alternatives to the values and practices of their organizations).

(p. 226)

Being a tempered radical is not easy by any stretch of the imagination. It means taking the risk that you might disrupt things around you and initiate backlash. It means constantly scrutinizing yourself to make sure that you are not compromising your own moral compass and becoming overly tempered by dominant culture. But it also means having the chance to be a leader, the possibility of making positive changes that are in line with your values, and the opportunity to lift up the voices of people who, by their own choice or not, do not operate within the system.

One last point to remember is that change does not always need to begin with you standing up and calling out others. Confronting injustice always begins by confronting ourselves, and one of the best ways of challenging ourselves is to learn how to listen. If you're concerned about the way a friend's misogynistic comments might be affecting women in your friend group, a first step can be to get curious about their experience. In particular, it is helpful to recognize that there are some voices that are much harder for us to hear. For instance, by reading this book, you're hearing from two well-educated White men. It often takes more effort to get the perspective of people who, because of systematic oppression, have not had their voices heard in public debates about men and masculinities. Given the way masculinity socializes men, male readers might find the idea of leadership more intuitively appealing than acknowledging blind spots and reaching out to others to fill in the gaps. Yet courage, when combined with curiosity, is all the more potent. To whom you decide to listen and whether and how you choose to lead is up to you. But one thing is for sure: you can't unknow what you've learned about the psychology of men and masculinities.

References

Beck, A. T., Rush, A. J., Shaw, B. F., & Emery, G. (1979). *Cognitive therapy of depression*. New York, NY: Guilford Press.

Clark, D. M. (1986). A cognitive approach to panic. *Behaviour Research and Therapy, 24*(4), 461–470.

Dardis, C. M., Murphy, M. J., Bill, A. C., & Gidycz, C. A. (2016). An investigation of the tenets of social norms theory as they relate to sexually aggressive attitudes and sexual assault perpetration: A comparison of men and their friends. *Psychology of Violence, 6*(1), 163–171.

Ellis, A. (1962). *Reason and emotion in psychotherapy*. Oxford, England: Lyle Stuart.

Hayes, S. C., Strosahl, K. D., & Wilson, K. G. (2011). *Acceptance and commitment therapy*. New York, NY: Guilford Press.

Kilmartin, C. (2017). Men as allies. In J. Schwartz (Ed.), *Counseling women across the life span: empowerment, advocacy, and intervention* (pp. 225–242). New York, NY: Springer

Kilmartin, C., Smith, T., Green, A., Heinzen, H., Kuchler, M., & Kolar, D. (2008). A real time social norms intervention to reduce male sexism. *Sex Roles: A Journal of Research, 59*(3–4), 264–273.

Meyerson, D. (2001). *Tempered radicals*. Boston, MA: Harvard Business School Press.

Prentice, D. A. & Miller, D. T. (1993). Pluralistic ignorance and alcohol use on campus: some consequences of misperceiving the social norm. *Journal of Personality and Social Psychology, 64*(2), 243.

Resick, P. A. & Schnicke, M. K. (1992). Cognitive processing therapy for sexual assault victims. *Journal of Consulting and Clinical Psychology, 60*(5), 748–756.

INDEX

Glick, Peter 112
Goffman, Erving 114
Goldberg, Herb 126–127
Good, Glenn 196, 228
Gowaty, Patricia Adair 110
Gramsci, Antonio 135
Gray, John 158
Greif, Geoffrey 155

Hacking, Ian 93, 99, 214–215
Hall, G. Stanley 16, 17–18, 21
Hammer, Joseph 228
Handsford, Suzanne 155–156
Harry, J. 143
health protective behavior 187–188
health risk behavior 188
hegemonic masculinity 135–136,
    139–140, 147
hegemony, concept 135
historiography, presentist/contextualist
    18–20
homohysteria 156
homosexuality: black masculinities 140;
    gay masculinities 143, 191; gender
    as relational 123–124, 140;
    homophobic bullying 177–178;
    male inversion as disorder 24;
    M–F scales, screening applications
    25–26; military aversion 24;
    relationship developments
    159–160; *Seinfeld*'s masculinity
    issues 97; socially constructed
    term 92
human kinds, concept 214–215
Hyde, Janet Shibley 54

Illinois Rape Myth Acceptance Scale
    (IRMA) 175
intersectionality: adoption challenges
    144–145; development impetus 137;
    emotional restriction 191;
    masculinity, aggressive assertion
    172; masculinity and voting
    behavior 145–146; race and gender
    137–138, 140
intimate partner violence (IPV)
    173–174

Jackass (TV show) 193

Kaufman, Michael 120–121, 191
Kilmartin, Chris 245–246
Kimmel, Michael 123, 141, 169
Korobov, Neill 97, 99
Kucharska, Justyna 55
Kuhn, Thomas 219

Lambert, Tracy 195
Levant, Ronald F. 79, 189
Lewis, Robert 156
Locke, Benjamin 174
Lu, Alexander 144
Luckmann, Thomas 92

MacKinnon, Catharine 110
Mahalik, James R. 81–82, 174, 193
male inversion (homosexuality) 24,
    25–26
male privilege: conferred male
    dominance 118; feminist-led
    disempowerment 118–119;
    fundamental attribution error
    119–120; men's pain, pressure point
    120–121; meritocratic beliefs 120;
    self-serving bias 119; unearned male
    advantage 118
masculinity: assertion through
    aggression/violence 171–173;
    avoidance learning and anxieties
    71–73; biological and gender
    distinctions 27; definition, various
    approaches 8–10; emotional
    restriction, health costs 188–191;
    femininity as asymmetrical 123;
    Freud's sexual identity theory
    21–22; good or bad, critical
    perspective 10–12; homosocial
    environments and learning 74–76;
    intersectional approach 134,
    137–138, 144–145; male bonding
    needs 62; man's body as
    performative machine 191–193;
    men's liberation movement 27–29;
    men's movements, diverging
    factions 29–30, 125–127; modeling,
    action imitation 73; multiple
    masculinities 33–34, 134–136; new
    psychology of men 32–35;
    precarious manhood research

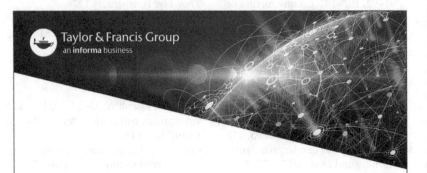